The Walter Berns
Constitution Day Lectures

The Walter Berns Constitution Day Lectures

2011–24

Edited by Gary J. Schmitt

AEI Press

Publisher for the American Enterprise Institute
WASHINGTON, DC

ISBN-13: 978-08447-5097-2 (Paperback)

Library of Congress Cataloging in Publication data have been applied for.

A≡I PRESS

Publisher for the American Enterprise Institute
for Public Policy Research
1789 Massachusetts Avenue, NW
Washington, DC 20036
www.aei.org

Printed in the United States of America

Contents

Introduction

In September 2011, AEI's Program on American Citizenship celebrated Constitution Day (September 17), the day 39 members of the Constitutional Convention signed a draft of the proposed Constitution in 1787. With that remembrance, we honored longtime AEI colleague Walter Berns with a panel dedicated to discussing his scholarship on the Constitution and the republican polity it supports. At this event, former AEI President Arthur C. Brooks announced that henceforth, AEI's annual Constitution Day celebration would be named in honor of Walter.

This volume is a collection of the 13 Walter Berns Constitution Day Lectures given since 2012. Walter's own work ranged widely, addressing issues on such diverse topics as civil and religious liberties, free speech, capital punishment, political philosophy, political science, presidential selection, Abraham Lincoln, and patriotism. It's fitting that the lectures named after him cover an equally broad array of topics related to the Constitution and the American republic.

Former federal circuit court judge and Stanford law professor Michael W. McConnell offered the first annual address, which focused on how the Constitution's design and words permitted deficit spending ("public debt") but attempted to cabin public spending by limiting it to expenditures that actually support the "common good." The following year, University of Notre Dame professor Michael P. Zuckert discussed how the Constitution's drafters dealt with the issue of slavery in crafting a republic that was federal in structure but whose legitimacy rested on a doctrine of natural rights.

In 2014, University of Virginia professor James W. Ceaser used his Constitution Day lecture to reflect on the Constitution's underlying political theory. His address considered the nature of political foundings, the role of choice in constructing a democratic government, and the methods the founders adopted to encourage reverence for the constitution they had created. Following Ceaser, Columbia Law School professor Philip Hamburger traced the underlying logic of the Fifth Amendment's due process requirement to its antecedent in the Magna Carta. Hamburger argued that in both instances, the goal was to preclude the ever-present problem of executives and administrations adjudicating disputes outside the courts and without the procedural rights associated with due process.

Former Attorney General Michael B. Mukasey delivered the 2016 Berns Constitution Day Lecture. His address focused on the "constitutional" criticisms of America's post-9/11 counterterrorism policies connected to secrecy, detention, interrogation, and surveillance—criticisms he contended were unfounded and more accurately understood as policy disagreements over national security policies. In 2017, AEI hosted then–US Court of Appeals Judge Brett M. Kavanaugh, whose Constitution Day address reflected on the late Chief Justice William Rehnquist's lasting impact in key areas of American jurisprudence. The following year, Loyola University Maryland professor Diana Schaub focused her lecture on Abraham Lincoln's account of the history of scientific progress, in which he subtly admonished Americans to combine their penchant for mastering nature with self-mastery.

AEI's Social, Cultural, and Constitutional Studies division began hosting the Berns Constitution Day Lecture series following the retirement of the Program on American Citizenship in 2019. The Constitution Day address that year was given by James R. Stoner Jr., professor of political science and director of the Eric Voegelin Institute at Louisiana State University. Stoner argued for understanding common law as the founders originally conceived it: infused with moral claims about the nature of justice and not, as Justice Oliver Wendell Holmes Jr. maintained, reducible simply to the long-term accretion of judge-made law.

The year 2020 marked the 100th anniversary of the 19th Amendment, giving women the right to vote. To mark that anniversary, University of Notre Dame professor Catherine H. Zuckert briefly reviewed the history of the suffragist movement and the proposed Equal Rights Amendment together with a reading of Henry James's *The Bostonians*, a novel that Zuckert argued depicts the inadequacy of general theorizing about relations between the sexes when it comes individual happiness.

Hillsdale College professor Wilfred M. McClay offered the 2021 Berns Constitution Day Lecture, in which he considered how the Constitution can and should be the most durable symbol of our national and civic identity. The following year's address was given by then-Representative Liz Cheney of Wyoming, who at the time was also vice chair of the House Select Committee to Investigate the January 6th Attack on the United States Capitol. Representative Cheney's remarks centered on elected officials' and party leaders' responsibility to devote themselves to the rule of law and, in turn, not elide behavior that undermines it.

Judge Neomi Rao of the US Court of Appeals gave the 2023 address. Judge Rao's lecture analyzed the connection between pluralism and our constitutional tradition, with a focus on how the modern administrative state short-circuits the American political system's ability to reconcile our diverse opinions and interests. Yuval Levin—director of Social, Cultural, and Constitutional Studies at AEI and editor of *National Affairs*—delivered the address the following year. Playing off *Taking the Constitution Seriously*, the title of a 1987 collection of Berns's essays, Levin asked that we see the Constitution "in full," understanding it not only as a legal document but also as a framework that, when broadly conceived, reflects and informs the American regime itself.

In the volume's afterword, we include the three presentations on Berns's scholarship that were delivered during AEI's Constitution Day celebration in 2011. In addition to presentations made by George Mason University law professor Jeremy A. Rabkin, AEI Madden-Jewett Chair Leon R. Kass, and former AEI President Christopher DeMuth, we have included Walter's own response to their remarks—remarks that are pithy, sharp, and simultaneously insightful about the US Constitution's exceptional character.

* * * *

On a personal note, I first "met" Walter as a graduate student through his writings on the First Amendment, in which he raised questions about American jurisprudence and the history behind that jurisprudence that few, if any, had raised before him. Not long after, I met him in person at the funeral of my mentor and his close friend, Professor Herbert Storing. There, without hesitation and without really knowing me other than the fact that I had been a student of Storing's, he asked how I was doing and what he could do to help me professionally. He never stopped asking.

One of my best Walter Berns moments happened without Walter even being involved. Not long after Storing had passed away and my tenure at the University of Virginia was coming to an end, I began a job search that included looking for a position on Capitol Hill. Having written a dissertation and articles on separation of powers, I saw that there was a staff opening on a subcommittee of the Senate Judiciary Committee dealing with separation of power issues. I sent my resume to the committee and, not long after, the committee clerk reached out to me and scheduled an interview with the staff's chief counsel.

When we met, it was clear from the start that he had no interest in hiring me. In truth, I wasn't even sure why he had gone ahead with the interview. His argument for dismissing my application was that I was not a lawyer. I responded that I had spent considerable time thinking about and writing on the American system of separated powers. He was not interested. Pretty quickly things got a bit testy as we went back and forth, fueled further by my aggravation of having made a worthless trek to DC. Finally, he'd had enough and suddenly blurted out that the only nonlawyer he would ever listen to when it came to the Constitution was Walter Berns. I responded a bit triumphantly, as I began to walk out of his office for the first and last time, "Well, I know Walter, and he's a friend."

So it was one of the great pleasures when I came to AEI some 20 years ago to be able to walk down the hall from my office, see if Walter was in his and, if he was, talk about whatever we each were working on at the time. These were not your typical quick and polite "how are you doing" exchanges. Walter wanted to know in some detail what you were working on—and even more probingly, why it was important to do so. He was a friend and a teacher.

* * * *

Walter Berns passed away 10 years ago at the age of 95. Walter's scholarship still provides insights about the Constitution and the American republic that remain as important today as when he first put pen to paper as a young scholar in the 1950s. It's our hope that readers will find this collection of Walter Berns Constitution Day Lectures of similar value.

Gary J. Schmitt
Senior Fellow, Social, Cultural,
and Constitutional Studies, AEI
September 2025

1

Spending, Public Debt, and Constitutional Design

MICHAEL W. MCCONNELL
September 13, 2012

You may have noticed we are in a presidential election year.
You can tell by the serious and sober analyses the candidates are offering for how to solve the nation's most pressing problems. Both sides have put forward detailed plans for bringing our fiscal house into order, and the essence of the campaign is a competition to persuade the people of why one plan will have better consequences than the other. The Framers would be proud of the way our democratic political system is working.

Just joking.

This year, the United States government will spend approximately $3.5 trillion. Over the past three years, federal spending has soared to peacetime record levels of over 24 percent of gross domestic product (GDP). We are borrowing 40 cents out of every dollar of that $3.5 trillion. For four years in a row, the federal deficit has exceeded $1.1 trillion. These annual deficits are adding up. As our two great political parties conducted their national conventions, the accumulated federal debt reached a total of $16 trillion.

Everyone agrees this cannot and must not continue. The word "du jour" means "unsustainable," which my handy political glossary defines as meaning the problem is too hard to solve.

What concerns many Americans most is not just the spending, and the taxing, and the borrowing, and the debt, but the political paralysis and ineptitude with which it is greeted.

At one great political convention, the debt clock was prominently featured, which was a sign of a certain level of seriousness about the problem.

And the party clearly has some ideas about what is necessary to bring it under control. But did they explain those ideas to the American public? Did they begin to build the political argument for taking serious action? Did they make clear what they would actually do about it?

Not so much.

But that was the responsible party. For the other party, the spending appears to be a virtue, the burgeoning debt somebody else's fault, and the deficit scarcely acknowledged as a problem. The nation is headed for fiscal catastrophe, but this scarcely warrants mention at the national convention of our largest political party.

Worse yet, the Senate has deliberately refused to pass a budget for the past three years—despite its legal obligation to do so—and Congress has not passed a single appropriations bill for the fiscal year that starts in just over two weeks. Apparently, they are afraid that if they revealed their plans for federal spending, the voters would not like what they see. So let's not budget at all.

This systematic inattention to fiscal problems makes many of us wonder whether ordinary democratic politics is capable of dealing with issues of spending and debt. Maybe we have a structural failure of institutions.

And indeed, looking around the globe at our fellow Western democracies, we are not alone. With a few honorable exceptions—Canada, for example, and maybe Sweden and a few others—Western democratic governments are drowning in sovereign debt, with little or no sign of political resolve to do much about it than to ask for bailouts from central banks and stronger economies.

Spending and debt are quintessential political issues, one might think. Political, not legal. Political, not constitutional. But is this necessarily so?

Just yesterday, the German constitutional court handed down one of the most significant decisions in its history, upholding the European Stability Mechanism over the constitutional claim that it yields German sovereignty to institutions that lack the essential attributes of democratic legitimacy. In Germany, there is no doubt that issues of public debt raise high questions of constitutional design.

And just last June, our Supreme Court handed down possibly the first decision in its history holding that the spending power under the United States Constitution is limited by principles of federalism.

So I want to talk about spending, public debt, and constitutional design in the United States Constitution.

Article I, Section 8, Clause 2 allows Congress to borrow money on the credit of the United States. It imposes no limit, but note that granting this power to the legislative branch denies it to the executive. Under the unwritten British constitution prior to the Glorious Revolution, the king could borrow money as a matter of his own prerogative authority, which kings frequently did, with disastrous results.

The British experience in the century prior to the Constitution suggested that parliamentary control over borrowing was a real, substantial, and effective check on excessive public debt. And so the Framers imitated that. Some people thought, last summer, that President Barack Obama should raise the debt ceiling on his own authority, which would have violated this fundamental constitutional principle. But Obama is only president of the United States. He is not King Charles II.

Some among the founding generation would have imposed more strenuous limitations. Thomas Jefferson argued that the federal government should have no power to borrow, which would have been an effective balanced budget amendment. More precisely, in a 1790 letter to James Madison, Jefferson argued that no generation had the right to impose debt on a subsequent generation.

"No man," Jefferson wrote, "can, by *natural right*, oblige . . . the persons who succeed him . . . to the paiment of debts contracted by him." He added:

> Suppose Louis XV. and his co[n]temporary generation had said to the money-lenders of Genoa, give us money that we may eat, drink, and be merry in our day; and on condition you will demand no interest till the end of 19. years you shall then for ever after receive an annual interest of 125/8 per cent. The money is lent on these conditions, is divided among the living,

eaten, drank, and squandered. Would the present generation be obliged to apply the produce of the earth and of their labour to replace their dissipations? Not at all.[1]

Jefferson was on to something. Democracies are subject to the temptation of looting the income of future citizens. Voters today may have some solicitude for the welfare of their grandchildren but not as much as they have for themselves. Borrowing money for current expenditures, and adding it to the public debt, is—as Jefferson recognized—nothing other than robbing the future of their equal rights.

Future generations will have all the needs we have for defense, social spending, education, health care, and the like. It will be no easier for them to finance their expenditures out of taxation than it is for us. But on top of those burdens, our children and grandchildren will have to pay the interest and maybe even the principal on the $16 trillion of public debt that we have run up through our failure to get the budget in order.

But future generations cannot vote. Current voters—current taxpayers—benefit by spending now and passing the bill to the future.

The underfunding of public pensions is a particularly egregious example. Future pensions are part of the pay of current public employees, and the cost of future pensions should be treated as part of the cost of current operations, paid for out of current taxes. The practice of underfunding pensions is nothing other than asking future generations to pay for our police, teachers, firefighters, and road crews. Jefferson would ask: "Why should they?"

If we believe that constitutions should be drafted to protect against systemic democratic maladies, Jefferson would seem to be right in suggesting that we need to use constitutional devices to protect future generations who cannot vote from being sacrificed to the interests of current voters. Balanced budget provisions are not merely an attempt to enshrine a particular economic philosophy into constitutional law—something I disapprove of—but a way to counteract an inherent bias of democracy in favor of the present at the expense of the future.

But Madison had an interesting and compelling response to Jefferson. Some expenditures, he pointed out, are incurred for the benefit of future generations. He pointed to the cost of "repelling a conquest."[2] He might have pointed to such things as purchasing Louisiana, which was done by borrowing—except he was writing in 1790, not 1803. When the government purchases a physical asset that will yield benefits for many years to come, there is nothing wrong with spreading the cost over those years of benefit, and the way to do that is through incurring debt. If governments cannot borrow for the purchase of infrastructure and other assets, then the same democratic preference for the present over the future would lead to significant underinvestment.

When I was a junior lawyer in the US Office of Management and Budget (OMB) in the early 1980s, I was tasked with drafting a sensible balanced budget amendment, or rather, several possible versions. The most difficult aspect was trying to incorporate Madison's insight that the purchase of valuable physical assets should be an exception. The trouble is that almost any expenditure can be called an investment and be characterized as producing future benefits. In principle, abusive borrowing is a proper subject for constitutional design, but it is very difficult to get it right.

Then there was Alexander Hamilton. Hamilton, the most sophisticated economist among the major Founders, recognized—as Jefferson and Madison did not—that public debt at a manageable level can serve the macroeconomic interests of the nation by supplying a store of value and easily transferrable medium of exchange—in short, a money supply.

It is probably not in the national interest for the public debt to be zero. US treasuries, effectively risk-free assets (at least for a while longer), are vital for just the reason Hamilton foresaw. Moreover, a growing economy requires an ever-larger pool of treasuries as a medium of exchange. So, a balanced budget is probably not quite right. As long as the deficit stays, on average, below the rate of growth of the economy, the public debt will be a "public blessing," to use Hamilton's language, and not a curse.[3]

Alas, the deficit today is careening toward 7 percent of GDP, which is a different matter altogether. Economists tell us that when sovereign debt exceeds 90 percent of GDP—ours is currently in the low 70s but rising fast—economic growth slows, interest rates rise, and it is very difficult to recover from the spiral. Ask the Greeks, if you do not believe the economists.

Keynesians will say that it is important to allow the federal government to engage in countercyclical fiscal policy, incurring debt in bad times and running surpluses in good. I am not sure whether I believe that, but even if I did, I would note that Keynesianism in practice seems to justify deficits in bad times but to tolerate deficits in good times as well. The United States has run a surplus only five times in the past half century—an era of unprecedented economic growth. Times never seem to be good enough to take away the punch bowl from the party, to use a well-known metaphor.

What about spending? Most people regard the spending power as a "plenary" power limited only by the political process. The Founders would have been surprised at this.

Spending from the national treasury presents a classic collective action problem—the veritable tragedy of the commons. Everyone who benefits from the spending gains a great deal while suffering only a tiny fraction of the burden of taxation to support it. No one will apply cost-benefit analysis to his or her political demands because the benefit will greatly outweigh the cost—even if the benefit is negligible in comparison to the total cost. This is an obvious problem that the Founders as practical politicians surely understood.

No one at the Founding—indeed, no one for the first century of the republic, as far as I can tell—thought that Congress had unlimited discretion to spend on whatever it wished. Article I, Section 8, Clause 1 limits Congress's use of tax funds to promoting the "general welfare." Today, this phrase has little or no meaning. But the term had actual limiting content at the time.

There were two competing interpretations. Madison argued that the general welfare was a quick way of saying that Congress could spend money only in service of the other enumerated federal powers. He had some support for this in the language and accepted interpretation of the Articles of Confederation.[4] I have to say, though, that as a matter of ordinary English usage, this interpretation strikes me as far-fetched.

Hamilton, in his Report on Manufactures, argued that the term "general" distinguished between genuinely national and merely local purposes. Thus, to be legitimate, "the object to which an appropriation of money is to be made [must] be *General* and not *local*; its operation extending in fact, or by possibility, throughout the Union, and not being confined to a particular spot."[5]

In the Founding period, the word "general" was used more precisely than we use it today. It was the term used for matters pertaining to the Union as a whole. Thus, they spoke of the "general" government (not the "national" government) and of "general" as opposed to "local" concerns. Hamilton's position was thus based on the ordinary meaning of the text.

Under Hamilton's interpretation, the clause addressed the collective action problem on a geographic basis. If merely local purposes are excluded, there will be no scrambling by particular representatives of particular places for maximum exploitation of the common fund. This may be an incomplete solution to the problem—there may be other forms of the tragedy of the commons than geographical—but it does address an important slice of the problem in a republic where representatives are elected on a local basis.

Hamilton's interpretation of the clause finds support in a debate at the Constitutional Convention in Philadelphia. Benjamin Franklin made a motion to give Congress the power to construct canals, a motion Madison supported on the ground that canals would foster "easy communication between the States" and thus promote economic integration in tandem with the political integration the new Constitution would bring.[6]

The immensely shrewd and practical Roger Sherman objected, saying that the benefit would "accrue to the places where the canals may be cut" while the expense would fall to the United States as a whole—an objection that many delegates apparently found persuasive. Franklin's motion lost eight states to three. It seems likely that the general welfare condition on the spending clause reflected the same distaste for allowing the general treasury to be tapped for localized benefit.[7]

In a moment, I will argue that this principle provides a partial solution to some of our contentious modern debates over spending. But first: How did it work?

The first appropriations statute, in 1789, contained no specific items. In its entirety, it appropriated $137,000 for the War Department, $190,000 to repay certain Treasury warrants, $96,000 for veterans' pensions, and $216,000 for the "civil list," meaning everything else.[8]

But the second appropriations statute, in 1790, contained an appropriation for the construction of a lighthouse on Cape Henry in Virginia. This seems to present the same problem as Franklin's canals, and the proposal set off the nation's first constitutional debate over the scope and meaning of the spending power. Following Madison's approach, the lighthouse might be defended as "incidental to commerce" or possibly in service of a navy (when the US would get a navy).

But what seemed to be decisive is the fact that the lighthouse had been authorized the previous year in a statute that would federalize all "lighthouses, beacons, buoys, and public piers" up and down the eastern seaboard.[9] In light of that statute, the Cape Henry lighthouse was part of a project that served the "general welfare" and not just local interests.

In the same year, Congress refused to fund the removal of obstructions to navigation in the Savannah River. That project was alone, divorced from any general legislation.

Perhaps the clearest example of this interpretation of the clause was President Andrew Jackson's veto of an appropriation to build a road from Maysville, Kentucky, to the Ohio River, a stretch of highway entirely within the state of Kentucky, coupled with his approval of an appropriations bill for the Cumberland Road, also known as the National Road, which linked the eastern seaboard with Ohio, Indiana, and Illinois. The National Road fell even within Jackson's grudging interpretation of the general welfare.

This does not mean that Congress must always allocate funds evenly among the states, but that its spending decisions must be based on criteria that "extend[s], in fact, or by possibility, throughout the Union."[10]

Distinctions of this sort may not be judicially administrable. Distinctions between "general" and "local" are matters of degree. But for almost the first century of the republic, these distinctions were vigorously debated and recognized by conscientious Congresses and still more conscientious presidents, who took seriously their duties to enforce the Constitution.

What might be the significance today of a limitation of congressional spending authority to projects whose benefits are "*General* and not *local*"?[11]

Well, for a start, what about earmarks, which are appropriations for specific projects not part of, or evaluated pursuant to, any broader or more general program? Are they constitutional?

I am not asking whether the courts would strike earmarks down. Presumably, no one has standing to challenge these appropriations in court. I am asking whether a conscientious legislator or president would regard these projects as serving a purpose that extends in fact, or by possibility, throughout the Union.

Earmarks are not a large part of the budget—they were not a large part even before the current supposed moratorium. But they are a gateway drug to irresponsible spending, and an invitation to corruption.

When the costs of a local project—let's say, for example, refurbishing a local park—and the benefits of the project are borne by the same set of taxpayers, we can assume that at some rough-and-ready level, the project will not be approved unless the benefits exceed the costs. But if someone else is paying the bill, the costs do not much matter. The benefits will get all the attention. Do you think Californians would pay their own good money to build a high-speed rail link between Bakersfield and Fresno?

Even if a project is not wasteful, it violates the terms of our national compact for the entire nation to pay for projects that benefit only one local area. That was Sherman's point, which carried the day at the

Constitutional Convention. Why should taxpayers all over the country fund a sewer improvement project for Modesto, California, when other cities have to fund such projects for themselves?

The general welfare limitation addresses the collective action problem that advocates of concentrated benefits will invest more in political effort than broadly dispersed bearers of the attendant costs.

Hamilton espoused the broadest understanding of the spending power among the major Framers. But even he would have said that modern earmarking is an abuse of our constitutional design.

The general welfare limitation may also provide a more satisfactory—if more radical—way of thinking about the Medicaid expansion in the 2012 health care decision *National Federation of Independent Business v. Sebelius*.

You will recall that Congress required the states to expand Medicaid eligibility to all persons, including childless adults, below 133 percent of the poverty line; if they did not, they would lose all their Medicaid funds. The US Supreme Court, in an impressive 7–2 majority in which Justices Stephen Breyer and Elena Kagan joined the more conservative justices, held that this threat of a cutoff was so coercive as to be unconstitutional.

But the *National Federation of Independent Business* Court's treatment of the issue is anything but crisp and clear. Indeed, the Supreme Court expressly declined to "fix a line" between permissible encouragement and impermissible coercion—it simply held that the Medicaid expansion was beyond the line.[12]

The Court framed the issue as whether a state has "a legitimate choice whether to accept the federal conditions in exchange for federal funds."[13] That question led the Court to make a series of shades-of-grey distinctions:

1. The size of the grant that would be withdrawn,

2. Whether the newly imposed conditions make the law "in reality a new program" rather than a "modification" of the old,

3. Whether the states are threatened with loss of "existing" funding or merely new sources of funding, and

4. Whether the attached conditions are ones that "govern the use of the funds" or instead "take the form of threats to terminate other significant independent grants . . . as a means of pressuring the States to accept policy changes."[14]

These considerations have a certain common sense to them, but the line-drawing problems are likely to prove intractable. It is particularly perplexing that the Court distinguished, instead of overruling, an earlier case in which Congress cut off 5 percent of the federal highway funds for any state that did not pass a 21-year-old drinking age. The Court called that a "relatively mild encouragement," in contrast to the Medicaid provision, which it called a "gun to the head."[15] But the two provisions are structurally and pragmatically indistinguishable.

Let me float an idea—more radical than the Court's holding, but possibly more administrable, and rooted in the constitutional text as originally understood. The idea may not be appropriate for judicial review, and it may not hold up to scrutiny. I am hoping to generate some thought.

My tentative suggestion is this: If Congress may spend only for the "general" welfare, it would be unconstitutional for Congress to set up a Medicaid system in which funds are spent in all states except for one (or some). It has to be a general program, extending throughout the Union.

And as with other equal-access regimes, it is presumptively unconstitutional for the government to exclude citizens on account of their exercise of a constitutional right—in this case, the state's constitutional right not to administer a federal program.

Justice Ruth Bader Ginsburg's dissent on the spending clause issue maintains that "a State . . . has no claim on the money its residents pay in federal taxes."[16] That is technically true. But if Hamilton was correct, the people of every state do have a constitutional right (whether judicially enforceable or not) to insist that federal spending be for general purposes, meaning extending to the entire Union. It arguably violates that principle to cut off a state's residents as a means of pressuring their state government to adopt policies Congress otherwise has no authority to compel the states to adopt.

We must not fall into the trap of thinking that federal grants are a "gift," as Justice Ginsburg misleadingly stated in her dissenting opinion.[17] The monies are forcibly extracted from the people of every state, and the people of every state are entitled to benefit from them. That is what the Court's conception of "coercion" seems to overlook.

This does not render Congress powerless to impose conditions that ensure that funds are properly spent. Congress need not grant funds to state governments that refuse to comply with clearly stated funding conditions. But, according to this theory, Congress's remedy if a state refuses to comply is not to cut the state's citizens off from the benefits of their tax dollars but to bypass the state government and administer the program directly—through federal agencies or nonstate grantees. The people of the state would not be cut out; only the government of the state would be cut out. The right of equal treatment belongs to the people of the states, not to the state governments.

This, interestingly, is the way Obamacare's "health benefit exchanges" work. If a state declines to operate such an exchange in accordance with the statute's dictates, the federal government will step in and do so in that state. This satisfies the constitutional requirement that spending be for the general welfare because taxpayers in every state will receive the benefit.

For Congress to cut off particular states and deny their citizens any benefit renders the program less than general, and hence unconstitutional.

Regardless of how any particular controversy might be resolved, I hope I have persuaded you that both the spending clause and the borrowing clause raise important issues of constitutional design, based on the collective action problems these powers present.

But recent events may give us reason to doubt that constitutional design can place a real restraint on political leaders determined to rack up more spending and more public debt. Europe's constitutional design appears to prohibit bailouts of its member states and prevent the central bank from purchasing sovereign debt. But once the political elite claimed that bailouts and central bank interventions were all that stood between Europe and the abyss, those restrictions were quickly disregarded.

Similarly, here the many state constitutional provisions requiring balanced budgets have easily been evaded, partly by clever devices and partly by, well, ignoring them. Who would know that California's constitution requires a balanced budget?

The 2011 Budget Control Act places a legal requirement on Congress to pass an annual budget well in advance of the new fiscal year and conform actual appropriations to the budget. In my day at OMB, this obligation was held sacrosanct and faithfully obeyed. Not so, anymore.

Madison warned that constitutional limits on governmental abuse would be mere parchment barriers if not reflected in the deep structure of accountable representation and separation of powers. The Anti-Federalists were even more pessimistic, saying that the only real restraint comes from an active and engaged citizenry—the very thing that Madison's Constitution sought to neutralize, on the assumption that the populace would generally favor shortsighted policies, like "spend now, pay later."

For a few important months in 2009 and 2010, an active and engaged citizenry were in the streets and at town halls demanding an end to the abuse. "Spend less, tax less, borrow less," they said.[18] Since that time, our government in Washington has spent more and borrowed more, and conventional wisdom says it should tax more, as well.

We have pretty much given up on constitutional design as a restraint. The general welfare limits on federal spending are completely ignored, and the Supreme Court did not even mention them in its Obamacare decision.

Will an active and engaged citizenry reemerge, and will they be heard? In the end, American citizens are the only protection that really counts.

Notes

1. Thomas Jefferson to James Madison, September 6, 1789, in *The Founders' Constitution*, ed. Philip B. Kurland and Ralph Lerner (University of Chicago Press, 1986; 2000), vol. 1, chap. 2, document 23, http://press-pubs.uchicago.edu/founders/documents/v1ch2s23.html (emphasis in original).

2. James Madison to Thomas Jefferson, February 4, 1790, in Kurland and Lerner, *The Founders' Constitution*, vol. 1, chap. 2, document 24, http://press-pubs.uchicago.edu/founders/documents/v1ch2s24.html.

3. Alexander Hamilton, "The First Report on Public Credit," January 14, 1790, Online Library of Liberty, https://oll.libertyfund.org/titles/banning-liberty-and-order-the-first-american-party-struggle#lf0464_head_074.

4. James Madison to Andrew Stevenson, November 27, 1830, in Kurland and Lerner, *The Founders' Constitution*, vol. 2, document 27, art. 1, § 8, cl. 1, http://press-pubs.uchicago.edu/founders/documents/a1_8_1s27.html.

5. Alexander Hamilton, "Report on Manufactures," December 5, 1791, in Kurland and Lerner, *The Founders' Constitution*, vol. 2, document 21, art. 1, § 8, cl. 1, http://press-pubs.uchicago.edu/founders/documents/a1_8_1s21.html (emphasis in original).

6. James Madison, "Records of the Federal Convention," September 14, 1787, in Kurland and Lerner, *The Founders' Constitution*, vol. 3, document 1, art. 1, § 8, cl. 7, http://press-pubs.uchicago.edu/founders/documents/a1_8_7s1.html.

7. Madison, "Records of the Federal Convention," in Kurland and Lerner, *The Founders' Constitution*.

8. Comm. on Appropriations, S. Doc. No. 110-14, at 3 (2008), https://www.govinfo.gov/content/pkg/CDOC-110sdoc14/pdf/CDOC-110sdoc14.pdf.

9. Richard Peters, ed., "An Act for the Establishment and Support of Lighthouses, Beacons, Buoys, and Public Piers," in *The Public Statutes at Large of the United States of America* (Charles C. Little and James Brown, 1845), 1:53–54.

10. Hamilton, "Report on Manufactures."

11. Hamilton, "Report on Manufactures" (emphasis in original).

12. National Federation of Independent Business v. Sebelius, 567 US 519, 55, compare 57 (2012).

13. *National Federation of Independent Business*, 567 US at 48.

14. *National Federation of Independent Business*, 567 US at 52, 50 (discussion of distinctions at 49–53).

15. *National Federation of Independent Business*, 567 US at 50, 51 (quoting South Dakota v. Dole, 483 US 211, 211–12 (1987) regarding the Court's judgment concerning "relatively mild encouragement").

16. *National Federation of Independent Business*, 567 US at 59n26.

17. *National Federation of Independent Business*, 567 US at 45 (citing and quoting College Savings Bank v. Florida Prepaid Postsecondary Education Expense Board, 527 US 666, 686–87 (1999)).

18. Matthew Bigg and Nick Carey, "Protesters Disrupt Town-Hall Healthcare Talks," Reuters, August 11, 2009, https://www.reuters.com/article/business/healthcare-pharmaceuticals/protesters-disrupt-town-hall-healthcare-talks-idUSTRE5765QH/.

2

Slavery and the Constitutional Convention

MICHAEL P. ZUCKERT

September 17, 2013

It is an immense honor to me to appear here at AEI to deliver the Walter Berns Constitution Day Lecture. This event also has great personal meaning for me because Walter Berns was my very first political science professor—more years ago than I think either he or I would care to count. He co-taught a course, Introduction to American Government, with a very newly minted PhD named Theodore Lowi. If any of you are familiar with the work and thought of these two men, you'll have some idea of what kind of experience it was to sit through a class taught by these two: It was exhilarating, but it was also in equal measure confusing—at least for a neophyte political scientist such as I was.

Walter Berns was also my first teacher in constitutional law, but in that subject he had a very capacious understanding of what ought to be covered. We spent a fair amount of time that semester reading James Madison's notes on the Constitutional Convention because Walter seemed to have this very quaint idea that constitutional law did have something to do with the Constitution. We also read parts of John Locke's *Second Treatise*, which he also thought had something to do with the Constitution. If it hadn't been for that course, I wouldn't be standing here today. I might be on Wall Street or in a law firm somewhere because that was my original plan. So Walter Berns was both an inspiring and a life-changing presence for me. But he was not always an easy person.

My first personal contact with him came at the end of my sophomore year when I, and all other Cornellians of that age, had to declare our major, and as a part of declaring our major, we had to take a little card and have it signed by somebody whom we had selected to be our adviser.

I chose Walter. And, with a good deal of trepidation, I went to his office—trepidation because this was the first time I had ever been in a faculty office at Cornell, so this was a new experience for me. Everything went very well—until I got to the office. I had just taken the only course I had had with him at that point, that very large introductory course, so he didn't really know who I was and I had to explain why I was there. I explained, "I'm declaring my major; I would like you to be my adviser." He looked me over and he asked, "Why me?"

This seemed like a completely unanswerable question; no answer I could come up with would be sufficient to answer this question. I stammered out something—I have no idea what it was, but he did sign the card. With great relief, I left his office, and I got halfway down the stairs and realized I had left this card in his office. I had to go back and get the card, and it is at that time I started to think, "Maybe another adviser would do better." In any case, I knocked on the door again, knowing that I was looking like an idiot, but Walter very kindly overlooked, or likely forgot, this less than auspicious beginning to our relationship. In any case, I still remember many things that I've heard or read by Walter, but what sits most in my memory is that "Why me?"

In any case, I am hoping that he did not say something similar when he heard that I was giving the Walter Berns lecture: "Why him?"

Now you probably did not notice this, but today we are celebrating the 226th anniversary of the day the delegates to the Constitutional Convention met for the last time and signed the document they had drafted. One of the reasons you did not notice this is that we don't usually notice 226th anniversaries of anything. This anniversary is nowhere near as visible as was the 200th anniversary of the Constitutional Convention in 1987. Chief Justice Warren E. Burger, as you may remember, was appointed head of something called the US Commission on the Bicentennial, which was put in place in order to encourage events related to the bicentennial. One of the things that the commission did was issue official seals of approval for events they felt were suitable for celebrating the bicentennial.

One activity of that year, which I do not believe got the bicentennial commission seal of approval, was a talk given by Supreme Court Justice Thurgood Marshall at a hotbed of constitutional studies—the San Francisco Patent and Trademark Law Association's annual seminar, which was held in Maui, Hawaii, of all places.

Burger, who was one of the most conservative justices on the court, and Marshall, who was one of the most liberal justices on the court, had clashed many times before this, but this time their disagreement really caught the attention of the entire thinking public. Rather than joining in the celebration of the Founders that Burger was sponsoring, Justice Marshall announced right off in his talk in Hawaii that he did not "find the wisdom, foresight, and sense of justice exhibited by the Framers particularly profound."[1] The issue that led Justice Marshall to his dissent, of course, was slavery.

While many people thought that it was a little bit indelicate for Justice Marshall to raise this awkward question at a time of great national celebration of the Constitution, nonetheless the issue of slavery and the Constitution had been much on the minds of historians, constitutional scholars, and many thoughtful citizens for quite a long time by then. And among the professionals, it seems to me, the ruminations about slavery had produced two factions—or schools of thought—about slavery and the Constitution: one sometimes known as "Neo-Lincolnian" and the other sometimes known as "Neo-Garrisonian." The latter is named for William Lloyd Garrison, the great abolitionist, activist, and thinker who had condemned the Constitution as a "covenant with death" and an "agreement with hell" because of its support for slavery.[2] The other group is, of course, named for Abraham Lincoln, who had rather a different view about the Constitution.

This is not the place to relate in any kind of detail the character of the debates between these different groups, but a brief summary will be useful. Two main issues separate these two groups. One is: How favorable was the Constitution produced in 1787 to slavery? The second is: What were the motives upon which the founding generation acted when they acted with regard to slavery?

Now the Neo-Garrisonians answer the first question by saying that the Constitution was very favorable to the institution of slavery—that the Constitution gave slavery a great deal of life-sustaining aid, including recognition of its moral legitimacy. To them, the Constitution was indeed an immoral compromise.

The Neo-Lincolnians, while conceding that the Constitution did indeed contain some accommodations to the institution of slavery, deny that these were nearly as substantial as the Neo-Garrisonians claim. And they particularly deny that the Constitution stamped the institution with some kind of recognition of its moral legitimacy.

The Neo-Garrisonians answer the second question about the motives behind the Founders' actions by saying that they were moved by the same complex of motives that led to the establishment and thriving of slavery in the first place: greed, racism, Christian triumphalism, and moral indifference.

The Neo-Lincolnians, on the other hand, emphasize the place of slavery in the constitutional order as due primarily to the press of necessity: They argue that without these concessions to slavery, the Union could not have been made, and so to them the Constitution was a moral, or at least a necessary, compromise. The Neo-Lincolnians frequently point at this connection to the expectation—or the hope, anyway—among many of the Founders that the process of abolition begun in the states during and just after the American Revolution would continue until slavery had been removed from the land.

The scholarly debates on slavery's place in the Constitution can be very heated. The topic is indeed so controversial that the parties cannot even agree on how many parts of the Constitution are relevant to slavery. One Neo-Garrisonian that I know found in the Constitution 18 clauses directly or indirectly supportive of slavery. The Neo-Lincolnians find far fewer (only three): the three-fifths formula for representation and taxation, the Slave Trade Clause, and the Fugitive Slave Clause.

Since these three clauses are important for my talk, I'll pause a minute and give you a quick idea of what's in them. The formulas for representation and direct taxes provided that each state would have seats in the House of Representatives in proportion to the number of "free Persons" in the state and, then they use the phrase, three-fifths of "all other Persons." "All other Persons" in this context is a roundabout way of saying "the slaves."[3] All free persons count for one, and all slaves count for three-fifths. So far as there would be "direct taxes," these also would be apportioned according to that same formula. The slave states would in effect get a bonus in representation for their slaves, but they would also be liable for more taxes for that same reason. As it turned out, direct taxes were not levied, so this formula turned out to be a bonus for the slave states, and they didn't have to pay any kind of particular penalty for it.

The Slave Trade Clause denied Congress the power to prohibit the slave trade until 1808, 20 years from the ratification of the Constitution.

The Fugitive Slave Clause provided, again in very roundabout language, that a slave escaping from one state into another would not become free by virtue of having done that but instead "shall be delivered up."[4]

Now, for the rest of my talk, what I would like to do is to go beyond the Neo-Garrisonian–Neo-Lincolnian battle and put forward a somewhat different account of slavery in the convention and in the Constitution.

I want to begin by saying a bit about the context of slavery at the time of the Constitutional Convention, because I think both the Neo-Lincolnians and the Neo-Garrisonians go astray by not taking sufficiently seriously that context. The historical circumstances in place at the time of the Constitutional Convention were very different from the subsequent history of slavery in America. Therefore, that subsequent history does not form an adequate basis for thinking about the expectations of the people who wrote the Constitution. But when we today—and this includes historians—think back to the problem of slavery at the convention, we too often think of it as if that history that subsequently unfolded was the history they foresaw, expected, or experienced—but it wasn't.

Paradoxically perhaps, achieving clarity on the history that occurred after the adoption of the Constitution is most important for accurately understanding our topic. The post-history—the history after the

Constitution was made—involved a real transformation of the slavery system. In the period around the time of the Constitutional Convention, the main use of slave labor in America was to produce tobacco in the upper South and rice and indigo in the lower South. But starting in the 1790s, the Southern economy shifted to cotton. And the shift to cotton was fueled by two technological developments.

First was the development of steam-powered machinery, which led to the development of the textile industry in Britain, which led to the production of cheaper cotton cloth, which led, in turn, to a rising demand for raw cotton. The second big technological breakthrough was the famous cotton gin. The cotton gin was particularly important in driving the transformation of the Southern economy because the kind of cotton that could be grown readily in the American South was a kind in which the fibers of cotton and the seeds of the cotton were very difficult to separate. The cotton gin made it possible to do this separation cheaply and relatively easily. With the cotton gin, cotton became an economically viable crop for the South, and with the ever-increasing demand for raw cotton, it became an economically lucrative crop.

The difference cotton production made after the Constitutional Convention is readily visible in a few simple statistics. In 1790, roughly at the time of the convention, the United States produced 3,000 bales of cotton. In 20 years, that figure increased sixfold, and by 1858, near the start of the Civil War, cotton production stood at four million bales—from three thousand to four million, more than a thousandfold increase. Cotton became the leading American export, and the dollar value of cotton was greater than that of all other American exports combined.

That the slave system that produced this cotton, which was so economically profitable, should be transformed by this immense growth in the cotton industry is therefore not a matter for surprise. And that the slave system should become larger and more important, more entrenched, I think should be relatively easy to see. But we cannot read back from the history of what did happen to cotton, and thus to slavery, in the post-1790 world to the expectations and plans of the men who wrote the

Constitution. That future, which we all see so clearly, was completely opaque and unexpected to them.

Instead, they looked back on a history and trajectory of slavery in America that was quite different—the history and trajectory before 1787. Of course, as is well known, slavery by the mid-18th century was well established on the American continent. All 13 colonies at the time of the revolution had slavery; slavery existed in French America and slavery existed in Spanish America. In 1750, according to the best estimates, about 20 percent of the population of what would become the United States was black, most of whom were slaves. But this population was very unevenly distributed. In the North, less than 5 percent of the population was black; in the South, on average 40 percent was black, with a high of 60 percent in South Carolina.

The situation of slavery, though, was much affected by the American Revolution and its aftermath. There was a combination of events and trends that actually set slavery back in those years. One cause was that the British, for example, offered freedom to slaves in the South who would come and fight on their side, and there were quite a few slaves who took them up on that. Moreover, there were many other slaves who took advantage of wartime chaos to flee from slavery. Beyond that, in a movement that one important historian has called "the contagion of liberty," all the northern states moved to abolish slavery in the years after the revolution.[5] Individual, voluntary manumission was occurring, and state laws were passed even in the South making it easier and easier to free slaves. In 1787, the Congress under the Articles of Confederation passed the Northwest Ordinance, prohibiting slavery in the Northwest Territory, which includes the present states of Ohio, Illinois, Indiana, Michigan, and Wisconsin. That's quite a large swath of land.

All these developments increased the number of free blacks in both North and South. In 1790, it's estimated that about 8 percent of all blacks in the United States were free. By 1810, 14 percent were free. The number of slaves was conversely affected, with the number of slaves dropping in those years.

These few facts should make clear that the world the men at the convention faced in 1787 was not the world the nation faced in the 1850s. These facts should make clear that the trajectory of slavery in 1787 was not the trajectory that led to the entrenching of slavery in the 19th century. To understand slavery at the Constitutional Convention, we must look at it as they did with their eyes, and not with our eyes, either enriched or clouded by our knowledge of subsequent history.

As I said, the two main ways of looking at this topic are the Neo-Lincolnian and the Neo-Garrisonian. I'm going to propose a third—the Neo-Madisonian approach, which is named for James Madison, who I think was the person at the time of the Founding who understood the Constitution best. I see the Neo-Madisonian position as a kind of middle ground between the Neo-Lincolnians and the Neo-Garrisonians, although not the kind of middle ground that just splits the difference between them.

One of the ways in which it's a kind of middle ground is that the Neo-Madisonian view holds the Constitution to be neither proslavery as the Neo-Garrisonians say nor quite antislavery in the way the Neo-Lincolnians say. The Neo-Madisonian position denies that the Constitution endorses the institution of slavery as legitimate and right. But it also denies that the Constitution made provisions to stamp out slavery—or, as Lincoln put it, that it consigned the institution to "ultimate extinction." Rather, the Neo-Madisonian position says a few things more subtle than these—three things in particular: First, slavery is legal but not legitimate in the Constitution; second, the Constitution postpones or defers any disposition of the issue of slavery; and third, it does so for reasons deep in the fundamental principles of the Constitution, so deep as to make it nearly inevitable that slavery was treated just as it was at the convention. Now, I want to take up those three things in turn.

It's undeniable that slavery is in some sense legal under the Constitution. It existed in many of the states at the time of the framing; the Constitution allows the continued importation of slaves for 20 years, and it provides for the recapturing of fugitive slaves. These are all ways in which the legal existence of slavery is recognized in the Constitution.

But the document itself is very careful not to endorse the institution it recognizes. The constitutional clauses that touch on slavery are all written in such a way as to establish unequivocally that slavery is an institution existing under the states, not under the Constitution's authority or with its blessing. The Fugitive Slave Clause, for instance, speaks of "persons held to service or labor in one state *under the laws thereof.*"[6] That is, the Constitution says forcefully that slavery is an institution under the laws of the states, not under *its* laws. The Slave Trade Clause is parallel: it speaks of "the importation of such persons *as any of the existing states shall think proper to admit.*"[7] The nefarious slave trade, then, is a trade of and by the states engaging in it, not of the government formed by the Constitution.

Moreover, as has been frequently noted, the words "slave," "slavery," and the like do not appear in the Constitution, nor are there any racial references. In fact, the first mention of the word "slave" or "slavery" in the Constitution is in the 13th Amendment, abolishing it. Instead of speaking of slaves directly, the Constitution uses awkward and wordy circumlocutions to refer to the slaves—it speaks of persons "held to service or labor" and of "such persons as any of the states now existing shall think proper to admit."[8] If you were parachuted down from Mars and read this, you would have no idea what this was all about.

Avoidance of the words "slave" and "slavery" and the like was altogether deliberate and intentional. At the convention, it was stated explicitly that such words should not appear in the document as a blemish on a system aiming to secure liberty. Moreover, when the Constitution does refer to slaves, it invariably refers to them as "persons." So far as the law of the Constitution is concerned, the slaves are persons, not property, only prevented from full recognition and enjoyment of their personhood by the state laws that treat them as property. The Constitution, then, never recognizes slavery as legitimate, even when it recognizes it as legal under the laws of the slave states.

In denying slavery legitimacy, the Constitution recognizes it as an imperfection, as a defect in the system. But it makes no provision to get rid of it, and indeed it contains many barriers to national action against it. Since slavery is recognized as an institution of the states, the most significant constitutional provision regarding slavery is the provision that isn't there.

The Constitution, as we all used to know, establishes a general government of limited and enumerated powers. None of the powers granted to this government remotely warrant action by the Union against slavery in the states. Slavery within the states is treated as a matter solely for the states themselves to deal with. This acceptance of the existence (if not legitimacy) of slavery in the states speaks against the Neo-Lincolnian theory. This was not something that was accepted only reluctantly. It was just taken for granted. Decisive action against slavery (or for it) was not provided for in the Constitution. Decisive action is deferred and displaced, both in time and place. If such action is to occur, it must occur in the states.

Many of the Founders hoped and expected that such action would be forthcoming, but they did not provide for it. The fact that antislavery sentiment was strong even in many of the states that had many slaves—states like Virginia—and the fact that men like James Madison and Thomas Jefferson—big slaveholders themselves—were cooking up schemes for gradual emancipation within the states seem to confirm the possibility that the institution could be eliminated inside the states. Thus at the Constitutional Convention, Connecticut's Roger Sherman noted "that the abolition of slavery seemed to be going on in the United States, and that the good sense of the several States would probably by degrees complete it."[9] Even some delegates from the Deep South joined in. Abraham Baldwin of Georgia surmised that his home state "if left to herself . . . may probably put a stop to the evil."[10] But if slavery was to end in America, it would not be eliminated by the government established by the Constitution.

The fact of facts about slavery in the Constitution, then, is that it is an institution of the states that have it and is neither established nor legitimated by the Constitution or government of the Union. However, as we have noticed, there are some places in the Constitution where slavery is somehow provided for, where some provision is made to deal with slavery. There are the Neo-Garrisonians' 18 clauses, for example.

I'm going to limit myself to the three clauses the Neo-Lincolnians emphasize and that are very clearly and directly involved with slavery. The presence
of these three clauses points to the fact that although slavery is an institution of the states, there are some places where it necessarily spills over
into the Union. Those are the places touched by our three clauses—places
where the Constitution necessarily had to do something about slavery. I
want to look briefly again at those three main clauses and see what they do.

Of the three, the Fugitive Slave Clause proved over time to provoke the
most difficulty and trouble. Paul Finkelman, a Neo-Garrisonian, thinks
this clause particularly reveals the falsity of the Neo-Lincolnian position
because, contrary to the Neo-Lincolnian way of explaining things about
slavery and the Constitution, the Southerners at the convention made no
threats to take their marbles, or their bat and ball, and go home if they did
not get this protection. Finkelman is, as a matter of fact, quite correct,
and he is also correct to see that this fact does stand in the way of some
aspects of the Neo-Lincolnian theory.

But I'd like to suggest a different interpretation of this clause that does
not lead to Finkelman's Neo-Garrisonian conclusion. According to the
Neo-Madisonian way of looking at this, the basic idea of making the Constitution was that they were trying to construct a federal union of states
with somewhat different domestic orders. One point of such a union was
to have open internal borders to facilitate commerce and other kinds of
intercourse among the member states or citizens of the member states.
Open borders means that there will of necessity be a certain porousness
that makes slaves' escape to free states more possible. The Union, in
order to be stable, however, should not be perceived by its members to
be subversive of their internal order or to be particularly burdensome to
them. One should attempt in making such a union to minimize predictable sources of friction among the members. The open borders and the
contiguousness of slave and free states produced likely threats to the harmony among the states.

Moreover, since many of the new free states had become quite hostile to slavery, they might adopt the very provocative policy of declaring

that all persons within their borders are free. Such is the prerogative of sovereign states to do—to declare or decide on the civil status of people within them. The Fugitive Slave Clause decrees as a matter of friendship or comity between the states that no state shall have the power to do that—that is, to declare escaped slaves free. That is why this clause is located in the part of the Constitution that deals with relations among the states. States have a duty not to become a refuge for fugitive slaves, just as under the Extradition Clause, they have a duty not to become a refuge for escapees from justice from other states.

Moreover, and this is maybe a little more controversial, the Fugitive Slave Clause contains no grant of power to Congress to enforce it. In my opinion, the best reading of this clause is to say that, originally, they did not intend a congressional power to enforce the Fugitive Slave Clause. The clause imposes a duty on the states not to attempt to change the legal status of fugitives, and indeed to "deliver them up," but it has no mechanism to enforce this other than the good faith of the states.

Here is another place where history moved off in a different direction from what the Founders expected. In 1793, Congress passed a Fugitive Slave Act, which was upheld by the Supreme Court in 1842 in the case of *Prigg v. Pennsylvania*—which, in my opinion, was wrongly upheld by the Court. If the Fugitive Slave Clause had been left as originally intended, it would not have been as effective an instrument for aiding slavery as it turned out to be. But in light of the potentially disruptive results of leaving some of the states free to undermine the domestic institutions of other states, it was easy for the convention to adopt the Fugitive Slave Clause, even without the prompting of threats of disunion. But the clause is not, I would maintain, meant as a support for slavery; it is rather a support for comity between the member states in the federal Union.

The Slave Trade Clause was a different matter. Here is a case where indeed some of the states did make threats about not joining the Union if they didn't get their way. So the reason why the Slave Trade Clause was important was that under the Constitution, Congress would be given the power to regulate commerce with foreign nations, and that power would include the power to regulate the slave trade. So here was a place where because of a certain power given to Congress, a certain aspect of the institution of slavery was just put in the hands of the general government—the Union government—and something would have to be said about that policy.

The Neo-Garrisonians concede that this was an area where threats of disunion were made. At the convention, representatives of both South Carolina and Georgia demanded that some provision be made for them to keep the slave trade open, and if not, they claimed they would be compelled not to join the Union. General Charles Cotesworth Pinckney of South Carolina insisted that "S[outh] Carolina & Georgia cannot do without slaves."[11] Another South Carolinian was even more pointed: "South Carolina can never receive the plan [for a constitution] if it prohibits the slave trade."[12]

Neo-Garrisonians believe that they were bluffing. There are many good reasons, the Neo-Garrisonians say, why Georgia and South Carolina wanted to be, and needed to be, part of the Union. Perhaps it was a bluff. But a factor we need to keep in mind when we think about that is how people were thinking about the future of America if this effort at making a Constitution did not succeed. It was already being said that perhaps one big union of all 13 states was not possible, and that instead of that one big union, maybe three smaller, partial unions would be preferable, or at least more possible: one, a New England confederacy; another, a middle states confederacy; and third, a southern states confederacy.

This idea disturbed many people. One of the reasons it disturbed them was because it played into their fears that Britain and other European powers were looking for a way to get a toehold back in this part of the continent. If they did that, and if there were different and competing confederacies, then the European powers would bring with them to America the balance-of-power and great-power politics competition the Americans wanted to avoid. In the face of the possibility that this union wouldn't include all 13 states, it's perhaps understandable why the convention did not wait to see whether South Carolina and Georgia were bluffing, and why they were willing, then, to accept a 20-year extension of the slave trade for those states—and only those states—that wanted to keep it.

Finally, I'd like to turn to the third big clause, the so-called Three-Fifths Clause that deals with taxation and representation. This is probably the clause in the Constitution that has had more nonsense said about it than any other. The usual point is captured in the title of a book, *Three-Fifths of a Man*, with the point being that counting the slaves as three-fifths was a statement of Americans' estimate of the degree of humanity of black people.[13] There are at least two facts that speak against that interpretation. First, free blacks were counted as full persons for purposes of representation, and as the statistics I cited earlier indicate, the number of free blacks was not negligible and was indeed, it seemed, growing. So this was not a racial matter per se. The second fact of significance is that the slave states and the slave owners at the convention were the ones pressing to count the slaves as full persons. And the Northerners, who were in the process of getting rid of slavery, were the ones who wanted to count the slaves for nothing, for zero. This fact I think is most inconvenient for the normally circulated account of the meaning of the Three-Fifths Clause.

The three-fifths formula, in fact, arose under the Articles of Confederation, and it was part of an attempt to come up with a formula that would allow Congress to calculate how much each state owed the general budget to pay into the Treasury of the United States at that time to offset the cost of the war. The original plan in the Articles of Confederation was to assess the total wealth of each state and then charge them in proportion to that. I don't know exactly how one would go about doing that—this would be a daunting task at any time—but imagine trying to do it during a war. After a while, they got the idea that this was not going to work, so they came up with the idea of using population as a surrogate for total wealth—the idea being, in part, that human labor (they were good Lockeans) is the chief source of wealth. But the question then came up: How should they count slave labor? Everybody agreed that slave labor was less productive than free labor because people work harder when they get to keep the fruits of their labor than when not.

So Southerners thought a slave was only half as productive as a free laborer. Northerners, who had a higher estimate of slave labor, thought it was two-thirds as productive as free labor. Remember, what's at stake here is the amount of taxes each state is going to have to pay. So, of course, the Southerners try to minimize it and the Northerners try to maximize it. Now the three-fifths formula arose as a compromise between one-half and two-thirds. That is the mysterious origin of that number.

At the Constitutional Convention, this issue came up because one of the early and most important decisions made provided that representation in the lower house would be in proportion to state population. Again, here was a necessary spillover effect of slavery because something would have to be decided about how to count the slaves when you counted the population. The idea behind population-proportional representation was, in part, that each state should be represented to a degree that reflected its relative wealth, relative power, and influence—that is to say, these were many of the same considerations that went into the original formulation of the three-fifths rule under the Articles. After some back and forth, they decided on three-fifths for many of the same reasons that it had been decided upon under the Articles.

In surveying the provisions that directly touch on slavery, what is striking is how few they are and how much they share one characteristic. They are the places where it was unavoidable that the Constitution take some stand on slavery, build in some power or some policy with regard to the institution of slavery. And when the Constitution dealt with the topic, it was very careful to hold it at arm's length as a matter for and within the states. Otherwise, it stayed away from the topic of slavery.

This arrangement should, I think, be called an acceptance of a certain sort—not the endorsement of slavery as the Neo-Garrisonians have it nor the rejection that the Neo-Lincolnians say—but an acceptance of the principle that, in a federal system, it is a matter up to the states. It is an acceptance only of a certain sort, though, and the embarrassed circumlocutions in the text, the frequent denunciations of slavery as unjust—inside and outside of the convention—show that this was not an acceptance of slavery in the states as a matter of official indifference or neutrality with regard to it. So, to give a sampling of that view, Luther Martin of the slave state Maryland called for abolishing the slave trade because it was "inconsistent with the principles of the revolution."[14] That, I think, was a fairly widely held view. Slavery is accepted as a state institution but, at the same time, regarded as an anomaly and as incompatible with the principles of right endorsed in the revolution and after. Nonetheless, the Constitution did little about this incompatibility. It in effect defers, postpones, or displaces any decision for later and elsewhere. The founding generation acted in the hope that somehow the issue would be taken care of in the future.

My point is that the way in which slavery was treated in the Constitution was inevitable, or at least nearly so, when we understand what the Founders were doing as they understood it. The first and really central point is this: In making a constitution, they were making a federation and not a nation—they were making a union of otherwise independent states for certain very important but still limited purposes. The internal ordering of the members of the federation was not one of the accepted purposes of such unions, and hardly anyone in 1787 thought that was what was at stake in making the Constitution. Almost no one thought that the convention or the union it was making had the power, right, or responsibility to settle questions of the internal ordering of the member states. Abraham Baldwin of Georgia made the point when he intervened in the discussion of the slave trade and said he thought "national objects alone to be before the convention, not [matters] such as [slavery, which] were of a local nature."[15] That in itself made the rest more or less inevitable.

But there was more to it than that, actually, and that more reinforced the same point. The two leading structural principles of the Constitution were to be a new kind of federalism and a new kind of republicanism. As I learned in Walter Berns's Introduction to American Government course, this new kind of federalism involved a direct interaction between the government of the Union and the human individuals within the member states in ways that had never been the case in previous federations. But the condition for this unprecedented kind of interaction is a very clear line of demarcation between matters of rightful concern to the general government and all the remaining matters that belong to the states. The new federalism reaffirmed the general idea that matters of internal governance are not matters for the general government. And that reaffirmation was particularly necessary because of the deep intrusiveness of the general government into the member states.

The republicanism of the Constitution, like every form of republicanism, is a commitment to self-government. Each unit should be republican—that is to say, a self-governing entity. That means that other units should not make decisions for it, and that's a thought that reinforced the division of authority demanded by the new federalism.

So the way slavery was treated in the Constitution was perfectly in accord with, and in a way required by, the nature of the task of union-making as they understood it and by the two chief principles of federalism and republicanism. So despite the Neo-Garrisonians' 18 or more clauses, slavery was not in fact a central theme at the convention, and all of what was done with respect to it was pretty much a side effect of other things that they were doing. That is not to say that they didn't see slavery to be important or that they thought it was insignificant—far from it—but that they saw it as a matter for the individual states and not for the Union. And as I've tried to suggest, in 1787, they at least had some good reason to believe that the states were on a trajectory to abolish this institution that had no place in a free country.

If we conclude that the best way to characterize the place of slavery in the Constitution and in the convention is in terms of inadvertence, deferral, and avoidance, this is not to deny that the issue played a major role in the travail of the American republic in the subsequent years, and perhaps it could have been predicted to do so. But strikingly, none of the leading men at the time of the Founding did so predict. It was not until the crisis over Missouri in 1820 that it became clear that slavery was going to be a major challenge to the constitutional order. The reasons why nobody foresaw this should be clear, I think, from my talk.

There was first the expectation or hope that the issue would take care of itself with the growth of enlightenment, liberal values, and "humanity" within the states. Second, the Founders thought they had provided for all these "spillover" places in the new order. In this they were much mistaken. Many more arose, requiring fresh constitutional-level decisions in a much less favorable environment for deciding. Questions like the fate of slavery in new territory, the role of the postal service in spreading anti- or proslavery opinion, the role of free states in relation to the unanticipated efforts to enforce the Fugitive Slave Clause—these and many other largely unprovided-for issues arose in the post-Founding era.

Finally, there was also the novelty of the federal republic that they created. It was more of a nation than any previous federation, but it was still thought of as a federal arrangement with limited need for a common moral sensibility. As was said at one point in the convention, referring to the Southern slaveholders: "Their consciences are their own."[16] That proved not to be possible. As Lincoln said: "A house divided against itself cannot stand."[17]

The original Founders, however, did not think of it as one house but rather as a subdivision with covered walkways joining the different states or units. The new federalism in time filled in those walkways so that eventually, it did feel more like a house than a subdivision. The result was that both the slave and the free states came to demand that the Union more unequivocally endorse their vision of moral truth. The political struggle became a struggle for recognition as much as for concrete gains and goods. The original arrangement regarding slavery—that is to say, legal but not legitimate—became increasingly untenable.

Political societies in general tend to work toward consistency between legality and legitimacy, and that effort proved to be much of the storyline for pre–Civil War America. So some—the abolitionists—demanded that the reigning legality be brought into conformity with the notion of legitimacy captured in the idea of a "natural rights republic." On the other side were those who tried to redefine legitimacy to match and justify the reigning legal presence of slavery. They rejected the central idea of the natural rights republic—the equal endowment of all human beings with natural rights to life, liberty, and pursuit of happiness. Thus, to the shame of Indiana, my home-state senator rose on the floor of that body to declare the propositions of the Declaration of Independence to be "self-evident lies."[18]

All of this brings us back to Thurgood Marshall and his bicentennial tirade against the Founders. As I hope I have made clear, he had a point, although I think not quite as much of a point as he thought. The Founders were not all-seeing or all-wise. Both history and their constitutional order developed in ways they did not foresee and for which they had not provided well. Yet he ought not to have been so harshly dismissive of them. Because the vision of racial equality in the name of which he denounced them is, after all, a vision built on their commitment to, and their construction of, a natural rights republic—a republic where all men are held to be created equal and endowed by their creator with certain unalienable rights.

Notes

1. Thurgood Marshall, "Remarks at the Annual Seminar of the San Francisco Patent and Trademark Law Association in Maui, Hawaii," May 6, 1987, https://scholarship.law.vanderbilt.edu/vlr/vol40/iss6/3/.

2. John L. Thomas, *The Liberator: William Lloyd Garrison: A Biography* (Little, Brown and Co., 1963), 330.

3. US Const. art. I, § 2, cl. 3.

4. US Const. art. IV, § 2, cl. 3.

5. Watson W. Jennison, "The Contagion of Liberty, 1776–1804," in *Cultivating Race: The Expansion of Slavery in Georgia, 1750–1860* (University Press of Kentucky, 2012), 41–88.

6. US Const. art. IV, § 2 (emphasis added).

7. US Const. art. I, § 9, cl. 1 (emphasis added).

8. US Const. art. IV, § 2, cl. 3; and US Const. art. I, § 9, cl. 1.

9. James Madison, "Madison Debates: August 22," August 22, 1787, Avalon Project, Yale Law School, http://avalon.law.yale.edu/18th_century/debates_822.asp.

10. Madison, "Madison Debates: August 22."

11. Madison, "Madison Debates: August 22."

12. James Madison, "Madison Debates: August 21," August 21, 1787, Avalon Project, Yale Law School, http://avalon.law.yale.edu/18th_century/debates_821.asp.

13. Floyd Bixler McKissick, *Three-Fifths of a Man* (Macmillan, 1969).

14. Madison, "Madison Debates: August 21."

15. Madison, "Madison Debates: August 22."

16. Oliver Ellsworth, "Landholder VI," Teaching American History, December 10, 1787, https://teachingamericanhistory.org/document/landholder-vi/.

17. Abraham Lincoln, "House Divided Speech," Teaching American History, June 16, 1858, https://teachingamericanhistory.org/document/house-divided-speech-3/.

18. *Canton Weekly Register* 8, no. 7 (October 28, 1856): 3, https://idnc.library.illinois.edu/?a=d&d=CWR18561028-01.

3

The Constitution as Political Theory: Between Rationalism and Reverence

JAMES W. CEASER

September 16, 2014

The Constitution of the United States of America is first and foremost a legal document. It serves as the supreme law of the land, establishing the basic structure or framework of the federal government, determining the powers of the federal government as well as certain powers of the states, and delineating a set of basic rights.

Yet, the Constitution has played another important, far less remarked upon role that is unrelated either to its status as law or to any connection it has to the United States. The body of thought that went into developing the Constitution, and then into explaining and defending it during the debate over ratification, comprises a notable contribution to political theory. The Americans who took the lead in this task engaged fundamental questions of political life, challenged a number of well-known philosophical positions, and offered new theoretical insights. The best of their work, which found its expression in the Federalist Papers, merits a place alongside such classics in political theory as John Locke's *Second Treatise*, Jean-Jacques Rousseau's *Second Discourse*, and Edmund Burke's *Reflections on the Revolution in France*.

One of the main topics of reflection in constitutional thought grew directly out of the practical business at hand: making a new government. Two questions attracted attention: First, what is the best or recommended way to go about forming a government? And second, how does a government, once formed, shape thereafter the public's epistemological premises? (By this last term I mean the way in which people conceive of and process the political world about them—whether, for example, people lay claim to being able to figure everything out by the use of their reason or whether they allow themselves space for revering things past and things noble.)

These questions are admittedly far removed from current concerns relating to the Constitution, such as the proper scope of the president's power or the degree of protection that should be afforded to businesses claiming a right of free exercise of religion. With the usual academic pride, I can therefore proclaim the irrelevance of the remarks to follow. Pushing perversity further, I can, in the Constitution's own language, solemnly swear (or affirm) to avoid mention this afternoon of any of the major constitutional principles commonly referenced in public discussions, whether it be separation of powers, judicial review, federalism, or checks and balances.

Beyond that, I pledge never to refer to the text of the Constitution—neither to an amendment nor to an article or a clause nor even to a single phrase or word. I include here the now-famous term "capitation," which Chief Justice John Roberts plucked from somewhere in Article I to salvage the Affordable Care Act. Needless to say, you will not hear a citation from any Supreme Court decision, current or past.

Perhaps, then, it would be appropriate at this time to pause in order to allow the law professors and policy experts in the audience to make a discreet exit. For those who have chosen to remain, who must be persons of a more theoretical disposition, I should offer a preliminary point of clarification about the meaning of political theory.

Political theory has been defined in a strict sense as the quest for truth or knowledge about political things. It has been distinguished from political thought, which is the exposition of political ideas, usually to support a given view or position. For example, most books and articles that appear on the subjects of liberalism and conservatism fall into the category of political thought, not political theory. Political thought may borrow arguments from political theory, but its goal is less the search for truth or knowledge than the furtherance of a political objective.

It turns out that by the exacting definition of political theory, many texts widely considered to be works of political theory are in fact works of political thought. Burke's *Reflections*, which derived from a speech meant to awaken people to the dangers of the French Revolution, is a case in point. The Federalist Papers, which sought first and foremost to secure ratification of the Constitution, are also a work of political thought. Yet, it has also been recognized that they relied greatly on arguments deriving from political theory and that they introduced many important theoretical ideas. In a preface to one of the earliest collected volumes of these papers, Alexander Hamilton concluded as follows: "The great wish is that it may promote the cause of truth and lead to a right judgment of the true interests of the community."[1]

The Federalist Papers, to which I will be referring mostly today, have two other features to commend them from the perspective of those interested in political theory. First, because they addressed a real-life political event, they were compelled to treat many interesting issues that theoretical writers, who have full control of the content of their work, have ignored. Consent by the new instrumentality of ratification of a written document is an example. Second, because The Federalist Papers hazard propositions of what will or will not take place depending on the decision of ratification, they allow us, looking back on the work, to assess the merits of some of the arguments. What we have is a kind of controlled experiment for analyzing certain ideas.

Government by Accident or Reflection?

The first question to be considered revolves around the preferred way to form governments. It is raised at the outset of the Federalist Papers, in the opening paragraph of the book, in a long and complex sentence, a part of which reads,

> It seems to have been reserved to the people of this country, by their conduct and example, to decide the important question, whether societies of men are really capable or not

of establishing good government from reflection and choice,
or whether they are forever destined to depend for their political
constitutions on accident and force.[2]

Setting aside for now some of the difficulties in this passage, the basic
issue posed seems clear enough. There are two possibilities: Either government can come into being by "reflection and choice"—that is, by some
individuals consciously making a plan to which the people consent—or
government can come into being by "accident and force"—that is, by
chance and without consent.

The authors of the Federalist Papers leave no doubt about which of
these alternatives they hoped to see confirmed. If the experiment in ratifying and implementing the proposed constitution succeeded, it would
lend support to the position that human beings—using their reason—can
make good government and that this is the preferred, perhaps even the
only, way of doing so. Let us notice, too, that the issue to be determined
here goes beyond the local matter of government in America to a general
question of political theory.

I confess that for many years, I read this passage without ever enter-
taining the possibility of the superiority of the alternative position. The
option favoring reflection seemed to me so obvious as not to require
further consideration. Nor, in fact, do the Federalist Papers at this early
point offer any argument on its behalf.

Obviously, I missed something crucial. Far from being universally accepted,
the position supported by the Federalist Papers had been questioned or
rejected by many political thinkers. Just a few years later, in the aftermath of
the French Revolution, a debate about the merits of the two positions became
one of the central points of controversy within political theory.

I will dispense for the moment with the dimension of whether choice
is better than force and focus on the dimension of whether reflection is to
be preferred to accident in the formation of governments.

On the side favoring reflection, the works of many of the theorists
who constructed models of government on the basis of philosophical or

scientific reasoning come immediately to mind. This tradition stretches all the way back to Plato's *Republic*, where Socrates builds a whole city in speech on the basis of such an analysis. Of course, some of these "imaginary republics and principalities," as Machiavelli refers to them, were never intended as realistic plans so much as intellectual exercises to teach about the possibilities and limits of political life.[3]

However this may be, the idea of making government on the basis of reason—ideally, from scratch—captured the theoretical imagination. By the time one gets to many modern philosophers, the plans offered to build political systems wholesale were often meant to be taken in earnest. Machiavelli himself dwelled on the best methods for new princes in a new territory to establish solid orders, although perhaps not by consent. A century later, we find René Descartes, the first great modern philosopher, contemplating the construction of cities in a manner akin to an engineer designing a great project. For modern rationalist thinkers, the point was to employ reflection—not to imagine a world but to change it.

On the other side, there is a whole school of thought, whose roots are found in the political theory of Montesquieu and David Hume, that challenges the wisdom of encouraging the making or remaking of governments. It does so not just on the prudential grounds that if a government is to be made, the project should be carried out with great care and perhaps only when absolutely necessary. No, the school I am referring to affirmed the alternative theoretical proposition that good government is more apt to result from growth and accretion, which is to say, from something akin to accident.

To be sure, most proponents of this position left room for the exercise of human agency at the margins, where political actors might inflect the development of government by making reforms. But it was a grave error, they insisted, to proclaim the superiority of the idea of wholesale making (or, in the terminology of the day, "new-modeling") government.

The best-known spokesperson of this position is Burke. In characterizing his beloved constitution of England—which of course has no written constitution—Burke observed that the English system was not "formed upon a regular plan or with any unity of design" but that it was developed "in a great length of time, and by a great variety of accidents."[4] The British constitution added parts "gradually, and almost insensibly, accommodated themselves to each other."[5] He noted that "the very idea of the fabrication of a new government is enough to fill us with disgust and horror."[6]

By this standard, a day that marks the formation of government by a plan, like Constitution Day, should be an occasion for mourning, not celebration. A law should be enacted to require that all flags be flown at half-mast as a sign of national repentance, not only for having dared to make a new government but also for having boasted about doing so.

Consider three of the arguments advanced in favor of what many today no doubt regard as a strange position.

First, the very act of conceiving of new-modeling government contains something fearful about it. It presupposes a central authority with power to make and remake a government. It thereby endorses, at least conceptually, the existence of a power without limits. Once acknowledged and accepted, what is there to prevent such a power from being invoked again?

Second, human reason is unequal to the task of erecting a plan of this magnitude. It is too big and complex a job. To cite Hume, "no human genius, however comprehensive, is able, by mere dint of reason and reflection, to effect" a project of this magnitude.[7] If, as some say today, you cannot remake one-sixth of the economy, what makes you think that you can remake nine-tenths of a political system?

Third, a public position in favor of creating a new model of government is destabilizing. New-modeling government sets a dangerous precedent. If a government is new-modeled once, why not new-model it again, just as those of a progressive temperament are inclined to tear down a house deemed old or obsolete and replace it with something new and modern?

The almost natural process of growth and accommodation that Burke described for the formation of government is often referred to in political theory textbooks as the organic model. The model is based on what is said to be the manner of development in biology as seen, for example, in the slow growth of a stately oak tree, its branches spreading out unsymmetri-cally in improbable directions. Nothing is planned, yet the result fits.

Applying this idea by analogy to the formation of government, a polit-ical system is said to evolve slowly by accidents and incremental adjust-ments, with customs and habits developing to support it. The people come to appreciate the resulting heritage or tradition, which adds another prop to preserve the system.

The organic theory in the historical version articulated by Burke pro-vides the premises for what many subsequently called conservatism or traditionalism. In a more analytic account of this process, some thinkers posited the existence of a general principle of spontaneous order at work in human affairs (and, by some accounts, in the physical world as well).

The principle of spontaneous order is nothing less than the idea that accident inevitably, over a certain period, assures a good result. The economist Friedrich Hayek based his whole social theory—as do many libertarians today—on this benign principle, the origin of which Hayek traced back to the thought of the 18th-century Scottish philosopher Adam Ferguson. "Nations," wrote Ferguson, "stumble upon establish-ments, which are indeed the result of human action, but not the execu-tion of any human design."[8]

The organic model stands in stark opposition to the idea of rational making, which has no similarly accepted name. To call it the inorganic model would probably be greeted as a provocation. Better to label it the synthetic or the rationalist model and, in its predominant modern form, label it the Enlightenment rationalist model. Proponents of this model also appeal to nature, but in a very different sense than that posited in the organic conception, with its tender picture of the growth of its beloved oak tree. Nature under the synthetic model refers instead to necessary relationships—abstract laws of nature—that are grasped by reason. This is not your garden variety of nature.

I am almost compelled at the American Enterprise Institute to digress a moment here to respond to a different provocation. If, as many continen-tal thinkers and a few Americans hold, the organic position is taken to be the definitive criterion for defining conservatism, then America, insofar as it accepts the Federalist Papers' preference for forming government by reflection and choice, cannot give birth to a genuine form of conservatism.

For American conservatives to accede without resistance to this European argument would be to allow others to determine the meaning of words and to govern us without our consent. We would do better to object to this long train of abuse and seek to teach our assuming brothers and sisters in Europe that there is an American form of conservatism that is no less worthy than the variant they espouse.

One fact, though, is undeniable. By underscoring the claim that good government is made by reflection, constitutional thought in America has promoted a rationalist mode of thought within the American mind. Some today, like Professor Sandy Levinson from the University of Texas, pursue this strand to its end and call for redoing the Constitution. Levinson rarely misses an occasion to quote approvingly from *Federalist* 1, adding for good measure a stirring passage from *Federalist* 14: "Is it not the glory of the people of America, that, whilst they have paid a decent regard to the opinions of former times and other nations, they have not suffered a blind veneration for antiquity [or] for custom?"[9]

It is also fair to conclude that the American claim of having made a government has had a profound effect on subsequent history. For better or worse, the American example has worked throughout much of the world to encourage efforts to write constitutions and new-model governments.

Political thought, as distinct from political theory, often abstracts from reality and simplifies in order to promote a given position. There may therefore be less theory and more rhetoric than meets the eye in the organic and rationalist positions. Many who claim that good government is made by reflection would no doubt concede that it sometimes comes about by accident, and many who argue that good government results from accident might allow that it sometimes can be produced by reflection.

What is at issue here is a dispute about doctrines. A doctrine is a firm conclusion put forward publicly as a general rule that is intended to influence the course of events. It is a political instrument. The organic model probably rests on the logic that because so much destruction and fanaticism have resulted from attempts to remake government, it is best to promote the doctrine that good government results from accident. The synthetic or rationalist model counters with the logic that because so much folly, ignorance, and superstition are embedded in tradition, it is best to support the doctrine that good government is established by reflection. Political theory is rarely rule bound, which is to say it is not doctrinaire.

To this point, I have presented only the beginning of constitutional thought on forming government. While the Federalist Papers come down on the side of remaking, their authors were nevertheless deeply sensible of some of the practical concerns raised by organic objectors. But they go further than that. In a way that I hope will become clear, they seek to qualify the synthetic view, not on the basic point of the possibility of making good government by reflection but on its possible derivative idea of encouraging the popular epistemological premise in favor of new-modeling government.

American constitutional thought aims in a certain way to combine—I refrain from saying synthesize—rationalism and traditionalism. It does so in part by reaching beyond the modern expressions of these positions and drawing on classical expressions of both positions. The forging of this combination marks the most important contribution of American constitutional thought to political theory.

Founders on Founding

I turn now to the Federalist Papers' treatment of another facet of the question of how governments are made: the theme referred to in the 18th century as "the lawgiver," which we today usually call "the founder." The two terms are not perfect synonyms, but they are close enough to proceed here as if they are largely the same.

The process of founding involves setting in motion the idea for a fundamental change, devising a plan for the new order of society (this is the law-giving activity strictly understood), and then acting to put the plan into effect. The founder—it could be founders—performs some or all of these tasks. The one—or ones—subsequently credited with having performed the most essential work wins the acclaim of being called a founder and joins a very exclusive club.

Before looking at the political thought on this subject, it is important to remind ourselves how often we Americans today speak about founding and founders. It is a huge theme in American discourse, both academic and popular, and is far more prevalent here than is the case in most other nations. For all of the attention given to the topic, however, the word is used with a certain imprecision. Are the Founders the leaders of the revolution or the makers of the Constitution?

For the most part, at public ceremonies and in speeches, the two are grouped together to form one august body of Founders. The names of some of the revolutionary figures, like Thomas Jefferson and John Adams, often receive greater attention than James Madison or Gouverneur Morris. Yet if pressed, most who write about this era consider the making of the Constitution as being more at the core of the general idea of the Founding.

The Founders overall enjoy a favorable reputation, although as anyone in the field of education knows, they encounter no shortage of criticism. The Founders are often charged, sometimes with an unseemly glee, with being defenders of wealth and privilege or of misogynists or racists or any combination of the three. However this may be, America does celebrate its Founders by building monuments in their honor and by naming buildings and streets after them. What, after all, could be more iconic of America than Madison Avenue?

What accounts for the prominence that is accorded in America to the Founders? One answer is that it is a simple result of the facts of history objectively considered. It is a reflection, no more and no less, of how things took place. Americans speak so much of the Founding and Founders because we had a founding and founders.

But there is another possibility: Americans pay so much attention to the Founders because of a theoretical treatment of this theme in constitutional thought. This treatment sets out the centrality of the concept of founding, ascribes to it a positive value, and attaches it to the act of making the Constitution.

The idea of founding derives directly from the aforementioned doctrine in favor of governments being made. If governments are made, then there must be a maker or founder. The elaboration of this concept encourages people to look for a founding and for founders. Absent this theoretical position, Americans might not view the Founders in the way that we have. Indeed, we might not call them founders at all.

It is easy to understand why a strand of traditionalist thought resists the use of the word "founder." If good government results from growth and accident, then it is unwise to speak of founders in an exalted sense. Some traditionalists, moreover, insist that not only is it unwise but also untrue. The American Revolution was never anything more than an effort to restore old English rights, and the Constitution represented an effort to preserve the revolution's objectives, which arguably were endangered by flaws in the first constitutions. What we had in 1787, then, was not a founding or founders but a reform and reformers.

The full view of founding runs throughout the Federalist Papers. It is treated most extensively in *Federalist* 38, which is the sequel to *Federalist* 1. It begins by picking up on its main theme, promising an analysis of cases "in which government has been established with deliberation and consent" (the equivalent of reflection and choice).[10] This theme is also now presented in more detail and with greater complexity.

America, we learn, is not the first example of a government formed by deliberation and consent. More importantly, the pair of deliberation and consent, far from being a unity or a whole, consists of two distinct and separable elements. There are, accordingly, four possibilities in establishing government, not two. Governments can be formed not only, as *Federalist* 1 implied, by reflection and choice or by accident and force but also by reflection, force, and, though this option is not discussed, accident and consent.

Federalist 38 provides one of the more complete treatments of the topic of the lawgiver in modern political thought. It merits study alongside of the surprisingly few other modern considerations of this theme, the most important of which are found in the writings of Machiavelli and Rousseau. These two authors also elevate the function, or office, of founding, discussing, among others, such notable figures as Moses and Romulus.

The Federalist Papers likewise survey some of the great lawgivers of antiquity, some 14 in all, including Lycurgus, the founder of Sparta, and Solon, who established the democratic constitution in Athens. America's founding is placed into the context of these other monumental foundings, with a comparison among them invited. Since the Founding had not yet been achieved in America when the Federalist Papers were written, it was premature to pronounce a final verdict. A judgment, in any case, would have been indelicate given that the authors of the Federalist Papers would qualify as being among the Founders.

The late-18th century was still an age, unlike today, in which leaders might have felt some reluctance at beginning every sentence with "I." Yet there is no doubt that the Federalist Papers sought to place in the reader's mind the possibility that America's founders should be considered the rivals of, if not indeed the replacements for, the founders of antiquity as the most esteemed models.

It is difficult to choose between the two possibilities mentioned: that we have founders because we had founders and that we have founders because of a theoretical argument that favored the idea of founding. As much as academics today prefer to wave around the little metaphysical talisman known as the social construction of reality, I cannot help but think that there is something to the notion that there is a real history. At the same time, it would be foolish to deny that theoretical doctrines greatly influence how we see and interpret events.

If it can be surmised that American constitutional thought had the effect of building up "founding," it is even more evident that alternative modern theoretical accounts about forming government have had the effect—at least they have tried—of diminishing the idea of founding. Under the organic theory, the function or office of founder all but disappears. Because governments are said to grow and not to be made, there is no maker. History is interpreted so that accident or an inevitable process replaces founders. If there ever were founders, they came in some ancient and heroic time no longer applicable to modern politics. Individuals today who aspire to the office of founder, far from meriting praise, are presented as fanatics bound to bring disaster.

Nor is it just the organic model that downplays founding. In the political thought from which Americans otherwise borrowed so much—I am referring to the work of Locke—the theme of founding is also largely absent. It is replaced by a theoretical construct: the idea that societies originate in a compact or contract. To be sure, this idea is presented as a theoretical supposition. Yet it is meant to have an effect on how we think about origins. It is meant to replace the historical efforts of a founder or founders—which is contingent or accidental—with a theory of contract, which is certain and universal. Liberal-contract political theory has little place for founding, and it has all but banished the figure of the founder from political analysis.

It is interesting to speculate about why the Federalist Papers diverge from most modern thought on the question of founding. Since founders and founding are so conspicuous in classical political theory—featured, for example, in the works of Aristotle, Plutarch, and Xenophon—it seems that American constitutional thought, along with the thought of Machiavelli and Rousseau, draws more from classical political philosophy.

In addition, since American constitutional thought arises from and is enmeshed in actual political events, it stays much closer to the phenomena of politics than does organic theory or compact theory, both of which abstract from political life. American thought in this respect is less doctrinal than the other modern approaches and more inclined to recognize the role of accident in human affairs, like the chance appearance of capable founders at a given place and at a given time. Such, after all, was the reality that these American leaders were experiencing.

Greatness and the Founding

Quitting such speculations, it is more important to ask why American constitutional thought embraced this view of founding and what effect it was intended to have. The Federalist Papers' account of founding and founders was above all meant to lend support to the idea of political greatness. It was meant to keep this idea alive inside of modern political life, not only, as the professional critics might say, for the self-interested reason that the American leaders themselves might be its beneficiaries—though there is nothing dishonorable in that—but also for the good that it would contribute to political life.

Some of the alternative modern theories, in their doctrinal bids to control the course of political life, sought to squeeze out the idea of greatness. The Federalist Papers do just the opposite, denying that politics can ever be controlled by a science or doctrine. It has been remarked that the American system of government was so constructed that institutional mechanisms might reduce the reliance on individual talent and that "enlightened statesmen will not always be at the helm."[11] This is true enough, but it does not obviate the fact that politics needed and would always need the contribution of great persons. The Federalist Papers emphasize—they certainly do not seek to obscure or hide—the fact that political talents and virtues are unequal.

The insistence on individuals of high rank in America is something of a paradox. The Constitution abolishes formal titles and establishes popular government. Yet those who took the lead in creating it showed no hesitancy in recognizing and underwriting the idea of hierarchy in the realm of political action. Far from being embarrassed by greatness, the authors of the Federalist Papers expand the scope of hierarchy. Greatness is an idea that bids us to look up to something that stands out as beyond the normal or the average. The idea of founding keeps alive an aristocratic idea.

As for the qualities that comprise greatness, it is impossible to supply an exhaustive checklist. Political greatness is distinct and particular, analogous to the genius of the most celebrated poets or musicians. The most that can be sketched are proximate qualities or models. The Federalist Papers celebrate the courage, both military and intellectual, of the leaders of the revolution. Their willingness to risk so much for what promised to be of benefit, not only for America but also "for the whole human race," is to be lauded.[12]

The Federalist Papers also, however, quietly emphasize another model, which is found in the figure of a certain kind of lawgiver. This figure possesses sagacity, which in modern times includes an in-depth knowledge of the science of politics; judgment and flexibility, which consists in the ability to take cognizance of the situation in which one acts and the capacity to fit scientific knowledge to the particular circumstances; and a combination of persistence and boldness, which is demonstrated in the account interspersed throughout the Federalist Papers of how those who undertook the project to create a new constitution did so with such commitment to the limits of the law and even a little bit beyond. While the Federalist Papers are a book about the Constitution, they are also a work of a different genre. They are a modern mirror of princes, in which the qualities of the lawgiver become a model of virtue.

Looking back, it is interesting to consider how well America's founders achieved the renown that the Federalist Papers sought for them. The American founding is widely considered today as the seminal event of modern constitutionalism, and America's founders, including the leaders of the revolution, are among the few in the world honored as great successes, sharing the stage with perhaps only Mahatma Gandhi and Nelson Mandela.

The founders of antiquity have largely been forgotten, eclipsed by the Americans. Among the moderns, many who have vied for fame, and who acquired it for a moment, have fallen by the wayside. In the former Soviet Union, the outsized statues of Lenin have mostly been torn down, their mighty stone ground to dust. In Russia, the anticipated monuments to Vladimir Putin, on horseback with shirt off and abs bulging, have yet to appear. Mao, though still formally credited as a founder in China, is no longer considered to supply the model for the system. Even in the case of Ataturk, the modern lawgiver who did so much to transform the habits and mores of the Turkish people, it would appear now that his project is under threat and at risk of being dismantled.

Why a Written Constitution?

I would like to turn now to the Federalist Papers' view of the way to go about forming a government. On this point, the authors go so far as to claim openly that America's lawgivers made improvements on "the ancient mode of preparing and establishing regular plans of government."[13] The Federalist Papers discuss three differences between the Americans and the ancients in their approaches to founding.

The first difference concerns the number of founders. The ancients always settled on a single person, "one illustrious citizen," whereas the Americans turned to a group, "an assembly of men."[14] The ancients, according to the Federalist Papers, rejected a group because it would more likely fall into discord and fail in the execution of the project. Other writers on the subject of founding, like Machiavelli and Descartes, seem to follow the ancients in adding the point that the most rational of plans emanate from a single mind.

The Federalist Papers acknowledge the risk of group discord, which may be more dangerous for successful founding than the possible perfidy of a single person. Where the Americans break with the ancients is on the question of whether the one or the few will produce the better plan. There can be more wisdom, they argue, deriving from discussions among a "select body" than from the work of a single mind. It is perhaps for this reason that the Federalist Papers refine their own position by changing the word "reflection," found in *Federalist* 1, to "deliberation," found in *Federalist* 38. The Americans introduce the concept of deliberation into the idea of founding and replace the founder with the founders.

It could be that the Federalist Papers were only justifying the fact that the task of remaking American government, from a legal standpoint, had been carried out by the Constitutional Convention. Yet, it seems clear that the real work of deliberation being referred to was that carried out by the prime movers involved in planning, writing, and explaining the Constitution—individuals such as Madison, George Washington, Alexander Hamilton, James Wilson, and Morris. It is this "select body" that comprises the persons we generally regard as the founders, not all the delegates who attended the convention in Philadelphia.

The second difference between the ancient and the American mode of establishing government involves the issue of consent. This difference was not absolute, since a number of the ancient founders proceeded by seeking consent. But the most famous among the ancient lawgivers—including Lycurgus, the founder of Sparta—relied on a measure of compulsion, whether by physical arms or by the manipulation of superstition.

Founding by the method of reflection and force has its obvious advantage. The perfection of the plan will not need to be sacrificed to the limitations of popular views. (The most vociferous advocates today of the idea of founding by reflection and force, though they do not seem to recognize this fact themselves, are the legions of critics of the founders, who berate them for failing to rid the nation of slavery in 1787.)

Acceptance by consent means that the lawgiver must settle for something less than perfect. Wisdom must bend to consent. The Federalist Papers here cite Solon, the lawgiver of democracy in Athens, who "confessed that he had not given his countrymen the government best suited to their happiness, but most tolerable to their prejudices."[15] The American founding in this respect appears to be closer to the methods of Solon than to those of Lycurgus. Founding by force was out of the question, not least because the American lawgivers in 1787 did not have physical arms at their disposal.

It was not the necessity of the case, however, that guided their decision. They chose choice because it was the supreme test of the viability of republican government. The ratification of the Constitution by consent arguably stands as the most important event in the establishment of modern republican government. In all human affairs, the initial act tends to be the most important one, setting the precedent for all that comes after.

Compare the American case in 1787 to the European one today, where various versions of the European Union (EU) have been submitted to referenda in a number of countries—including Denmark, France, Ireland, and the Netherlands—and where the EU has routinely been rejected. Never mind! The elites continue to build Europe and even to pass a constitution by other means. Does that not reveal something about the spirit or manner in which governance in Europe takes place?

The third difference between the ancient mode of founding and the American method turned on the use of a written constitution. The Americans set out in one document the basic structure of government and its basic powers and limitations. The ancients, apparently, did not.

The instrument of a written constitution is now so much taken for granted that few even recognize it as a chosen instrument. It is known, of course, that a nation can have an unwritten constitution in the sense of a known set of stable laws, customs, and understandings that structure and limit government. Great Britain is an example. It is the oldest and arguably the most constitutional of the constitutional governments in the world. But it is widely regarded as a relic or a curiosity. It has been all but forgotten that there were once no written constitutions and that theoretical objections were once advanced in opposition to the whole idea.

Among these objections, to mention only the most prominent, is the argument that a written constitution can never be law in a true sense. Necessity or reason of state will dictate that the most basic elements of the law may need to be set aside or ignored for the good or survival of the nation. The highest, or supreme, law will need to be violated, with the dangerous consequence that respect for law as a whole will be undermined. Better, then, not to make the fundamental structure of governance a matter of written law.

In looking back on the original period of American constitution making, which includes the writing of the state constitutions immediately after the break from Britain in 1776, it is surprising to learn that some American leaders counted the idea of a written constitution as one of their great theoretical innovations. Jefferson contended that Virginia was

the first of the nations of the earth, which assembled its wise
men peaceably together to form a fundamental constitution, to
commit it to writing, and place it among their archives, where
every one should be free to appeal to its text.[16]

Jefferson may have been in error in placing Virginia before South
Carolina, but on the main point about the novelty of written constitutions, I do not know that his claim has ever been definitively controverted.

Given the commitment to the idea of popular consent, which had
already become accepted in some of the states, a written document in
1787 was necessary. The ratifying bodies had to consent to something, and
it was only by referring to a common text that people assembled in different places at different times could conduct the exercise. The history of
the ratification process bears this out. The main features of the proposed
constitution were discussed and debated not only in the ratifying conven-
tions but also in pamphlets and in the popular press, as was the case with
most of the essays in the Federalist Papers.

Yet, the significance of a written text went far beyond the requirements
demanded by the procedure of consent. Conceived as supreme law, the
Constitution marked an innovation in the form of government. It placed
a written law above the ordinary government, meaning that no statute
passed and no act taken by any official can rightfully claim to stand if it
is inconsistent with the Constitution. To fortify this legal hierarchy, the
Constitution derives its legitimacy from what is said to be the people.

It was enacted not by the ordinary processes of government but by a
distinct process of ratification defined in the Constitution. Subsequent
additions to it were to be made through a special process of amendment
distinct from the ordinary method of legislation. The Federalist Papers
speak of the novel character of this plan:

The important distinction so well understood in America,
between a Constitution established by the people and unalterable by the government, and a law established by the

government and alterable by the government, seems to have
been little understood and less observed in any other country.[17]

The decisive principle is that the will of governing bodies and government officials is subordinate to a written law that government itself cannot alter.

Ratification was a historical event that has affected subsequent political theory. One of the great inventions of modern political theory, beginning in the 16th century, was the social contract. It is fundamental to the
thought of Locke, and by the 18th century many viewed the contract as
the juridical source of legitimate government.

Yet as critics of this idea pointed out, the contract was never more
than a hypothesis, written about in theoretical books but rarely or
ever to be found in practice. The American innovation of popular ratification of a written constitution gave this theoretical idea a concrete
legal-institutional form. It operationalized the social contract. This development has had an enormous impact on the growth of modern constitutionalism, notwithstanding the many abuses of ratification by resorts to
outright fraud and threats of force.

Reverencing the Constitution

The idea of a written constitution, if it was indeed an American discovery,
is coupled in the Federalist Papers with an equally important contribution
that relates to the way in which people are to regard the document. The
issue here is fundamental: What kind of thing is a written constitution?
From a legal standpoint, as we have seen, a written constitution is higher
law. But is it merely law, or does it perform a further function and have a different status? Is the Constitution something to be venerated—something
that endows government with respect and contributes to its stability
and endurance—and that provides a bond that connects the people to
the nation?

Federalist 49 develops the doctrine of attaching the sentiment of reverence to the Constitution. As with the idea of a written constitution, many today can easily overlook the originality of this doctrine, so widely is it accepted today that the Constitution is supposed to be looked up to (a little bit, anyhow).

Yet there is nothing logical that connects veneration with what are, after all, just words on a page. Nor, apparently, was it originally conceived that it should be so regarded. Historians whom I have queried on this point, since I have not found it extensively researched, have confirmed that there likely was no expectation in 1787 that the Constitution would be revered. Further evidence for this contention may be seen in how people look at other constitutions. It is a strange kind of person who professes reverence for, say, the constitution of Illinois or of California. Not only do these constitutions not possess this status, but they also do not, so to speak, seem to ask for it.

The idea of reverence for the Constitution was thus a creation of the Federalist Papers. Once promulgated, it was by no means universally accepted. Jefferson, among others, strongly resisted it. Though Jefferson fully subscribed to the legal view that a written constitution was higher law, he deplored the slightest movement toward endowing such a code of law with higher status. With disdain he wrote:

> Some men look at constitutions with sanctimonious reverence, and deem them like the arc of the covenant, too sacred to be touched. They ascribe to the men of the preceding age a wisdom more than human, and suppose what they did to be beyond amendment.[18]

In line with the spirit of this view, Jefferson had earlier proposed that all constitutions should expire after 19 years, roughly a generation by his calculation, and that a new document be prepared and submitted to the people for ratification. Just like any other law, constitutions should change and keep pace with the times. Though Jefferson's proposal may strike many today as quixotic, it reflected what was no doubt a widespread understanding of the nature of a written constitution.

Even today, some 14 state constitutions include provisions that require a periodic remake. As the political scientist John Dinan has shown, America has developed two distinct views about constitutions: a Jeffersonian view, found in many states, of a charter that is easily changed or rewritten and a Federalist view, found at the national level, of a permanent document that changes only rarely. The one is regarded in a utilitarian light; the other carries additional symbolic qualities that engage the sentiments.

Why did the Federalist Papers create the doctrine of constitutional reverence? One set of arguments rested on practical considerations, though practical in the most expansive sense of the term. The experience of the leading figures in writing and promoting the Constitution led them to appreciate just how difficult it was to secure a happy outcome for this kind of venture. The odds of success, they concluded, would always be slim, and there were always grave risks in trying. Every attempt at remaking government creates instability and threatens to divide the nation.

These leaders were also aware of how favorable, relatively speaking, the circumstances were in their day for accomplishing their objective. The proposed constitution was being considered at a time when the people still had unusual confidence and trust in their leaders, most notably Washington, and when there was a lingering unity of purpose stemming from the revolution. A fact of still greater importance was one that the Federalist Papers could not openly avow: that the main figures involved were persons of exceptional talents, rare devotion to the public good, and, in the case of a few, extensive knowledge of the science of politics. Chance or accident, though it did not take the place of reflection in the making of the Constitution, played a critical, perhaps decisive, role in its ratification.

Given these facts, the conclusion drawn was that it would be best to lock in the gain. Veneration of the Constitution was a means to assure its durability and avoid the temptations to engage in experiments of new-modeling the government. Durability would not exclude changes, which the

Constitution allows for by the process of amendment. But amendment is not made easy, as this would defeat the objective of durability.

Although the Federalist Papers acknowledged that there would be a need for occasional changes, their authors worried about the quality of amendments. Because each amendment focuses on one object, there was a danger of ignoring the relation between the part and the whole system. Overall, the goal was to ensure the continuing integrity of the general design. Veneration of the Constitution, even more than the high legal threshold for change imposed by the Constitution, was the primary means to this end.

The Federalist Papers second these practical reasons for creating the doctrine of constitutional veneration with an important theoretical consideration. A main concern in forming any government is its effect on shaping the public's epistemological premises. The fate of the whole system may rest on identifying and inculcating the premise or combination of premises suited to maintaining it. Premises cannot be enacted directly by law. To the extent that they are chosen, they are put into effect by means of political ideas or doctrines.

American constitutional thought sought to combine elements of rationalist and traditionalist epistemological premises. The rationalist epistemological premise is that the public can and should decide matters by the standard of reason. As Jefferson wrote to John Tyler, "No experiment can be more interesting than that we are now trying, & which we trust will end in establishing the fact that man may be governed by reason and truth."[19] This premise includes not only the idea that individuals are capable of proposing good plans of government but also the claim that the public can judge and endorse these plans. The age-old problem of securing consent for wisdom is not so difficult as was once thought. It has begun to be resolved and will prove less and less an obstacle as mankind progresses.

The traditionalist premise calls attention to the limits of reason. In one respect, it may question whether human beings can ever plan a good government; in another, it has doubts about the ease of public acceptance of such a plan. The Federalist Papers reject the first point of the traditionalist argument but are partly sympathetic to the second. The extreme rational-ist view looks to be a prejudice. Governments rest on opinion more than on reason. Popular consent to wisdom is and will always remain a huge problem that no degree of enlightenment, its boast notwithstanding, can overcome. The acceptance of good government inevitably will depend in some measure on chance.

This conclusion opens the door in the Federalist Papers to the need to shape a people who have a capacity to revere. Reverence is an epistemo-logical premise to be valued in its own right. If a disposition to venerate was seen as instrumental for supporting the Constitution, so it can be said that the Constitution was seen as instrumental for promoting a dis-position to venerate. Venerating the Constitution becomes a means for promoting other desired ends, chief of which is an appreciation of the Founding and the Founders. The Founders only become founders if they create an enduring fundamental law. If there is no enduring constitution, there are no founders.

The Federalist Papers recommend the doctrine of veneration on the basis of reason or reflection, not on the basis of ancestor worship or piety. It contends that the rationalist epistemological premise is not entirely reasonable and argues for why it makes good sense to instill a disposition to venerate. That disposition, while it may have natural roots in human psychology, is in danger of being eliminated by the ideology of rational-ism. Those with the inclination and ability to consult these arguments will understand the case for the doctrine of veneration. For those who venerate, of course, it will be more the disposition than the reason of the matter that operates.

The combination of rationalism and traditionalism sought in American constitutional thought is not easy to realize. These two public epistemo-logical premises pull the public mind in different directions. They cannot be fully reconciled, certainly not in their extreme versions. But arguably the best place for the public mind to be is somewhere suspended between them. The system should be so conceived that one premise of public epis-temology counteracts another.

To support this combination, I chose upon solemn reflection to place "Fed 49" on my Virginia license plate. By this means I hope to impress on all who venture on our roads the importance of fidelity to the Constitution. I wish especially to remind the willful who tailgate of the need for restraint and of the importance of reverence.

Such, I think, is the proper spirit in which to observe Constitution Day.

Notes

1. *Federalist*, no. 1 (Alexander Hamilton), https://guides.loc.gov/federalist-papers/text-1-10#s-lg-box-wrapper-25493264.

2. *Federalist*, no. 1 (Hamilton).

3. Niccolò Machiavelli, *The Prince*, 2nd ed., trans. Harvey C. Mansfield (University of Chicago Press, 1998), xv, 61.

4. Edmund Burke, "On the Genius and Character of the French Revolution as It Regards Other Nations," in *Selected Works of Edmund Burke* (Liberty Fund, 1999), 3:129, https://oll.libertyfund.org/titles/canavan-select-works-of-edmund-burke-vol-3#lf0005-03_head_006.

5. Edmund Burke, "Letter to a Member of the National Assembly, in Answer to Some Objections to His Book on French Affairs," in *The Works of the Right Honorable Edmund Burke*, 3rd ed. (Little, Brown, and Company, 1869), 4:50.

6. Fordham University, "Modern History Sourcebook: Edmund Burke: Reflections on the Revolution in France, 1791," https://origin-rh.web.fordham.edu/halsall/mod/1791burke.asp.

7. David Hume, "Part I, Essay XIV: Of the Rise and Progress of the Arts and Sciences," Library of Economics and Liberty, www.econlib.org/library/LFBooks/Hume/hmMPL14.html.

8. Adam Ferguson, *An Essay on the History of Civil Society*, 5th ed. (T. Cadell, 1782), § II, http://oll.libertyfund.org/titles/1428.

9. *Federalist*, no. 14 (James Madison), https://avalon.law.yale.edu/18th_century/fed14.asp.

10. *Federalist*, no. 38 (James Madison), https://avalon.law.yale.edu/18th_century/fed38.asp.

11. *Federalist*, no. 10 (James Madison), https://avalon.law.yale.edu/18th_century/fed10.asp.

12. *Federalist*, no. 14 (Madison).

13. *Federalist*, no. 38 (Madison).

14. *Federalist*, no. 38 (Madison).

15. *Federalist*, no. 38 (Madison).

16. Thomas Jefferson to John Cartwright, June 5, 1824, Founding.com, https://founding.com/founders-library/american-political-figures/thomas-jefferson/letter-to-john-cartwright/.

17. *Federalist*, no. 53 (James Madison), https://avalon.law.yale.edu/18th_century/fed53.asp.

18. Thomas Jefferson to Samuel Kercheval, July 12, 1816, Teaching American History, https://teachingamericanhistory.org/document/letter-to-samuel-kercheval/.

19. Thomas Jefferson to John Tyler, June 28, 1804, Founders Online, https://founders.archives.gov/documents/Jefferson/01-43-02-0557.

4

Magna Carta, Due Process, and Administrative Power

PHILIP HAMBURGER
September 17, 2015

W hat is Magna Carta? Does it still matter? And why? It cannot matter as law, because even in England, almost none of it is still binding. It is an ancient document, written in a language few can read, on parchments that are brittle and decaying, and even its historical significance is elusive. If ever there were a dead constitution, this is it!

In fact, Magna Carta has often been an object of disdain. Those who like centralized power have long treated Magna Carta as irrelevant. Medieval English kings regularly ignored Magna Carta and therefore were repeatedly asked to reissue it. In the 16th century, the High Commission—an early prerogative or administrative agency—rejected arguments from Magna Carta, saying they were "obsolete and worn out of use."[1] In the 17th century, Oliver Cromwell allegedly disparaged the document as "Magna Farta."[2]

Although Magna Carta is nowadays merely an object of historical inquiry, many commentators go out of their way to question whether it ever was really a constitutional charter. They say that it protected not the freedom of the people as a whole but merely the specialized grievances of the barons. As one *New York Times* opinion piece put it, "Magna Carta was a result of an intra-elite struggle, in which the nobles were chiefly concerned with their own privileges."[3]

It thus merely protected the privileges of the privileged. In most academic and otherwise enlightened circles, it therefore is considered naive to think of it as a constitutional document. One would sound unsophisticated or unknowing if one took it too seriously for constitutional purposes or if one suggested that it addressed enduring problems or principles.

And this brings us to Walter Berns. Writing of another constitutional document—one that is not yet *quite* dead—he urges us to take the Constitution seriously. Walter was a man of incorruptible integrity. A man not swayed by intellectual fashion and its rewards. A man devoted to intellectual inquiry into enduring truths. A man who understood the importance of our Constitution. A man who recognized the danger of attempts to disparage virtue, liberty, and law. With his example in mind, I want to take Magna Carta seriously as a constitutional document.

Magna Carta still matters, not so much for what it says as for what it reveals—about an enduring danger and the repeated constitutional responses. Magna Carta was the beginning of the long struggle in common-law countries to rein in the threat from absolute power and substitute rule through and under law. It thus allows us to trace the long ebb and flow of absolute power on the one hand and law on the other.

Of particular interest for purposes of this talk, it opens up a window onto a principle that developed shortly afterward—the principle that came to be known as "the due process of law." Nowadays, the due process of law is most basically a procedural protection for what happens in court, not against what happens elsewhere—not, in particular, against what is done in administrative agencies. Thus, in court you are guaranteed the full due process of law, but in an administrative tribunal, you get only administrative process—a minimal process that is justified as "the process that is due."

Due process once was more robust. Prerogative adjudication—what nowadays is called administrative adjudication—was an evasion of adjudication in the courts, and due process was the primary response. Rather than merely setting a standard for what happened in court, it required the government, when it engaged in binding adjudication, to work through the processes of the courts.

Magna Carta was the most prominent manifestation of the beginning of this robust response to administrative adjudication, and it thus illuminates the real meaning of due process. It reveals the beginning of a long history in which binding administrative adjudication has been a recurring danger and in which the due process of law has been the primary means of rejecting such adjudication.

There are four parts to this talk. I will discuss, first, Magna Carta; second, the development of due process; third, the destruction of due process; fourth, some counterarguments.

Magna Carta

Magna Carta is a charter or grant in which King John made concessions to his barons. So, how did he come to meet them at Runnymede and accede to such a document?

King John acquired power after a civil war or a contest for the throne. Already then, the barons and the Church worried about his rapaciousness, and therefore, at his coronation in 1200, he had to issue a coronation charter, promising to limit taxes and takings of church revenues.

John soon distinguished himself with a series of foreign failures. He fought a losing war against France, where by 1204 he had lost Normandy and Anjou. He quarreled with Pope Innocent III about the appointment of bishops and especially that of Archbishop Steven Langton—a dispute that in 1209 led to John's excommunication. And again, in 1214, he was defeated by the French at Bouvines. John therefore was mocked as "King Lackland" and "King Softsword."

These dismal foreign adventures led him into domestic trouble. For example, to support his army, John demanded exorbitant amounts of scutage—a payment (in lieu of military service) from barons who did not fight—and in stretching his authority to raise this money, he revived the concerns that had led to his coronation charter.

Unfortunately for John, he quarreled with both his barons and the Church at the same time. His foreign policy and taxation annoyed the barons; his disputes with the pope over the appointment of bishops annoyed the Church. Most prominent of John's clerical opponents was Stephen Langton—a former academic (known to his students as

"Tongue of Thunder"). In 1207, after being elected and appointed over John's objections, Langton became the new Archbishop of Canterbury, and together with some other bishops, he provided the intellectual heft for the ensuing rebellion. John's reign may therefore be considered a vivid illustration of the danger of provoking both the men of power and the men of intellect.

The eventual result in May 1215 was a brief civil war. The key place to be controlled was London, and after Baron Robert FitzWalter seized it, John had few options. On June 10, 1215, at Runnymede, alongside the Thames, John made concessions in the Articles of the Barons. Five days later, these were formalized in Magna Carta.

* * * *

What was the content of Magna Carta? It contained 63 articles, most of which concerned matters that nowadays seem so antiquated that their meaning is obscure, except to a small number of medievalists. Nonetheless, it was a broadly written and ambitious document.

It is often said that it merely protected the barons in their particular liberties, not the broader populace in their general liberty, but this is mistaken. Consider these articles:

- Article 7: "A widow, after the death of her husband, is immediately ... to have her marriage portion and her inheritance"—thus protecting women's property.[4]

- Article 10: "No one is to be distrained to do more service for a knight's fee or for any other free tenement than is due from it"—thereby preventing a sort of taking.[5]

- Article 20: "A free man is not to be amerced for a small offence except in proportion to the nature of the offence, . . . and a villein [an unfree man] is to be amerced in the same manner, saving to him his growing crops"—thus protecting even serfs.[6]

- Article 40: "To no one will we sell, to no one will we deny or delay right or justice."[7]

All of these were general provisions, which secured basic freedoms for wide segments of English society.

One of the broadest articles was number 39, and this talk will later devote much attention to it. Article 39 declared that "no free man shall be . . . imprisoned or disseised [that is, dispossessed] . . . except by the lawful judgment of his peers or by the law of the land."[8] This laid down principles that were not yet trial by jury and the due process of law but that were the foundation of these rights.

* * * *

Before turning to due process, let's conclude our examination of Magna Carta by considering its afterlife. Magna Carta was not the last word on its assurances, because in the Middle Ages, what we would consider constitutional documents were merely the personal assurances of a monarch. Successive kings therefore reissued Magna Carta to show their commitment to it. On John's death in 1216, his nine-year-old son, Henry III, acting with his advisers, sought to avoid further unrest by reissuing Magna Carta (with some provisions omitted), and it was reissued again in 1217 and 1225 in exchange for grants of taxes to the king. The 1225 version was copied in later reissuances, the last of which occurred in 1300.

Much later, in the 17th century, Parliament reasserted portions of Magna Carta. Parliament recited Article 39 in 1628 in the Petition of Right and again in 1641 in the statute abolishing the Star Chamber. The latter (together with statute of the same year abolishing the High Commission) was the mid-17th-century equivalent of an abolition of administrative agencies.

Thereafter, however, Magna Carta becomes a matter of history. So let's stop talking generally about Magna Carta and focus instead on Article 39 and where it led.

The Development of Due Process

My argument is that Article 39 and later concepts of due process developed precisely in order to defeat prerogative or administrative adjudication—that is, to defeat the binding adjudications that rulers tried to impose outside the courts of law. Thus, rather than merely setting a standard for the courts, the due process of law also, perhaps even more centrally, bars binding administrative adjudications.

The origins of due process can be found in Magna Carta's Article 39. It did not use the phrase "due process of law." Instead, remember, it stated that "no free man shall be . . . imprisoned or disseised . . . except by the lawful judgment of his peers or by the law of the land."

The meaning of this clause is much disputed. For example, what was "the lawful judgment" of one's "peers"? Some say it refers to juries; others point out that the English adopted juries only slowly over the next century and that it therefore must have referred to only barons. In fact, trial by one's peers was a widely admired ideal, not only for barons but for all free men, and tellingly, Article 39 begins: "no free man." Thus, although Article 39 did not narrowly refer to juries, it apparently referred to the underlying principle.

Why did Article 39 emphasize these two principles: judgment by peers and by the law of the land? Article 39 was designed to bar binding adjudication outside the courts—in other words, it took aim at the prerogative or administrative adjudication by which rulers evaded the regular processes of the courts.

How can one know this? There is not space here to examine all the evidence, but two examples should suffice. In letters patent (a grant) of May 10, 1215—a month before Magna Carta—John assured his opponents that he would "not take or disseise or go against" them "by force or by arms" except "by the law of our realm or by the judgment of their peers in our court."[9]

Other evidence comes from the "Unknown Charter"—so-called because it was unknown until the late 19th century. The Unknown Charter records talking points in the negotiations for Magna Carta, and the very first clause begins: "King John grants that he is not to arrest a man without judgment."[10] This became Article 39's guarantee that "no free man shall be . . . imprisoned or disseised . . . except by the lawful judgment of his peers or by the law of the land."

Article 39 thus took aim at adjudications outside the courts—what civilian commentators would call "extralegal" adjudication and what we would call administrative adjudication. Of course, much of John's administrative adjudication was more vigorous, even violent, than that which prevails today, but it was similar in being a means of doing justice outside the courts of law. As put by J. C. Holt (the most distinguished historian of Magna Carta), Article 39 was "aimed" primarily against "arbitrary disseisin at the will of the king," against "summary process," and against "arrest and imprisonment on an administrative order."[11] Or as put by another historian, W. L. Warren, Article 39 targeted "executive action" against offenders.[12]

This focus on administrative adjudication is important. Although Magna Carta is merely history, administrative adjudication is now even more common than in 1215, and this suggests that, whether one calls it prerogative or administrative adjudication, it is a recurring danger. Governments are never content to govern through the law and the decisions of the courts but repeatedly seek other, extralegal modes of power, and just because we have replaced a monarchy with a republic does not mean the problem has gone away. The central danger that Magna Carta addressed thus remains very much alive.

* * * *

How did Article 39 become the due process of law? This happened through a series of 14th-century statutes, and these due process statutes confirm that due process was an obstacle to administrative adjudication.

The statutes were prompted by the prerogative or administrative misconduct of Edward III. Edward was not satisfied to hold subjects to account in the courts; he also summarily called them before his council for questioning and punishment. In 1354, Parliament therefore enacted the first due process statute, which echoed Magna Carta's Article 39: "no man of what Estate or Condition that he be, shall be put out of Land or Tenement, nor taken, nor imprisoned, nor disinherited, nor put to Death, without being brought in Answer by due Process of the Law"—meaning the process of the courts of law.[13]

Of course, Edward, being a king, failed to live up to this statute; within a decade, he once again hauled men into his council instead of working through the courts. So in 1368, Parliament passed another due process enactment. The preamble recited that the attempts to hold subjects accountable "before the King's Council" were "against the Law." The statute then provided that "no Man be put to answer without Presentment before Justices, or Matter of Record, or by due Process and Writ original, according to the old law of the Land."[14]

As summarized on the margin of the Parliament roll: "None shall be put to answer without due Process of Law."[15]

All of this is interesting, for it makes clear that any attempt to bind subjects in the king's prerogative or administrative council was unlawful. Even merely an attempt to summon them to answer questions was unlawful. Due process barred all binding administrative adjudication.

One of the most curious aspects of the 1368 Due Process Statute is its final clause about the judges. It instructs them: "If any Thing henceforth be done to the contrary, it shall be void in Law, and holden for Error."[16]

This has long puzzled commentators. Some have suggested that Parliament was inventing judicial review. This, however, is nonsense. The judges already were willing to hold unlawful royal acts unlawful and void—as when they encountered royal grants of previously conveyed land. The judges therefore did not need statutory authorization to hold royal acts void.

Why, then, the statute's final clause? It would appear that the judges had previously deferred to the king's prerogative adjudications. Therefore, to prevent any such deference, Parliament added that "if any Thing henceforth be done to the contrary, it shall be void in Law, and holden for Error."

In a 1368 case, the judges made clear that they understood what was required of them. After a commission established by Edward seized and imprisoned a man and took his goods, the judges held the commission void, saying it was "against the law" because it authorized the commissioners "to take a man and his goods without indictment, suit of a party, or due process."[17] Adjudication outside the courts was contrary to due process, and the judges held it unlawful without any deference. How times have changed!

This role of due process in precluding administrative adjudication remained familiar because of the Petition of Right. Charles I came to the throne in 1625, and he soon was demanding money not only as authorized by law but also based on prerogative or administrative edicts. And to enforce his administrative demands, he penalized noncompliant men in administrative proceedings—that is, outside courts.

Parliament responded in 1628 with the Petition of Right, which echoed Magna Carta and the 1368 Due Process Statute. The petition recited Magna Carta to the effect that "no freeman may be taken or imprisoned . . . but by the lawful judgment of his peers, or by the law of the land."[18] The Petition of Right also quoted the 1368 statute that "no man" should be "taken, nor imprisoned . . . without being brought to answer by due process of law."[19]

* * * *

Let's now move up to the 18th century. When the Fifth Amendment to the US Constitution guaranteed the due process of law, it continued in the tradition of Magna Carta, the due process statutes, and the Petition of Right. Although it set a standard for the courts, it more basically barred any binding adjudication outside the courts.

Consider the words of the Fifth Amendment: "No person shall . . . be deprived of life, liberty, or property, without due process of law."[20] If the amendment merely limited what the courts could do, it would have stated in the active voice: "*No court* shall deprive any person of life, liberty, or property, without due process of law." Instead, it was written in the passive voice, and it thereby limited all parts of government.

This is true of much of the federal Bill of Rights. Most of the Bill of Rights guarantees procedural rights, and most of these rights—including the Fifth Amendment—traditionally were barriers to adjudication outside the courts. The Bill of Rights had to limit not merely the courts but all parts of government. Most of its amendments therefore had to be stated in the passive voice.

Not only the text but also the location of the Fifth Amendment is revealing. To bar administrative adjudication—that is, binding adjudication outside the courts—the Fifth Amendment and the other procedural rights could not have simply modified Article III of the Constitution, because then they would have limited only the courts. These guarantees also had to limit the executive in Article II of the Constitution. The drafters of the Bill of Rights therefore changed how they wrote it.

Originally, they drafted amendments to particular articles of the Constitution. Ultimately, however, they added amendments at the end of the whole Constitution, and this mattered because it allowed the amendments to limit all parts of the government. For example, the Fifth Amendment at the end of the Constitution limited not only the courts but also Congress and the executive.

In these ways, both the text and the location of the procedural rights make clear that they limit all parts of government. And in limiting not only courts but also Congress and the executive, they bar prerogative or administrative power.

The implication for due process was recognized by the earliest surviving academic commentary on the Bill of Rights. St. George Tucker—a Virginia judge—began teaching constitutional law at William & Mary in 1791, and some of his notes, apparently added to his lectures in early 1796, are revealing. After quoting the Fifth Amendment's Due Process Clause, he concluded: "Due process of law must then be had before a judicial court, or a judicial magistrate."[21]

The Fifth Amendment thus bars the government from holding Americans to account outside courts and their processes. This was the breadth of the principle from its very beginnings, this was how the Fifth Amendment was drafted, and this was how the amendment was understood.

The development of ideas of due process thus runs directly from Magna Carta's Article 39 in 1215, to the 1368 Due Process Statute, to the 1628 Petition of Right, to the Fifth Amendment in 1791. Throughout this history, due process was a guarantee against not only abuses by courts but also binding adjudication outside the courts. Whether prerogative or administrative, binding adjudication outside the courts violated guarantees of the due process of law.

So, how did this change? We now have administrative adjudication on a vast scale, and the Supreme Court tells us that this does not violate due process. How did the concept of due process come to permit what it once centrally forbade?

The Destruction of Due Process

The creation of ideas of due process was one of the great achievements of the past. The destruction of due process is an accomplishment of our own times.

The destruction has occurred primarily through administrative adjudication. Administrative adjudication evades courts, judges, juries, the privilege against self-incrimination, and most other procedural rights, and all of this can be summed up as the evasion of due process.

Just to be clear, when I criticize administrative adjudication, I mean binding adjudication outside the courts—the issuance, in particular cases, of administrative edicts that bind or constrain persons subject to the law of the United States. My argument therefore does not include the adjudication of benefits, unless they have become legal rights. Nor does it ordinarily include any adjudication on the status of illegal or enemy aliens.

Instead, the problem is binding or constraining adjudication that evades the due process of law and most other procedural rights. On account of this evasion, administrative adjudication is the most serious assault on the Bill of Rights in the nation's history.

The practical result of this administrative evasion of due process is ambidextrous enforcement. When due process was still understood, the government could constrain Americans in particular cases through only the courts and their judges and juries. Now the government can instead choose administrative adjudication. It thus has the choice to proceed through the courts and their due process or through administrative adjudication and its faux process.

The US Securities and Exchange Commission (SEC) offers a timely illustration. It can refer cases to the Justice Department to prosecute defendants criminally, or it can proceed against them in-house through its administrative law judges (ALJs). When the SEC does not expect to win in court (with juries and regular due process), it can simply proceed through its ALJs (without juries and regular due process). In the summer of 2014, indeed, the SEC's enforcement director candidly explained that the SEC could pursue cases administratively when it did not expect to persuade a jury.[22]

The problem, however, is much broader, for it is not merely that an *agency* can chose between enforcement in court and out of court. The problem includes all administrative evasion of due process, and it thus most basically occurs whenever *Congress* authorizes agencies to work through administrative adjudication. It therefore makes no difference whether or not the decision to proceed administratively rests in the agency. Regardless, whenever an agency engages in administrative adjudication, the government has chosen to evade the courts, judges, juries, and the due process of law.

The problem, in other words, is not agency discretion but government evasion. It is not simply that a particular agency (such as the SEC) can choose to enforce its regulations through either the courts or its own proceedings; instead, the problem more generally is that Congress can choose to establish paths of enforcement outside the courts, and the government as a whole can thereby evade due process. And in evading due process, including most of the procedural rights, the government evades much of the Bill of Rights.

But it gets worse, for in addition to allowing the evasion of due process, the Supreme Court has eviscerated the very concept of due process. To accommodate administrative adjudication, the due process of law has been reconfigured as "the process that is due," which surely is one of the most misleading phrases in American law. Whereas due process once was the due process of law (meaning the process of the courts of law), it now legitimizes the administrative evasion and its ambidextrous vision.[23] Now, due process means *either* the process of the courts of law (when the government chooses to proceed in the courts) *or* merely administrative process (when the government chooses to authorize administrative adjudication in agencies).

Due process thus is now bifurcated into the government's choice between judicial due process and administrative faux process. Whereas due process of law once was a guarantee against government, it now is merely an option for the government—an option it can choose or not, as it pleases.

Counterarguments

Before concluding, I want to consider some counterarguments. These counterarguments turn out to be less than persuasive, but they need to be taken seriously.

One counterargument is that administrative adjudication is actually very fair. Administrative adjudication often comes with ALJs, most of whom are conscientious and who are protected in their salary and tenure. It also often comes with hearings, evidence, and often a formal record. In theory, therefore, it is not really so bad. In theory.

Consider the personnel—the "judges." Many administrative adjudicators are not ALJs and thus lack any independence. Even ALJs are not really independent. They can be demoted or have their salary docked if they reject administrative regulations as unconstitutional. In a 1992 survey of ALJs, 15 percent complained of threats to their independence, and 8 percent said this was a frequent problem.[24] Just recently, Lillian McEwen—a former ALJ at the SEC—protested about intimidation at the SEC by superiors. [25] Even after ALJs adjudicate, their decisions often are subject to review (or being finalized) by heads of agencies, who did not hear the cases, who are political appointees, and who usually lack even the pretense of independence.

Now consider the process. Agencies rely on subpoenas for discovery without usually allowing the same discovery for defendants. There are no juries, even when agency proceedings are criminal in nature. And the burden of proof and persuasion is often reversed, so that defendants have to prove their innocence—a common problem in many licensing proceedings and also in other administrative proceedings when an adjudicator takes "official notice" of facts. Rather than the due process of law, all of this is a pale imitation of it.

Another counterargument is that one always can get due process later, in judicial review of administrative adjudications. This delayed due process argument, however, runs into difficulties.

For one thing, due process, juries, and other procedural rights are rights in the first instance, not merely on review. Some of the earliest state constitutional cases—such as those dealing with the Ten Pound Act in New Hampshire in 1786 and 1787—repeatedly held that judicial review (even with a *de novo* hearing before a jury in court) cannot cure an initial administrative violation of jury rights. From this point of view, the administrative adjudication already violates procedural rights, regardless of any review.

The delayed due process argument is also unpersuasive because of the doctrine of exhaustion of administrative remedies. For practical purposes, this means the exhaustion of administrative defendants before they get to court. An agency in its administrative proceedings will often exhaust the defendant's finances, and the defendant then cannot afford to appeal to the courts.

The delayed due process theory is ultimately rather comic, because after administrative proceedings, you cannot get due process in the courts. When you appeal an administrative decision to the courts, the judges do not call a jury but instead simply defer to the government's administrative record—in other words, to the government's version of the facts. The judges also defer to the government's interpretation of ambiguous statues—that is, to its legal position (this being the *Chevron* doctrine).

Even when lower court judges reject an agency interpretation, the Supreme Court allows the agency to disregard the court decision (this being the *Brand X* doctrine). And even when the judges hold an agency action unlawful, they often hesitate to declare it void, instead remanding it to the agency. All of this is deference to the government, and when the government is a party, it is systematic judicial bias in favor of one party and against other parties.

Thus, even if judicial review were a cure for the administrative denial of due process, judicial review of administrative adjudication is very different from other judicial review. It offers much less than due process, and where the government is a party, it is marred by systematic bias. Rather than delayed due process, this is a gross violation of due process. The courts, in other words, are no cure for the administrative evasion of due process. Instead, too often, after the initial administrative evasion of due process, the courts engage in their own denial of due process.

Another counterargument is that due process has been expanded, and it has in some ways. But much of its core has been destroyed.

For example, on account of *Goldberg v. Kelly*, there now is some minimal due process right against the denial of some benefits, and in these cases, it can be mildly advantageous to have the process that is due. *Goldberg*, however, offers only a smidgeon of process for denials of some *benefits*, and it is part of a broader jurisprudence that accepts a profound denial of due process for government *constraints*.

The sort of doctrine evident in *Goldberg* therefore strains at a gnat and swallows the proverbial camel. It secures negligible administrative process in some benefit cases while accepting serious denials of the due process in constraint cases. The overall effect is not so much to expand due process at the edges as to legitimize administrative violations of due process at the core.

Yet another counterargument is that we now have substantive due process and the use of due process to "incorporate" the Bill of Rights against the states. The use of due process, however, to protect substantive rights cannot justify the denial of the core procedural due process.

The reality for the core of due process—the procedural right—is grim. Due process has shifted from something guaranteed to something merely optional. It once was a guarantee against the government—that the government could not bind anyone in a particular case without proceeding against them in a court, with its due process. Now due process is merely an option for the government. *If* the government proceeds against you in a court, you get the due process of law, but if it chooses to proceed against you in an agency, you merely get administrative process—"the process that is due."

Conclusion

In the nearly 1,000-year common law struggle for government under and through the law, extralegal power (whether prerogative or administrative) has repeatedly evaded the paths of law, thereby provoking constitutional responses. The constitutional barriers have included Magna Carta, the 14th-century due process statutes, 17th-century English constitutional developments, and 18th-century American constitutions.

Extralegal power, however, has repeatedly returned, and in the resulting ebb and flow of law, most procedural rights now are at an ebb tide. The current administrative evasions escape courts, judges, juries, and—in general terms—the due process of law. They thus make a mockery of the Bill of Rights.

In these circumstances, the US Constitution has never been *less* relevant, and Magna Carta has never been *more* relevant. Our right of due process and other procedural rights increasingly look as if they are as lost in the mists of time as the provisions of Magna Carta. And Magna Carta is therefore especially relevant, for it is a reminder that extralegal power, including the judicial power exercised outside the courts, is an enduring danger—a danger that is nearly 1,000 years old. Constitutional documents repeatedly have interred this threat, but it always comes back from the grave.

In 1590, when protesting against the High Commission, the prominent lawyer James Morice protested: "Where is now . . . the great Charter of England? . . . Where is now the [due process] statute?"[26] We might ask the same questions. Where is now the Constitution? Where is now the Fifth Amendment's guarantee of due process? Times have changed, but the danger endures.

And this brings us back to Walter Berns. He recognized the enduring problems of human nature, and he therefore understood the recurring character of the threats to law and liberty. For this reason (and many, many others), he will be sorely missed.

Never in this nation's history has law been more at risk. Because of administrative power, most of the guarantees in the Bill of Rights, including due process, have become merely optional. No longer guarantees of rights, they have become simply options for power. More than ever, therefore, we need to follow Walter's example: We need to keep our eye on the Constitution and the enduring dangers to it.

Notes

1. Simonds D'Ewes, "Journal of the House of Lords: October 1597," in *The Journals of All the Parliaments During the Reign of Queen Elizabeth both of the House of Lords and House of Commons*, ed. Paul Bowes (John Starkey, 1682).

2. Tom Ginsburg, "Stop Revering Magna Carta," *The New York Times*, June 14, 2015, https://www.nytimes.com/2015/06/15/opinion/stop-revering-magna-carta.html.

3. Ginsburg, "Stop Revering Magna Carta."

4. Magna Carta, art. 7.

5. Magna Carta, art. 10.

6. Magna Carta, art. 20.

7. Magna Carta, art. 40.

8. Magna Carta, art. 39.

9. Nicholas Vincent, "'By the Law of Our Realm or by Judgment of Their Peers,'" Magna Carta Project, https://magnacartaresearch.org/read/itinerary/_by_the_law_of_our_realm_or_by_judgment_of_their_peers__.

10. Magna Carta Project, "Clause 39—Commentary for Academic Researchers," https://web.archive.org/web/20240522053536/https://magnacartaresearch.org/read/magna_carta_1215/Clause_39/aca.

11. See J. C. Holt, *Magna Carta*, 3rd ed. (Cambridge University Press, 2015).

12. See W. L. Warren, *King John* (University of California Press, 1978).

13. Liberty of Subject 1354, 28 Edw. 3.

14. Observance of Due Process of Law 1368, 42 Edw. 3, c. 3.

15. Observance of Due Process of Law 1368, 42 Edw. 3, c. 3.

16. Observance of Due Process of Law 1368, 42 Edw. 3, c. 3.

17. Y.B. 42 Edw. 3, fol. 258b, pl. 5 (1368). Reprinted in Nathan S. Chapman and Michael W. McConnell, trans., *Year Books: Liber Assisarum 1327–1377* (George Sawbridge, 1678–80), 258. See also Nathan S. Chapman and Michael W. McConnell, "Due Process as Separation of Powers," *The Yale Law Journal* 121, no. 7 (2012): 1684n23, https://www.yalelawjournal.org/pdf/1080_y4si0of3.pdf.

18. The Petition of Right 1628, 3. Car. 1, c. 3.

19. The Petition of Right 1628, 3. Car. 1, c. 4.

20. US Const. amend. V.

21. St. George Tucker, "Structure and Organization of the Federal Government," in *Blackstone's Commentaries: With Notes of Reference to the Constitution and the Laws, of the Federal Government of the United States; and of the Commonwealth of Virginia* (William Young Birch and Abraham Small, 1803), vol 1., note D, part 2, https://lonang.com/library/reference/tucker-blackstone-notes-reference/tuck-1d2/.

22. Since then, under political pressure, the SEC has partly backed away from this ambidextrous policy, but only partly, and legally it remains free to pursue it.

23. Although courts of equity and admiralty are often contrasted with courts of law, these specialized courts increasingly were understood to operate within the common law system, not merely as alternatives to it, and in this sense they are included here among the courts of law—meaning the courts that applied the law.

24. For the 1992 survey, see Charles H. Koch Jr., "Administrative Presiding Officials Today," *Administrative Law Review* 46 (1994): 271, 278.

25. Ed Beeson, "SEC Subpoenaed for Docs on Ex-Judge's Intimidation Claims," Law360, May 22, 2015, https://www.law360.com/articles/659272/sec-subpoenaed-for-docs-on-ex-judge-s-intimidation-claims.

26. Philip Hamburger, *Is Administrative Law Unlawful?* (University of Chicago Press, 2014), 179, 485.

5

Terrorism and the Bill of Rights: Suicide Pact or Not?

MICHAEL B. MUKASEY

September 15, 2016

I t's an honor to be invited to this podium, particularly considering those who have preceded me here. It's also a pleasure.

One of the most pleasurable features is the chance to say that I think Walter Berns, for whom this talk is named, was the person with the deepest understanding of the US Constitution—its structure, its meaning, and its purpose—of anyone who has written or spoken on the subject in modern times. I should add that in saying that, I don't mean to diminish the importance of the late Justice Antonin Scalia, whose originalism brought a lot of lawyers and others in and out of government to a better understanding of the Constitution and who wrote a book each on constitutional interpretation and statutory interpretation. But his intellectual strength was focused mainly on issues related to courts and lawyering and displayed mainly in the cases and controversies that happened to pass before the Supreme Court.

Professor Berns was not encumbered by a law degree. It's been said that the law sharpens the mind by narrowing it. Professor Berns's books and essays are especially important today because the Constitution itself and the framework that it established are in danger of disappearing from the consciousness of the people who should be its principal custodians and defenders, and that is lawyers and government officials, including but certainly not limited to judges.

Consider, for example, that there's hardly any law school in this country that teaches a course in the Constitution itself and the system of governance that it establishes. Rather, constitutional law consists of studying cases, mostly Supreme Court cases, revolving around one or another provision of the Constitution, involving only the Commerce Clause from the body of the document itself or some of its amendments, mainly the first, the fourth through the sixth, and of course the fourteenth.

Professor Berns made the revolutionary suggestion that law schools should include the study of the Constitution itself in their constitutional law courses. The idea, however, doesn't seem to have caught on. In fact, the author of one casebook on constitutional law, who heard that his book was criticized for including the text of the Constitution only as Appendix H, is said to have responded that he was going to cure that and make the Constitution more prominent. He moved it up to Appendix A.

Unseriousness about the Constitution, which Professor Berns targeted in the title of one of his books, *Taking the Constitution Seriously*, has been so pervasive that when the Speaker of the House heard that the Affordable Care Act was going to be challenged in Court as a violation of the Constitution, her response was "The Constitution, really?," accompanied by a rolling of the eyes in case anyone missed the condescension.

* * * *

Just as knowledge of the actual Constitution seems to fade, expressions of concern from both the left and the right over what is said to be unconstitutional behavior by the government seem to get constantly sharper, particularly in response to measures the government has taken to safeguard the country in the face of a worldwide campaign of terror being waged by Islamists.

One manifestation of that particular concern was the successful campaign by libertarian Republicans and liberal Democrats in Congress to end the government's practice of gathering telephone metadata so as to better track foreign terrorists. The phenomenon has been widespread, and it's not limited to legislative efforts.

One law school professor and dean just published a book in which he traces what he regards as government infringement on a broad range of constitutional rights to what he regards as the Supreme Court's undue deference to the political branches—mainly the executive—and the courts' refusal in general to exercise what he regards as their proper role. He condemns not only the Supreme Court but also the Foreign Intelligence Surveillance (FISA) Court. He criticizes that court not only for the outcomes it produces, by giving the government what he argues is free rein to conduct electronic surveillance, but also for reaching results at least part of the time in decisions that are themselves kept secret, thus creating a body of "secret law."

The criticisms of our counterterrorism efforts focus mainly on three topics: secrecy, detention and the closely related topic of interrogation, and surveillance, mainly but not exclusively electronic surveillance.

It's a regular feature of panels and seminars on the government's response to Islamist terrorism that what we must do is strike a balance between safety and the liberties protected by the Constitution and that, of course, studying the Constitution itself is essential to doing that. I believe that the Constitution actually has very little to do with these disputes. I believe that what we are faced with here is a political and national security problem that's been constitutionalized in certain aspects, in part so as to avoid dealing with it. I also believe that in this process we trivialize the real Constitution. At some point, we are going to have to pull up our socks and deal with this problem, or it's going to deal harshly with us.

* * * *

I think part of taking the Constitution seriously, as Professor Berns taught us we should, involves recognizing the choices that it does *not* make for us and that we, therefore, have to make for ourselves.

Let's start with secrecy. The need for secrecy in pursuing the ends of government was something that was well-known to those who wrote the Constitution and to those who first declared our independence. The first Continental Congress convened under rules that required that the doors be shut during the transaction of business and that members keep deliberation secret until a majority authorized them to be released. The second

Continental Congress imposed an oath of secrecy on each member to be relaxed only when Congress gave its explicit permission.

The Constitution itself was drafted under conditions of strict secrecy, in summertime in Philadelphia in 1787, before air conditioning. The doors and windows were shut; the delegates sworn to secrecy. James Madison, the principal architect of the Constitution, recognized the obvious conflict between secrecy and democracy when he wrote that a popular government without popular information, or the means of acquiring it, is but a prologue to a farce, a tragedy, or perhaps both. Knowledge will forever govern ignorance, and "a people who mean to be their own governors must arm themselves with the power which knowledge gives."[1] On the other hand, he also wrote that no constitution would ever have been adopted by the Constitutional Convention if the debate had been public.

The body of the Constitution explicitly accommodates the need for secrecy. It provides that each house of Congress "shall keep a journal of its proceedings, and from time to time publish the same, excepting such parts as may, in their judgment, require secrecy."

George Washington himself fully understood the need for secrecy in gathering intelligence. He wrote in 1777 to one of his colonels that

> the necessity of procuring good intelligence is apparent and need not be further urged. All that remains for me to add is that you keep the whole matter as secret as possible, for upon secrecy success depends in most enterprises of the kind, and for want of it they are generally defeated, however well planned and promising a favorable issue.[2]

The Constitution, of course, built into the government a system of checks and balances between branches of the federal government and between the federal government and the states, but it provided little in the way of a mechanism other than the power of the purse for Congress to oversee and check the power of the executive, requiring only that the president report to Congress from time to time on the state of the union.

Here I think it's important to recall that the reason for the creation of the FISA Court to oversee collection of intelligence was simply to provide yet another layer of supervision, not to open intelligence gathering to public scrutiny or turn it into an adversary proceeding. It was simply to assure that the surveillance of those people protected by the Fourth Amendment—all people present in the United States and American citizens traveling abroad—was reasonable.

The creation of the FISA Court was certainly not constitutionally mandated. The only court provided for in the Constitution is the Supreme Court, which was given judicial power along with, as the Constitution puts it, "such inferior courts as the Congress may from time to time ordain and establish."[3]

However, the very existence of the FISA Court has led to demands that its deliberations be conducted under adversary conditions, which, it is suggested, is the main attribute of a real court, and opened up to greater public scrutiny. Critics of the FISA Court are fond of pointing out that the government has above a 95 percent success rate in its applications to the FISA Court, and so they conclude that the court must simply be rubber-stamping the applications.

Those critics do not consider the real reason for that success rate, which is quite simply that the national security division lawyers who prepare those applications are well aware that their main stock and trade is credibility and, therefore, prepare their applications as conservatively as possible. They avoid aggressive requests so as not to incur the criticism of the court and, thereby, risk having applications generally subjected to more searching and hostile review with the possibility that applications that should be granted may be delayed, in the effort to assure that the court does not grant one that shouldn't be granted.

Also, the process of securing approval is sometimes iterative. The government submits an application, the court raises one or more issues, and the application is scaled back or otherwise changed. The suggestion that the court rubber-stamps government applications is simply a grotesque distortion.

Because the 1978 statute gave the judiciary a role in supervising the gathering of intelligence and did it through the creation of a court, some have used the existence of a court itself as a basis for demand that the supervision be provided through an adversary process. After all, most court proceedings (at least in the popular imagination) involve adversary encounters between two parties. Some have suggested that the FISA Court is not a real court because only the government appears in connection with applications for authority to conduct surveillance. Of course, for the government to notify each target of intelligence gathering that such gathering is proposed, and then to permit each such target to contest the issue, would destroy intelligence gathering altogether and notify our adversaries and enemies of what we're doing.

One proposal has been to create an office that will stand constantly in potential opposition to any application for authority to conduct surveillance and litigate the issue before the FISA Court. Apart from burdening each application, we should wonder in which branch of government this office would be located. Because its function is in essence executive, this would create the constitutional absurdity of an executive litigating against itself to no end other than creating the appearance of an adversary proceeding. Notably, the judges of the courts themselves have said that they find this proposed office burdensome and unnecessary.

In the same way, requiring that the work of the Foreign Intelligence Court be open to the public or that decisions of the Foreign Intelligence Court be disclosed publicly, uniformly, so as to respond to the criticism that the court is applying secret law in secret, would mean that one of the main features of intelligence gathering—maintaining secrecy—would be compromised.

Whether applications before that court are reasonable or not turns on the facts underlying them and not on any insight that could be gained by examining the text of the Constitution or its amendments. The FISA Court was not called into existence as a matter of constitutional necessity, but as a matter of perceived—and, I happen to think, highly debatable—prudence.

There is no reason why it has to be decked out to look like an Article III court, with public adversary proceedings, to fulfill the function for which it was created, which is simply to add the judiciary to the supervisory apparatus within the executive and the intelligence committees of both Houses, so that all three branches would be involved in monitoring the reasonableness of electronic surveillance gathering—sort of a Madisonian trifecta.

This is not the traditional role of a court or, more relevantly, the constitutional role of a court, which is to decide cases and controversies. It is fairly close, however, and it involves issues that could easily generate cases and controversies.

* * * *

The detection and interrogation of suspected and confirmed terrorists have also generated what purport to be constitutional controversies. We're told that it's a violation of the Constitution to detain anyone without a trial and that interrogation presents constitutional concerns both in the means used to get the information and in the possibly incriminating effect of any information that is obtained.

In fact, there's a whole range of situations, some related to wartime powers and some not, in which detention without trial is entirely permissible so that the person or people detained do not cause harm to others or to themselves. In each of the wars that we've fought, we detained at times hundreds of thousands of prisoners of war, some in the United States and some elsewhere, and none of them were tried. Furthermore, none of them were permitted even to file a habeas corpus petition.

The Constitution's Suspension Clause permits Congress to suspend the writ of habeas corpus entirely, when it is deemed necessary to protect public safety such that people detained would not even have the means to challenge the lawfulness of their detention.

Our criminal laws provide for pretrial detention of those who may be charged with crimes but not convicted when necessary to protect public safety or to assure that those defendants will appear for trial. And detention of material witnesses who have been convicted of no crime and who stand charged with no crime is permitted to make sure that their testimony is available when necessary if they present a risk of flight. Aliens who face deportation may be detained, and the mentally ill may be detained to protect society or themselves. Pregnant addicts may be detained to protect their unborn children. And sex offenders who are found likely to repeat their offenses may be detained even after they have completed their sentences—all of those detentions occurring without offense to the Constitution.

Many of these authorities, these detention authorities, predate the Constitution itself. So it's not that we started out with an absolute ban on detention without trial and have created exceptions over time. Some individual powers have expanded, notably detention of sex offenders; others have narrowed, notably detention of the mentally ill, but they have existed over time without successful constitutional challenge.

As to unlawful combatants—those who do not follow rules of war that were designed to protect civilians—it was permissible at one time to deny them any legal protection whatsoever. The laws of war offer combatants essentially the following bargain: If you wear a uniform so that you can be distinguished from civilians, if you carry your arms openly, if you follow a recognized chain of command so that you act only on orders so that your superiors can be held accountable for your conduct, and most importantly, if you do not target civilians, then you're assured that if you're captured, you must be treated humanely and consistently with your rank, and you may not be forced to divulge your side's secrets. However, you may be detained without trial for the duration of the conflict.

As I said, at one time if a combatant did not adhere to those standards, they received no protection at all. It was permissible to treat them (as it's put in the international law treatise that I have on my shelf) summarily, which is to say, to shoot them. In fact, there were Germans tried after World War II for executing partisans who were acquitted of that charge because executing partisans who did not fight in uniform or carry their arms openly was not a war crime.

Current law still permits US citizens who violate the laws of war to be treated just the same as noncitizens, on what seems to me the entirely plausible theory that if they throw in their lot with unlawful enemies, they can be treated like unlawful enemies.

However, the distinction between lawful and unlawful combatants appears to be wearing down to the point where some have suggested that although those who follow all the laws of war may be detained without trial for the duration of the conflict, we should actually offer a better deal to those who violate all the rules. Rather than being held indefinitely or at least until it's clear that they no longer present a danger, they should have the right to a trial in civilian court with appointed counsel, the presumption of innocence, and the possibility that if acquitted, they will be released.

In fact, one terrorist, a man involved in planning the bombing of the US embassies in Kenya and Tanzania, nearly did just that. Ahmed Ghailani was acquitted after a trial in New York of the hundreds of murders that resulted from those bombings, but he was convicted of one count of conspiracy to damage US property, for which, despite the innocuous-sounding charge, he was sentenced to life in prison.

Before he was tried, Ghailani had been detained at Guantanamo. And although he had been charged before he was captured and detained there, his case was apparently supposed to be the thin end of the wedge to show that we can bring detainees from Guantanamo to the mainland and try them here with no adverse consequences. His near-total acquittal in New York somewhat undermined that gambit.

We have captured and detained many people who in fact violated the laws of war, some of whom we have evidence against that's sufficient to charge them with war crimes—the defendants charged in the 9/11 attacks are a good example—and others of whom we do not have such evidence against, but who nonetheless present enough of a threat to our security that simply releasing them would assure that they return to the fight and inflict more casualties than they have already, even assuming that there's a jurisdiction that will have them.

Of all those detainees, some may have information that's still valuable despite their long period of confinement, information not simply about particular plots but about relationships between and among terrorist groups and even individual terrorists that can be used to help dismantle those groups and capture people who mean us harm. The Supreme Court has ruled that even detainees not charged may continue to be held.

However, the current administration is unwilling to rely simply on laws of war detention, with the result that interrogation of newly captured detainees, when there are such detainees and they're not killed by a drone, is truncated, and they are either turned over to other countries or charged in civilian courts.

For example, when a defendant involved in the attack on our embassy in Benghazi, Ahmed Abu Khattala, was caught in Libya, he was held for 19 days aboard a Navy vessel, where he was interrogated in an effort to get any intelligence he may have had. Now, I have no idea whether the government got anything of value from him, but 19 days is a ludicrously short time in which to get useful information from even a willing subject. And it does not appear that Abu Khattala was a willing subject.

Intelligence gathering from human sources is usually an incremental process in which information is gathered and checked, new information is gotten, and the interrogator returns to the detainee, sometimes over a period of months, to obtain additional information. In any event, at the end of the 19 days, Abu Khattala was brought before a court, formally charged, and assigned a lawyer. That ended his use as an intelligence source. Whatever information was obtained from him, as well as any leads from that information, may not and will not be used in connection with his prosecution.

What we now have are some detainees held at Guantanamo without charges, some held with charges that are pending before a military commission, and still others held in US prisons who have been convicted of federal crimes or are charged with such crimes and awaiting trial. This patchwork of detention is not a constitutionally dictated outcome but rather a result of a series of political accommodations. Although I am describing this situation in the present tense, I certainly do not intend to absolve the administration in which I served from responsibility or, if appropriate, from blame.

When we first responded militarily after the attack on September 11, 2001, it appears that great reliance was placed on World War II–vintage authority in determining how detainees would be treated. Recall that even prisoners of war who followed the rules of war were held indefinitely and without recourse to the courts. When two groups of German saboteurs landed on mainland United States territory, one group on Long Island and the other in Florida, and fatally for them, shed their uniforms, they were rounded up and on the direct orders of President Franklin D. Roosevelt were tried before a military commission convened in Washington, even though the civilian courts of the country were still open and functioning. They were convicted and executed, all within three months of the time that they landed, despite the claim of at least one that he was a US citizen. Their convictions were affirmed by the Supreme Court in an opinion that was actually filed after they were already dead, the Court having affirmed the convictions so as to permit the executions to proceed with the opinion to follow.

It was anticipated, based in part on that history, that the executive could set up military convictions to deal with detainees who would be charged with violating the laws of war and simply hold the rest indefinitely. However, as detentions lengthened, the Supreme Court has pared back that history mightily. It held, first, that the president did not have the authority to establish military commissions on his own—a gap that Congress quickly filled with the Military Commissions Act. And then the Court held that even unlawful combatants who are detained by the United States in a location that's outside the theater of war have a right at least to challenge the lawfulness of their detention in a proceeding that should resemble the rudimentary challenge brought in a habeas corpus case.

Habeas corpus is a right that actually preceded the Constitution and that the Constitution recognizes by restricting its suspension to situations in which Congress determines that public safety requires it, due to invasion or rebellion. However, the Constitution does not provide substantive standards that describe what conduct must be proved to detain someone as an unlawful combatant or what level and type of proof is necessary to justify continuing to hold a prisoner as an unlawful combatant and for how long. Interrogation techniques used on some detainees have been objected to on constitutional grounds, although constitutional objections have been secondary to the claim that the techniques violated the statutory ban on torture, which they did not.

In any event, nothing in any clause of the Constitution provides even a clue as to what is permitted when there is reason to believe that a detainee has information that, if disclosed, can save lives. The Eighth Amendment's ban on cruel and unusual punishment has no application here, because interrogation techniques are not applied as punishment but rather as coercion to bring about a cooperative state of mind.

The only hint of a constitutional standard comes from a line of cases that started with *Rochin vs. California*, which bars the government from doing anything to a prisoner that "shocks the conscience"—not a real rigorous standard, considering not only the range of sensibilities that lie under the thousand or so black robes on the federal bench and the thousands more that populate the state courts but also the range of situations that law enforcement officers confront.

Pumping the stomach of a prisoner may shock the conscience if it's done to retrieve evidence in a drug offense, as happened in the *Rochin* case. But later cases have made it clear that the standard is situational. So the same conduct may not shock the conscience if it were done to find the whereabouts of a kidnapped child or the location of a bomb.

One thing the Constitution does do is to provide a response to those who argue that we should have a direct voice in the interrogation techniques that are applied in our name, as they like to put it. That answer is that the Constitution establishes a representative democracy, not a direct democracy. Decisions made by those who hold executive or legislative office are reviewable, if at all, at election time, not otherwise.

* * * *

Until the creation of the FISA Court, it appeared that there was enough protection for the Fourth Amendment's general command that the right of the people to be secure in their persons, houses, papers, and effects against unreasonable searches shall not be violated and that there was enough protection for that in the amendment's Warrant Clause, which provides that no warrant could be issued except upon probable cause—meaning a showing of probable cause that a crime has been committed and probable cause to believe that evidence would be found in a particular place or on a particular person to detect it. Absent a warrant or showing of probable cause and exigent circumstances that excuse obtaining a warrant, evidence could not be introduced in court, and so a principal source of damage from unlawful surveillance could be avoided.

However, after Watergate it was felt necessary to subject even intelligence gathering to supervision by not only the executive itself and Congress but also the judiciary—the Madisonian trifecta that I referred to before—so as to assure that there would be no abuse.

The need for such assurance seems to have stemmed in part from a few lines in the White House tapes in which the president is heard urging that the Watergate break-in be concealed behind a claim that it involved national security and from another passage in which he seems to suggest that if the president authorizes what would be regarded as an unlawful course of conduct, it is by that authorization rendered lawful.

Now, I don't want to get into a long discussion here or try to defend the indefensible, but Richard Nixon was, after all, a lawyer and a fairly serious one. So he may have had in mind a doctrine that does exempt the sovereign from the reach of criminal laws that are not intended to prevent harm or injury of a private citizen, although burglary and wiretapping are not within that doctrine. It may have been arguable that wiretapping for national security purposes might not have been within it, at least until Congress definitively occupied that field with the Foreign Intelligence Surveillance Act in 1978.

The actual collection of electronic intelligence itself has incurred the anxiety of people who claim they are concerned about constitutional violations. Until last year, there was in place a program whereby the government collected what is known as metadata of calls in the United States, the record of the calling number, the called number, the date, and the time—the same information that telephone companies keep track of to generate a bill, which does not include the content of the call.

The purpose for doing that was to permit the government—when it got word of, say, a telephone at a safe house used overseas by terrorists—to run the number of that telephone against the database of calls in the United States to see whether it had called or been called by any telephone in this country. The government could then focus on that telephone number and try to gather enough other information about the subscriber to apply to the court for a wiretap order under conventional standards with a showing of probable cause. That was the only purpose to which this database was put. There were fewer than 30 people at the National Security Agency (NSA) who were authorized to query the database, and they could do so only after getting permission from their supervisors, and most recently from the FISA Court. They were not permitted to engage in data mining or any other exploitation of this database.

Nonetheless, opponents of the program mounted a successful scare campaign that subscribers' privacy was being violated, a scare campaign based not on what NSA employees actually did as they followed the rules under the program but on what they could do if they broke the rules. This makes about as much sense as disarming the police because some officer might run amok and decide to turn his gun on a civilian.

And yet a coalition of self-professed libertarians and self-professed progressives combined to terminate the program. They argued that assembling data in this fashion violated the subscribers' Fourth Amendment rights because it amounted to a general search in violation of the Fourth Amendment's particularity requirement, notwithstanding that the records in question do not belong to the subscribers at all but rather to the carriers, and that the searches of data in the hands of the carriers, assuming that they can be carried out successfully, are intended to be and are as broad as searches of the same data in the hands of the government.

The result is that the government can no longer gather metadata itself; it must consult individual carriers, each of which organizes the metadata as it wishes, and each of which may simply stop maintaining it. There is now afoot a move to curtail the gathering of information from foreigners abroad, who have no rights under the Constitution, by treating them as if they were protected by the Fourth Amendment. This in essence turns the Constitution from a document that protects citizens and residents of the United States into a treaty with the entire world.

The wording of the Fourth Amendment itself provides no clue as to which precautions may be necessary and which are unduly burdensome to preserving the integrity of the persons, houses, papers, and effects of citizens and residents of the United States. If Congress chooses to extend protection to nonresident noncitizens, it does not tell us how far to extend those protections.

* * * *

All of this would be of largely academic interest if not for the fact that whether we acknowledge it or not, we have been for decades the main targets of a war being waged by a death cult. It didn't start on 9/11. Nor did it start in February 1993 with what we now know as the first World Trade Center bombing.

It actually started back in the 1940s, when one of the leading lights of the Muslim Brotherhood—Sayyid Qutb, an Egyptian working in the Egyptian ministry in Cairo—was awarded a traveling fellowship that was meant in large part to get him out of the country, and he chose to travel to Greeley, Colorado. When he encountered Western society in postwar Greeley, Colorado, in the late 1940s with jazz music, crew cuts, and dancing (he is reputed to have walked in on a church social when people were dancing to a recording of "Baby, It's Cold Outside," and he was scandalized), he decided that Islam as he knew it would have to be eternally at war with such a society.

He went back to Egypt and continued to agitate in the same way that in the late 1940s had gotten him a traveling fellowship—except this time, in the late 1960s, it got him hanged. Many of his followers left Egypt for Saudi Arabia, where Qutb's brother wound up teaching the spoiled son of a wealthy Saudi construction family, a young man named Osama bin Laden. And the rest, as they say, is history.

To fight this ideology, it's going to take not only force, although it's certainly going to take that, but also support for those within the Muslim world who favor reform. And they are there. In 2014, President Abdel Fattah el-Sisi delivered a remarkable speech at Al-Azhar University in Cairo, the seat of Sunni learning and the venue for President Barack Obama's 2009 outreach to the Muslim world. President Sisi addressed the imam of Al-Azhar University, looking right at him and the other imams who were assembled; told them that Islam as being preached was bringing death and destruction on Muslims; and urged them to put an end to it. He urged that curricula in Egypt must be reformed to eliminate the teaching that strict Islam must dominate the world by force, if necessary, and that it is the personal duty of each Muslim to bring about that domination.

The imam, Ahmed al-Tayeb, followed up with his own speech, which he delivered not in Cairo or in Chevy Chase, Maryland, but in Saudi Arabia, arguing that Muslim young people were being misled and ruined by an erroneous interpretation of Islam. Although latest reports from Egypt indicate some backsliding from that position by those in control of Al-Azhar University, the government itself apparently remains committed to the reform effort.

There are those in our own country who preach the same message, but they are not the focus of the government's outreach, which has gone instead to organizations like the Conference on American-Islamic Relations (CAIR) and the Islamic Society of North America (ISNA), both of which are affiliated with the Muslim Brotherhood.

Now, the Muslim Brotherhood sounds like a fraternal organization, such as the Elks or the Rotary Club. It's not. The slogan of the Muslim Brotherhood from the time of its founding until now has been "Allah is our objective, the Prophet is our leader, the Koran is our law, Jihad is our way, and dying in the path of Allah is our highest hope."[4] CAIR, as a matter of fact, was named as an unindicted co-conspirator in a terrorism-financing case against the Holy Land Foundation, the largest such case ever tried in the United States. They are the people who are regularly invited to the White House and recognized as representative of Muslims in the United States.

As recently as last week, the secretary of homeland security attended and spoke at the annual meeting of ISNA and thereby credentialed that organization. He waved off any criticism of what he did, saying that he was merely reaching out to a large audience of Muslims. His blindness to the secondary effect of his outreach is stunning.

Imagine what the reaction is bound to be for the average Muslim resident of the United States, when high government officials confer on ISNA the mantle of respectability that comes with being wooed by such officials. How likely do you think it is that such an average resident would reject the council of CAIR and ISNA and opt instead for the teaching of those who believe that those organizations are intent on subverting the values of this country? Not very likely at all.

No doubt the claim would be made that, if our government favored reform-minded Muslim groups and enhanced their credentials by engaging them rather than organizations like CAIR and ISNA, the government would be picking winners and losers in a religious dispute and thereby violating the First Amendment's establishment clause.

The point here, however, is not a matter of religion but a matter of politics and national security. Is it lawful for the government to favor, for political and national security reasons, people who accept our constitutional system of governance and to oppose those who don't? It was entirely permissible to do that during the Cold War, when our adversaries were communists who wanted to subvert our constitutional system and replace it with a totalitarian system.

In fighting this war against such an enemy, one who thinks that not only dancing but also the very idea that people can choose their own government is a sacrilege, perhaps we should follow the example and take the advice of our greatest president, certainly our greatest lawyer president, who said this in 1862 about how to deal with an unprecedented crisis that threatened the existence of our country at that time. He said: "As our case is new, so we must think anew and act anew. We must disenthrall ourselves and then we shall save our country."[5]

Make no mistake about it. The ideology that motivates the Muslims who are at war with us is a totalitarian ideology. It rules every aspect of life—economics, family law, whatever. It transcends allegiance to any nation-state. Does this ideology's use of religious symbols—its call to a God and to a prophet and its reliance on a book—mean that even to the extent it touches on politics and seeks to impose obligations on non-Muslims (and even to the extent it endangers our national security by encouraging Muslims to commit violence) that we can't fight it the same way that we fought other forms of totalitarianism? Do the free exercise and establishment clauses of the First Amendment tie our hands and prevent us from doing that, simply because this ideology can claim to be rooted in a religion? The answer to that hasn't yet been definitely written, at least not in a case or series of cases, and no doubt if we try there will be cases, just as there have been cases about intelligence gathering under the Fourth Amendment and cases about detention under the Fifth.

But if we take the Constitution seriously—not just one or two of its amendments but the political architecture it put in place for a government that can, among other things, preserve the state and protect its citizens—if we take that Constitution seriously, maybe we can fight the ideology that I described in the way that I've suggested to save the country that the president I quoted a moment ago called the "last best hope of earth."[6]

At least I think it's worth a try.

Notes

1. "Selected Quotes of James Madison," Constitution Society, http://www.constitution.org/jm/jm_quotes.htm.

2. George Washington to Colonel Elias Dayton, July 26, 1777, Founders Online, http://founders.archives.gov/documents/Washington/03-10-02-0415.

3. US Const. art. III, § 1.

4. Andrew C. McCarthy, "Hamas Is the Muslim Brotherhood," *National Review*, January 29, 2011, https://www.nationalreview.com/corner/hamas-muslim-brotherhood-andrew-c-mccarthy/.

5. Abraham Lincoln, "Second Annual Message," The American Presidency Project, https://www.presidency.ucsb.edu/documents/second-annual-message-9.

6. Lincoln, "Second Annual Message."

6

From the Bench:
The Constitutional Statesmanship
of Chief Justice William Rehnquist

BRETT M. KAVANAUGH
September 18, 2017

I'm honored to be at the American Enterprise Institute with friends and scholars I've known for many years. This organization has been a place of learning and thinking, and I applaud it for its many continuing contributions to public debate and discourse.

I'm honored to speak at a lecture named for Walter Berns. I was fortunate to become friends with Walter after I was appointed as a judge on the DC Circuit in 2006. As many of you know, Walter was a great storyteller, he possessed a keen sense of poker odds, and he loved the Constitution.

He had the belief, considered naive in some circles, that the meaning of the Constitution is related to the actual words of the Constitution. To use the title of one of his books, he took the Constitution seriously. Walter exuded wisdom and seriousness of purpose. He wrote and taught well. He was a patriot and a great American. I miss him, and we all miss him in these turbulent times. I'm honored to be here at the Berns Lecture.

* * * *

We're here to celebrate Constitution Day, so I'll start with a few words about the Constitution itself. The Constitution was signed by the delegates at Philadelphia on September 17, 1787—230 years ago yesterday. The Framers believed that in order to protect individual liberty, power should not be concentrated in one person or one institution.

To preserve liberty, they created a system of federalism with dual national and state sovereigns. And, furthermore, within the new national government, they separated the legislative, executive, and judicial powers. As William Rehnquist later stated, the Framers devised two critical innovations for the new national government: a president who is independent of and not selected by the legislative branch and a judiciary that is independent of both the legislative and executive branches.

It is sometimes said that the Constitution is a document of majestic generalities. I view it differently. As I see it, the Constitution is primarily a document of majestic specificity, and those specific words have meaning. Absent constitutional amendment, those words continue to bind us as judges, legislators, and executive officials.

And if I can be so bold as to suggest an initial homework assignment from my talk today, it is this: In the next few days, block out 30 minutes of time and read the text of the Constitution word for word. I guarantee you'll come away with a renewed appreciation for the Constitution and for its majestic specificity.

We revere the Constitution in this country, and we should. We also, however, must remember its flaws. And its greatest flaw was the tolerance of slavery. That flaw cannot be airbrushed out of the picture when we celebrate the Constitution. It was not until the 1860s, after the Civil War, that this original sin was corrected in part, at least on paper, by ratification of the 13th, 14th, and 15th Amendments to the Constitution.

But that example illustrates a broader point as well. When we think about the Constitution and we focus on the specific words of the Constitution, we ought not to be seduced into thinking that it was perfect and that it remains perfect. The Framers did not think that the Constitution was perfect. And they knew, moreover, that it might need to be changed as times and circumstances and policy views changed.

And so they provided for a very specific amendment process in Article V of the Constitution. The first 10 amendments, as we all know, came very quickly after the new Congress met in 1789. And those amendments were ratified in 1791. The 11th and 12th Amendments followed soon thereafter, and that process has continued.

Indeed, the amendments have altered fundamental details of our constitutional structure. The 12th Amendment changed how presidents and vice presidents are elected. The 22nd Amendment changed how long presidents can serve. The 17th Amendment altered how the Senate is selected, changing it from a body selected by state legislatures to a body directly elected by the people. The 13th, 14th, and 15th Amendments altered the autonomy of the states and created new constitutional rights and protections for individuals against states.

Many think we could use a few more constitutional amendments: term limits for Supreme Court justices, term limits for members of Congress, an equal rights amendment, a balanced budget amendment, abolition of the death penalty. Different people have different views. But here, as elsewhere, the Constitution already focused on the specific question that lies at the foundation of this and so many other constitutional disputes: Who decides?

In this instance, the question is this: Who decides when it is time to change the Constitution? Who decides when it is time to create a new constitutional right or eliminate an existing constitutional right or alter the structure of the national government? The Constitution quite specifically tells us that the people decide through their elected representatives. An amendment requires the approval of two-thirds of both houses of Congress as well as three-quarters of the states.

But the amendment process is slowed in part because it is so difficult to garner the congressional and state consensus needed to pass constitutional amendments. Because it is so hard, and because it is not easy even to pass federal legislation, pressure is often put on the courts, and the Supreme Court in particular, to update the Constitution to reflect the times.

In the views of some, the Constitution is a living document, and the Court must ensure that the Constitution adapts to meet the changing times. For those of us who believe that the judges are confined to interpreting and applying the Constitution and laws as they are written and not as we might wish they were written, we too believe in a Constitution that lives and endures and in statutes that live and endure. But we believe that changes to the Constitution and laws are to be made by the people through the amendment process and, where appropriate, through the legislative process—not by the courts snatching that constitutional or legislative authority for themselves.

* * * *

That brings me to my primary topic today: William Hubbs Rehnquist. William Rehnquist served on the Supreme Court for 33 years, from 1972 until his death in September 2005. Appointed by President Richard Nixon, he was an extraordinary associate justice from 1972 to 1986. Then in 1986, President Ronald Reagan appointed William Rehnquist as the 16th chief justice of the United States. He served with distinction in that role for 19 more years. If he were still alive today, the chief would be 92 years old.

William Rehnquist died on Saturday, September 3, 2005. I remember it vividly. At the time, I was working as staff secretary to President George W. Bush. Hurricane Katrina had hit earlier that week. I was distressed about how the week had unfolded for the people of New Orleans and the Gulf Coast, for the country, and for the president himself. I sat late that Saturday night on my couch at home with my then-two-week-old daughter, Margaret, on my shoulder and a college football game on TV. I got a call on my cell from Dan Bartlett, who was communications director for the president. He said simply, "Rehnquist just died; the president wants to meet tomorrow morning." I was profoundly sad, but I had no time to dwell on it.

As staff secretary, I was responsible for hustling into the White House right away, contacting the president, immediately getting out a presidential written statement, and working with the speechwriters to help prepare the president's remarks for the following morning, which he delivered from the White House at 10:00 a.m. that Sunday morning.

At that time, John Roberts was the pending nominee for the vacancy created by Sandra Day O'Connor's retirement earlier that summer. Roberts had been a Rehnquist clerk and would be a pallbearer at his funeral. When all of us met with the president in the Oval Office on Sunday morning, it did not take long for the president to settle on nominating John Roberts for the Rehnquist vacancy; he decided that he would worry about the O'Connor vacancy after Roberts was confirmed. The president then publicly announced John Roberts's nomination early on Monday morning before we all took off for another trip to New Orleans and the Gulf Coast.

The enormity of it all—Katrina, Rehnquist, Roberts—still hits me when I think about it in retrospect. But my focus today is Rehnquist. And I've chosen to speak about William Rehnquist for three reasons.

First of all, he and Walter Berns were friends, and they shared a tremendous appreciation for the Constitution and for each other. So it is appropriate, I believe, to remember William Rehnquist at the Berns Lecture.

Second, it pains me that many young lawyers and law students, even Federalist Society types, have little or no sense of the jurisprudence and importance of William Rehnquist to modern constitutional law.

They do not know about his role in turning the Supreme Court away from its 1960s Warren Court approach, in which the Court in some cases had seemed to be simply enshrining its policy views into the Constitution, or so the critics charged. During Rehnquist's tenure, the Supreme Court unquestionably changed and became more of an institution of law, where its power is to interpret and apply the law as written, informed by historical practice, not by its own personal and policy predilections.

When Rehnquist died, Linda Greenhouse of *The New York Times*, who would probably not describe herself as an especially big fan of conservatives, said that Rehnquist had "one of the most consequential" tenures in Supreme Court history. She said that Rehnquist's tenure was marked by "a steady hand, a focus and commitment that never wavered, and the muscular use of the power of judicial review."[1] Well said by Linda Greenhouse.

And it is incumbent on us, I believe, to remind ourselves of the importance of Rehnquist and to teach the younger generations to appreciate that legacy as well.

Third, I want to speak about William Rehnquist because he was my first judicial hero. He was not my last judicial hero. But in the fall of 1987, as I started my first year at Yale Law School and as the Bork hearings unfolded that fall, Justice Antonin Scalia had been on the Court for only a year and not yet written any important opinions as a justice. Justice Clarence Thomas was not even a lower court judge yet. My future boss and future mentor, Justice Anthony Kennedy, was still a Ninth Circuit judge. And that fall, in the confines of my constitutional law classroom and in other classrooms and other classes later in my law school career, I became exposed to the landmarks of American constitutional law.

In case after case after case during law school, I noticed something. After I read the assigned reading, I would constantly make notes to myself: Agree with Rehnquist majority opinion. Agree with Rehnquist dissent. Agree with Rehnquist analysis. Rehnquist makes a good point here. Rehnquist destroys the majority's reasoning here.

At that time, in 1987, Rehnquist had been on the Court for 15 years, almost all of it as an associate justice. And his opinions made a lot of sense to me. In class after class, I stood with Rehnquist. That often meant in the Yale Law School environment of the time that I stood alone. Some things don't change.

For a total of 33 years, William Rehnquist righted the ship of constitutional jurisprudence. To be sure, I do not agree with all of his opinions. No two people would agree with each other in all cases. *Morrison v. Olson* in 1988 comes quickly to mind as a Rehnquist opinion I still have some trouble with, and there are others as well. I must also confess that I don't fully understand why he put gold stripes on the sleeves of his judicial robes in his later years as chief justice, but we all have our quirks, I suppose.

Rehnquist moreover would be the first to say that he did not achieve full success on all the issues he cared about. But it is undeniable, I believe, that he brought about a massive change in constitutional law and how we think about the Constitution.

To begin with, Justice Rehnquist was a judge who contributed to the public debate not only through his judicial opinions but also through his books and articles.

He wrote four very readable books: one about the Supreme Court, one about impeachment (which became helpful a little later in his career), one about civil liberties in wartime (which also became helpful), and one about the election of 1876. When asked why he liked to write books, he said that it was very nice to be able to write something that you don't have to get four other people to agree with.

My Rehnquist story begins with an extraordinarily important law review article Justice Rehnquist wrote in 1976 in the *Texas Law Review*. It's titled "The Notion of a Living Constitution."[2] In that article, Justice Rehnquist sought to alter the debate about the proper role of judges, especially on the Supreme Court, in response to the Warren Court's jurisprudence and to the changing times and the changing mores of the people.

Rehnquist noted with his characteristically understated wit that a living Constitution was surely better than a dead Constitution. He added that only a necrophile would disagree. In response to the straw-man argument often raised by opponents of originalism, Rehnquist first noted, importantly, that the principles of the Constitution apply to new activities.

In his words,

> Merely because a particular activity may not have existed when the Constitution was adopted, or because the framers could not have conceived of a particular method of transacting affairs, cannot mean that general language in the Constitution may not be applied to such a course of conduct.[3]

Consistent with Rehnquist's point there, the Fourth Amendment today applies to searches of cars, even though cars did not exist at the time of the Founding; the First Amendment applies to speech on the internet; and so on. Put simply, Rehnquist believed that the constitutional principles do not change absent amendment. But the principles may and indeed must be applied to new developments and activities unforeseen by the Framers.

The straw man dispensed with, Rehnquist then addressed what he described as a quite different living Constitution philosophy, which then was being espoused in certain circles. Under that version of the living Constitution, as Rehnquist described it, nonelected members of the federal judiciary may address themselves to a social problem simply because other branches of government have failed or refused to do so. These same judges, responsible to no constituency whatever, are claimed as the voice and conscience of contemporary society, Rehnquist wrote.

Rehnquist set forth what he saw as three serious difficulties with this vision of the living Constitution. First, it misconceives the nature of the Constitution, which was designed to enable the popularly elected branches of government, not the judicial branch, to keep the country abreast of the times. Second, that vision ignores, Rehnquist said, the Supreme Court's disastrous experiences in the past, in cases such as *Dred Scott*, when the Court embraced contemporary, fashionable notions of what a living Constitution should contain. Third, he said, however socially desirable the policy goals sought to be advanced might be, advancing them through a freewheeling, nonelected judiciary is quite unacceptable in a democratic society.

In short, Rehnquist stated, the Constitution does not put the popular branches

> in the position of a television quiz show contestant so that when a given period of time has elapsed and a problem remains unsolved by them, the federal judiciary may press a buzzer and take its turn at fashioning a solution.[4]

It's important to emphasize that Rehnquist's notion of the Constitution was not one in which courts simply deferred to legislative choices. One early critic of Rehnquist in 1976 wrote that Rehnquist's vision of the

Constitution meant that in cases involving conflicts between the government and individuals, the government would win.[5] That was wrong. That was not Rehnquist's philosophy or the point of his article.

His point was that it was not for a judge to add to or subtract from the individual rights or structural protections of the Constitution based on the judge's own views.

I read Rehnquist's *Texas Law Review* article when I was a first-year law student, and it's impossible to overstate its significance to me and how I first came to understand the role of a judge in our constitutional system. The article stood then as a lonely voice against the vision of the Supreme Court that was being promoted by most Supreme Court justices and by virtually all law professors at the time.

In my view, Rehnquist's article is one of the most important legal articles of all time. It is short and straightforward, and if I can be so bold as to give you a second reading assignment from this lecture, it is to read Rehnquist's article titled "The Notion of a Living Constitution."

Of course, he was not only a scholar. He was a jurist. He put his views not only into law reviews and books but also into the *United States Reports*. I can't possibly touch on all or even most of his enormous body of judicial work, but I'm going to briefly summarize five areas of Rehnquist's jurisprudence where he applied his principles and where he had a massive and enduring impact on American law: criminal procedure, religion, federalism, unenumerated rights, and administrative law.

The first topic is criminal procedure, including the death penalty. When I clerked for Justice Kennedy in 1993–94, the Kennedy clerks as a group had lunches with each of the other justices at some point during the year. When we had our lunch with Chief Justice Rehnquist, one of my Kennedy co-clerks (and it wasn't Neil Gorsuch) somewhat boldly asked the chief justice what kinds of cases he liked the most. And without missing a beat, the chief said cases involving the rights of criminal defendants.

In a 1985 *New York Times* interview, Rehnquist said that one of the achievements during his first 13 years on the Court had been to call a halt to the number of sweeping rulings of the Warren Court.[6] In the field of criminal procedure, Rehnquist fervently believed that the Supreme Court had taken a wrong turn in the 1960s and 1970s, and nowhere was he more forceful on this point than in the Fourth Amendment context, especially in cases involving violent crime and drugs. He led the charge in rebalancing Fourth Amendment law to respect the rights of the people and victims of violent crime as well as of criminal defendants. He wrote the 1983 opinion in *Illinois v. Gates*, still cited often today, that made the probable cause standard more flexible and commonsensical. He wrote opinions expanding the category of special needs searches, those that could be done without a warrant or individualized suspicion—for example, the 1990 case of *Michigan v. Sitz* upholding drunk-driving roadblocks.

Perhaps his most vehement objection to Warren Court Fourth Amendment law concerned the exclusionary rule by which courts would exclude probative evidence from criminal trials because the police had erred in how they obtained the evidence. At the time Rehnquist took his seat on the Court in 1972, *Mapp v. Ohio*, which had extended the exclusionary rule to states, was only 10 years old. But Rehnquist was obviously not sold on it. In his 1979 separate opinion in *California v. Minjares*, Rehnquist called for the overruling of *Mapp*. He disagreed with the idea that, in his words, "'the criminal is to go free' solely because of a good-faith error in judgment on the part of the arresting officers."[7] This judge-created rule in Rehnquist's view was beyond the four corners of the Fourth Amendment's text and imposed tremendous costs on society.

He advocated for other remedies for police mistakes or misconduct, but he believed that freeing obviously guilty violent criminals was not a proper remedy and, in any event, was surely not a remedy required by the Constitution. Rehnquist of course did not succeed in calling for the overruling of the exclusionary rule, and not many people today call for doing so, given its firmly entrenched position in American law.

But it would be a mistake to call his exclusionary rule project a failure. On the contrary, Rehnquist dramatically changed the law of the exclusionary rule. Led by Rehnquist, the Supreme Court created many needed exceptions to the exclusionary rule that endure to this day. Probably the most notable is the 1984 decision of *United States v. Leon*, where the Court held that exclusion would rarely be appropriate if an officer conducted a search with a warrant in good faith. And there were many others.

The same basic story occurred with *Miranda v. Arizona*. Justice Rehnquist was for years the most vehement critic of *Miranda*, and he wrote numerous opinions limiting its application. For example, in *New York v. Quarles* in 1984, Rehnquist wrote for the Court that there was a public-safety exception to *Miranda* so that *Miranda* warnings need not be given in situations where the officers sought information to protect the public from harm.

To this day, as with the exclusionary rule, courts apply *Miranda* based on many precedents that Rehnquist authored. Those precedents and cases authored by Rehnquist have ensured that *Miranda* is applied in (as Rehnquist would say) a more commonsensical way that is closer to the proper constitutional meaning and that avoids the extremes of the Warren Court holdings.

The story is similar with respect to the death penalty. Just a few days after Rehnquist took his seat on the Supreme Court in January 1972, the Court heard argument in a series of cases, known by the lead case *Furman v. Georgia*, about the constitutionality of the death penalty. The Court that June ultimately struck down, by a 5–4 decision, all of the death penalty laws in the United States. Rehnquist dissented, joined by Chief Justice Warren Burger and Justices Harry Blackmun and Lewis Powell. Burger wrote the main dissent, but Rehnquist's dissent also packed a punch.

A mere five and a half pages in the *US Reports* deftly summarize the fundamental problems he saw in the core of the Court's holding. As he explained, the decision "brings into sharp relief the fundamental question of the role of judicial review in a democratic society."[8] He continued,

> The most expansive reading of the leading constitutional cases does not remotely suggest that this Court has been granted a roving commission, either by the Founding Fathers or by the framers of the Fourteenth Amendment, to strike down laws

that are based upon notions of policy or morality suddenly found unacceptable by a majority of this Court.[9]

The Court's ruling, Rehnquist stated, was "not an act of judgment, but rather an act of will."[10]

But the story did not end there. In the wake of *Furman*, many states enacted new capital punishment statutes. In 1976, the Court turned around and upheld many of them. To this day, the death penalty remains constitutional. Many judges and justices no doubt have policy or moral concerns about the death penalty. But Rehnquist's call for the Court to remember its proper and limited role in the constitutional scheme has so far proved enduring in the death penalty context.

In short, today's constitutional jurisprudence in the field of criminal procedure and the death penalty has Rehnquist's fingerprints all over it. Those are the cases that Rehnquist cared about most. That was his mission primarily, and it is fair to say that he had a dramatic and enduring effect on the course of constitutional law in those areas.

The second topic is religion. When Justice Rehnquist joined the Supreme Court in January 1972, the Court was in the midst of erecting a strict wall of separation between church and state. Religious institutions could not receive funds from government, even pursuant to neutral government benefits programs. William Rehnquist was instrumental in reversing that trend. He persuasively criticized the wall metaphor as "based on bad history" and "useless as a guide to judging."[11] Rehnquist said that the true meaning of the Establishment Clause can be seen only in its history.

To be sure, his views of the Establishment Clause did not always prevail. He dissented in a 1985 case, *Wallace v. Jaffree*, which struck down a moment-of-silence law. He asked, reasonably enough, how a law that allowed students a moment of silence could be deemed an establishment of religion. He was in dissent in several other cases involving prayer in public schools, such as *Lee v. Weisman* and *Santa Fe Independent School District v. Doe*, involving prayer at graduation ceremonies and before football games.

Of course, all of those cases involved prayer in the public school setting. And it is fair to say that a majority of the Court throughout his tenure and to this day has sought to cordon off public schools from state-sponsored religious prayer. But Rehnquist had much more success in ensuring that religious schools and religious institutions could participate as equals in society and in state benefits programs, receiving funding or benefits from the state so long as the funding was pursuant to a neutral program that, among other things, included religious and nonreligious institutions alike.

In the critical 1983 case of *Mueller v. Allen*, he wrote the opinion for a 5–4 Court upholding a Minnesota program that allowed taxpayers to deduct expenses for the education of their children at private schools, including parochial schools. In 1993, again in an opinion written by Rehnquist in the *Zobrest v. Catalina Foothills School District* case, the Court reinforced that *Mueller* holding. And then in 2002, the Court in *Zelman v. Simmons-Harris* (again, a majority opinion by Rehnquist) upheld an Ohio school voucher program that allowed vouchers for students who attended private schools, including religious schools.

In the Establishment Clause context, Rehnquist was central in changing the jurisprudence and convincing the Court that the wall metaphor was wrong as a matter of law and history. And that Rehnquist legacy continues, as we see in recent cases such as *Town of Greece v. Galloway*, which upheld the practice of prayer for local government meetings. And without the line of Rehnquist cases beginning with *Mueller v. Allen*, we never would have seen last term's 7–2 decision in *Trinity Lutheran Church of Columbia v. Comer*. In that case, only two justices found an Establishment Clause problem in a state program that provided funds to schools, including religious schools, for playgrounds. There again, the Rehnquist legacy was at work.

Third is federalism. Justice Rehnquist led a federalism revolution in a variety of areas—including federal commandeering of state officials and state sovereign immunity. I'm not going to speak more about those two issues today, but I will focus on federalism in terms of Congress's power to regulate interstate commerce.

As of the early 1990s, it was widely assumed that there was no real limit to the scope of the authority Congress could exercise under the Commerce and Necessary and Proper Clauses. Although other clauses may impose limits on the scope of congressional power, few expected that the Court would ever rely on a lack of Commerce Clause authority as the basis for invalidating a federal law. That was certainly what I was taught at Yale Law School. But it was not just in New Haven. It was widely believed that no such limits existed.

Enter the case of *United States v. Lopez* in 1995. The case involved the federal Gun Free School Zones Act of 1990. That law made it a crime to possess a firearm within 1,000 feet of a school. The defendant, who was convicted of violating that law, raised a seemingly Hail Mary argument that the law exceeded Congress's authority under the Commerce Clause. And in an unexpected 5–4 decision written by Chief Justice Rehnquist, the Supreme Court agreed with the defendant's position.

Laws like this, the Court said, should be and were being passed by the states. They could not be passed by the federal government. In the chief's opinion, he stated:

> We start with first principles. The Constitution creates a Federal Government of enumerated powers. As James Madison wrote: "The powers delegated by the proposed Constitution to the federal government are few and defined. Those which are to remain in the State governments are numerous and indefinite." This constitutionally mandated division of authority "was adopted by the Framers to ensure protection of our fundamental liberties."[12]

Rehnquist then described the arc of the Court's Commerce Clause jurisprudence, which had expanded the clause significantly over the years. But he said there still had to be outer limits. And he noted that all the precedents involved regulation of economic activity where the activity substantially affected interstate commerce.

The government's theory was that possession of a firearm may result in violent crime, which may in turn affect the economy. Rehnquist was having none of it. Under that theory, he explained, federal regulation of family law and local educational curriculum could be justified on the ground that such activities affected the national economy. And he stated, "If we were to accept the Government's arguments, we are hard pressed to posit any activity by an individual that Congress is without power to regulate."[13] Congress, Rehnquist emphasized, does not have "a general police power."[14] He concluded that the activity being regulated had to be commercial in nature, and he stated that possession of a gun in a local school zone is in no sense an economic activity.

Five years later, Rehnquist again wrote the majority opinion of the Court in *United States v. Morrison*, holding that a 1994 statute creating a federal civil cause of action against gender-motivated violence likewise exceeded Congress's Commerce Clause power. He repeated, Congress's Commerce Clause authority extends to regulation of economic activity, not to noneconomic conduct such as traditional violent crimes. Regulation of that kind was limited to the states.

Those two decisions were critically important in putting the brakes on the Commerce Clause and in preventing Congress from assuming a general police power. After Rehnquist had left the Court, in the health care case in 2012, although it is not often the first thing discussed about that case, we do remember that a five-justice majority said that the Commerce Clause did not give Congress authority to require citizens to purchase a good or service.

Congress's Commerce Clause power undoubtedly remains very broad, but there are limits. Congress does not have a general police power, and William Rehnquist is largely responsible for that important feature of modern constitutional law.

Fourth is the Court's power to recognize unenumerated rights. A few months after he joined the Court in 1972, Justice Rehnquist faced an oral argument about the constitutionality of a state law prohibiting abortion in the case of *Roe v. Wade*. Rehnquist, along with Justice Byron White, ultimately dissented from the Court's 7–2 holding recognizing a constitutional right to abortion.

Rehnquist's dissenting opinion did not suggest that the Constitution protected no rights other than those enumerated in the text of the Bill of Rights. But he stated that under the Court's precedents, any such unenumerated right had to be rooted in the traditions and conscience of our people. Given the prevalence of abortion regulations both historically and at the time, Rehnquist said he could not reach such a conclusion about abortion. He explained that a law prohibiting an abortion even where the mother's life was in jeopardy would violate the Constitution. But otherwise he stated the states had the power to legislate with regard to this matter.

In later cases, Rehnquist reiterated his view that unenumerated rights could be recognized by the courts only if the asserted right was rooted in the nation's history and tradition. The 1997 case of *Washington v. Glucksberg* involved an asserted right to assisted suicide. For a 5–4 majority this time, Rehnquist wrote the opinion for the Court, saying that the unenumerated rights and liberties protected by the Due Process Clause are those rights that are deeply rooted in the nation's history and tradition. And he rejected the claim that assisted suicide qualified as such a fundamental right.

Of course, even a first-year law student could tell you that the *Glucksberg* approach to unenumerated rights was not consistent with the approach of the abortion cases such as *Roe v. Wade* in 1973—as well as the 1992 decision reaffirming *Roe*, known as *Planned Parenthood v. Casey*.

What to make of that? In this context, it is fair to say that Justice Rehnquist was not successful in convincing a majority of the justices in the context of abortion either in *Roe* itself or in the later cases such as *Casey*, in the latter case perhaps because of stare decisis. But he was successful in stemming the general tide of freewheeling judicial creation of unenumerated rights that were not rooted in the nation's history and tradition. The *Glucksberg* case stands to this day as an important precedent, limiting the Court's role in the realm of social policy and helping to ensure that the Court operates more as a court of law and less as an institution of social policy.

Fifth and last is administrative law. Here, too, I can't possibly cover all of his many significant contributions. For example, in *Vermont Yankee Nuclear Power Corporation v. NRDC* in 1978, he wrote a textualist and important opinion for the Court. The Court should not be making up new procedural requirements for agencies to meet, beyond those requirements specified in the Administrative Procedure Act.

But the case I want to focus on in this context is Justice Rehnquist's separate opinion in the 1980 case of *Industrial Union Department v. American Petroleum Institute*, popularly known as the "Benzene Case." In that case, the statute gave the secretary of labor expansive authority to promulgate standards to regulate harmful substances such as benzene. In a separate opinion, Justice Rehnquist, speaking for only himself, would have held that the act was an unconstitutional delegation of legislative power to the executive branch.

He operated within the confines of precedent. And the precedent did allow some delegation of rulemaking authority to agencies. Rehnquist did not suggest that agencies lacked any power to issue binding rules. But applying the precedents, Rehnquist argued that Congress may not delegate *important* choices of social policy to agencies. He summarized the point this way: "It is the hard choices, and not the filling in of the blanks, which must be made by the elected representatives of the people. When fundamental policy decisions underlying important legislation about to be enacted are to be made, the buck stops with Congress and the President" in the legislative process.[15]

Rehnquist's opinion on the nondelegation issue has not become the law, but it nonetheless has had a major impact in laying the foundation for the Court's modern major rules doctrine, sometimes referred to as the major questions doctrine. In the 2000 decision in *FDA v. Brown & Williamson*, the Supreme Court, with Rehnquist in the majority, adopted a principle of statutory interpretation under which Congress may not delegate authority to agencies to issue major rules unless Congress clearly says as much. In

Professor Abbe Gluck's words, *Brown & Williamson* applied "a presumption of *non*delegation in the face of statutory ambiguity over major policy questions or questions of major political or economic significance."[16]

In recent years, the Supreme Court has applied that major rules doctrine in an important Environmental Protection Agency case written by Justice Scalia. And lower courts, including this judge, continue to apply that doctrine in significant ways. The major rules or major questions doctrine is critical to limiting agencies' ability to make major policy decisions that belong to Congress, at least unless Congress clearly delegates that authority. Rehnquist is ultimately responsible for that rule.

* * * *

In sum, few justices in history have had as much impact as William Rehnquist. He did so by dint of his personality and the force of his intellect. He was a humble man. He was not flashy. The 1970s book *The Brethren: Inside the Supreme Court* by Bob Woodward and Scott Armstrong was highly critical of many justices for being too arrogant or too aloof or too lazy or not up to the job. The book was unsparing and caused a sensation in the country. More than any time since then, the individual justices themselves were the talk of the country.

But that negativity did not extend to Rehnquist. Although the book was arguably critical of his jurisprudence as being too conservative, at least in the eyes of the book's sources or authors, Rehnquist was referred to with the following descriptions sprinkled throughout the book: easygoing, good-natured, thoughtful, diligent, a crisp intellect, a solid conservative, well-reasoned, sophisticated analysis, a clever tactician, very casual, friendly toward clerks, a team player, remarkably unstuffy, and affable. Pretty good for a book critical of virtually everyone on the Supreme Court. But that reflected the man.

He loved to play tennis with his clerks. He played once a week with his clerks. He only hired three clerks because he wanted to have a set doubles game every week. Asked if he hired clerks based on their athletic ability, he said, "Of course not. It's only one of several factors."

He wrote clever lines. Here's one lengthy passage from a 1977 case:

> Those who valiantly but vainly defended the heights of Bunker
> Hill in 1775 made it possible that men such as James Madison
> might later sit in the first Congress and draft the Bill of Rights
> to the Constitution. The post–Civil War Congresses which
> drafted the Civil War Amendments to the Constitution could
> not have accomplished their task without the blood of brave
> men on both sides which was shed at Shiloh, Gettysburg, and
> Cold Harbor. If those responsible for these Amendments, by
> feats of valor or efforts of draftsmanship, could have lived to
> know that their efforts had enshrined in the Constitution the
> right of commercial vendors of contraceptives to peddle them
> to unmarried minors through such means as window displays
> and vending machines located in the men's room of truck
> stops, notwithstanding the considered judgment of the New
> York Legislature to the contrary, it is not difficult to imagine
> their reaction.[17]

Rehnquist was at the helm of major national events. He presided over
the impeachment trial of President Bill Clinton. Of his experience presiding over that trial, he later said he did nothing of note and did it very well.
He presided over and kept the Court intact after perhaps the single most
controversial episode in modern Supreme Court history, *Bush v. Gore.*
In that case, he wrote a concurring opinion joined by Justices Scalia and
Thomas that was based on the precise text and history of Article II, and
that was more persuasive to many than the *per curiam* majority opinion.

Despite suffering badly from cancer, he valiantly made his way to the
inauguration stand in 2005 to administer the oath to President George W.
Bush. He led the Court and the federal judiciary with a firm hand on the
wheel, but without seizing the spotlight. One senses that his former clerk
John Roberts is following the Rehnquist model and seeking to lead the
Court and the judiciary with that same firm but humble touch.

Despite his affability, Rehnquist was efficient. He hated wasted time. He bristled at logistical messes. The year I clerked at the Court, I was put in charge of organizing a baseball game outing to Camden Yards with the Rehnquist, Scalia, and Kennedy clerks. The Washington Nationals did not exist yet, so we were off to Baltimore. But not just the clerks. The chief justice decided he wanted to go as well, along with Justice Kennedy. I bought all the game tickets; I arranged the train transportation to Baltimore from Union Station. At the time, there was a direct train to the stadium.

It seemed simple, but I was scared that some screwup would occur. "What was I doing in charge of the chief justice?" I thought to myself. Happily, the whole day went off without a hitch, although I can't say I enjoyed any of it until we were all safely back in DC and went our own ways.

But I do remember when the chief said to me as we left Union Station at the end of the day that the trip had been enjoyable and very well organized. Maybe it was just a throwaway line, but I was excited. From the chief, that was the highest praise. It was as if Walter Berns had told you that you were an excellent constitutional scholar. It doesn't get any better than that.

For those who saw him only in oral argument, Rehnquist could seem tough and gruff at times. When I argued an attorney-client privilege case in the Supreme Court in 1998, Rehnquist quickly asked me if anyone supported the position I was advocating. I quickly cited two academic commentators, Christopher Mueller and Laird Kirkpatrick. Without missing a beat, Rehnquist, with evident disdain, said, "Who are they?" When I explained that they had written a treatise on evidence, Justice John Paul Stevens unhelpfully chimed in, "We usually rely on Wigmore."

Later in the argument, Justice Stephen Breyer returned to the theme and asked whether anyone supported another position I was advocating in the case. And I said: "With hesitation at raising their names again," and I then paused and turned my head to look at the chief justice. He smiled and laughed. And then I proceeded to repeat that Professors Mueller and Kirkpatrick supported that position, too.

The bar for humor at the Supreme Court is admittedly pretty low, but I was nonetheless pleased that I somehow cleared it that day and did so without irritating the chief justice. Indeed, in the official transcript of the oral argument, which I double-checked this morning just to make sure I was not imagining things, the transcript says, "Laughter." Thank God.

That moment made it a little easier for me when Chief Justice Rehnquist wrote the majority opinion rejecting my position in the case. But, by the way, he cited Mueller and Kirkpatrick.

As we celebrate Constitution Day, I am honored to have been able to say a few words about my first judicial hero, William Rehnquist. Working on these remarks has been a labor of love and a sign of my deep appreciation and respect for Walter Berns and for William Rehnquist, two constitutional statesmen.

Notes

1. Linda Greenhouse, "William H. Rehnquist, Chief Justice of Supreme Court, Is Dead at 80," *The New York Times*, September 4, 2005, http://www.nytimes.com/2005/09/04/politics/william-h-rehnquist-chief-justice-ofsupreme-court-is-dead-at-80.html.

2. William H. Rehnquist, "The Notion of a Living Constitution," *Harvard Journal of Law & Public Policy* 29, no. 2 (2006): 401–15, http://ejtn6r2.episerverhosting.com/Documents/About%20EJTN/Independent%20Seminars/Human%20Rights%20BCN%2028-29%20April%202014/Rehnquist_Living_Constitution_HJLPP_2006.pdf. Originally published in *Texas Law Review* 54 (1976): 693–707.

3. Rehnquist, "The Notion of a Living Constitution," 402.

4. Rehnquist, "The Notion of a Living Constitution," 408.

5. David L. Shapiro, "Mr. Justice Rehnquist: A Preliminary View," *Harvard Law Review* 90, no. 2 (1976): 293–357, https://www.jstor.org/stable/1340157.

6. John A. Jenkins, "The Partisan," *The New York Times*, March 3, 1985, http://www.nytimes.com/1985/03/03/magazine/the-partisan.html.

7. California v. Minjares, 443 US 916, 918–19 (1979) (Rehnquist, J., dissenting from denial of stay).

8. Furman v. Georgia, 408 US 238, 466 (1972) (Rehnquist, J., dissenting).

9. *Furman v. Georgia*, 408 US at 467.

10. *Furman v. Georgia*, 408 US at 468.

11. Wallace v. Jaffree, 472 US 38, 107 (1985) (Rehnquist, J., dissenting).

12. United States v. Lopez, 514 US 549, 552 (1995) (parenthetical references omitted).

13. *United States v. Lopez*, 514 US at 564.

14. *United States v. Lopez*, 514 US at 567.

15. Industrial Union Department v. American Petroleum Institute, 448 US 607, 687 (1980) (Rehnquist, J., concurring).

16. Abbe R. Gluck and Lisa Schultz Bressman, "Statutory Interpretation from the Inside—An Empirical Study of Congressional Drafting, Delegation, and the Canons, Part I," *Stanford Law Review* 65, no. 5 (2013): 1003, http://www.stanfordlawreview. org/wp-content/uploads/sites/3/2013/06/Gluck_Bressman_65_Stan._L._Rev._901.pdf (emphasis in original).

17. Carey v. Population Services International, 431 US 678, 717 (1977) (Rehnquist, J., dissenting).

7

Emancipating the Mind: Lincoln, the Founders, and Scientific Progress

DIANA SCHAUB
September 17, 2018

The American founders, the US Constitution, and Abraham Lincoln were dear to Walter Berns, as his entire career testified and as I learned firsthand when I took an American political thought seminar with him, way back in the early 1980s, when he visited for a semester at the University of Chicago. In Walter's honor, I will touch upon all three of his favorites, but on a topic that I don't believe he ever addressed—namely, the meaning and status of science and technology in our political order.

Let me begin, as I believe Walter might have, by drawing a contrast between ourselves and the ancient Greek city-state of Sparta. Our regime is uniquely friendly to science, as can be seen from Article 1, Section 8 of the US Constitution, which grants Congress the power "to promote the Progress of Science and useful Arts."[1] Unlike us, Sparta didn't believe in promoting progress (scientific or otherwise) because it didn't believe there was such a thing as progress, at least not after the great leap forward of its dramatic founding by Lycurgus. If the political community is already in the best of health, then change can only mean decline. To stave off decline, Sparta disallowed the great agents of change: trade and technology. Interestingly, this devotion to fixity also entailed hostility to the written word. Sparta's fundamental ordinance, called the Great Rhetra, which came direct from the Delphic oracle, was that the laws should never be put in writing. Instead, Sparta sought to imprint its unwritten laws on the young through "good discipline." Sparta aimed to write indelibly, on the heart itself, thus creating incontestable agreement—the kind of homogeneity that repels questioning. The avoidance of the written word affected the spoken word too. We still call a terse, uninquisitive style of speech "laconic" after Laconia, the region of the Peloponnese where Sparta was located.[2]

Opposition to written laws has not been as pronounced in other nations or traditions. Certainly, the adherents of the Abrahamic religions, often called the Peoples of the Book, managed to embrace writing without sacrificing reverence. Moses and the biblical God took a different route to obedience than Lycurgus and the Delphic oracle, but both sought obedience. Yet it seems that the written word, even when the Writ is regarded as Holy, does invite quarrels over interpretation. The exegetes of the Torah, Bible, and Quran are the precursors of our schismatic schools of constitutional interpretation.

Even after the advent of written scripture, it took an awfully long time for the innovation of a written constitution to appear. Ours, as we all know, was the first. The idea caught fire: Of the almost 200 nations in the world today, only the merest handful are without a codified constitution, and those few (e.g., Israel, Saudi Arabia, and the UK) do, as a matter of course, have statutory laws, not simply customs.

It shouldn't be surprising that the world's first written constitution contains an explicit acknowledgment of progress as a human possibility. The progressive assumption is there not only with general reference to science and technology but politically as well. The Preamble asserts that the Constitution aims to achieve "a *more perfect* Union" and to "*promote* the general Welfare"; both phrases emphasize improvement—indeed, the literal meaning of "pro-mote" is "to forward move."[3] Likewise, the provision for constitutional amendments welcomes a search for further political improvement, and the provision for "new States" encourages the country's enlargement.[4] "Bigger and better" is the American way. The project "to institute new Government," first called for in the Declaration of Independence and finally realized in the US Constitution, is defended in the Federalist Papers, where the word "new" is repeatedly invoked.[5] The authors of the "new science of politics" pursued "a new and more noble course" incorporating "wholly new discoveries" into the "new modelled" "new Constitution." "New" is the oldest word in the American political lexicon.[6]

Arguably, the greatest generator of newness is that clause I began with, a clause that is known not as "the science clause" or "the progress clause" but as "the patent and copyright clause," although neither the word "patent" nor "copyright" appears in the text. Here's the full sentence: "The Congress shall have Power . . . To promote the Progress of Science and useful Arts, by securing for limited Times to Authors and Inventors the exclusive Right to their respective Writings and Discoveries."[7] Of the 18 paragraphs in Section 8, each one specifying a power of Congress, this one is unique. All the other paragraphs simply state, without elaboration, what power is being granted—for instance, Congress shall have power "to borrow money" or "to establish Post Offices."[8] The means for "carrying into Execution" each of the enumerated powers is left up to Congress under the general guidance of "the necessary and proper" clause, which concludes Section 8.[9]

However, in the case of the power to promote the progress of science, the means to attain the object are spelled out. Issuing patents and copyrights seems to be the sole constitutional means by which the federal promotion of science can be pursued. Thus, what could have been a very far-ranging grant of power became instead a narrow one. Accordingly, we refer to the clause by its restricted means rather than its more expansive aim; it is "the patent clause" rather than "the progress of science clause."

According to Madison's records of the Constitutional Convention, the initial suggestions for this section detailed many other modes of promoting the arts and sciences, such as offering research grants and prize money to inventors, as well as establishing public institutions of learning.[10] All the suggestions were sent, by unanimous vote, to the Committee of Detail. We know nothing about the discussions that took place there. All we know is that the final wording was approved by the full body, unanimously and without discussion, during the last two weeks of the convention.[11]

It might be worth noting that the limits expressed in the clause flow in two directions, by which I mean that, just as the promotion of science is limited to patents, the rationale for patents is limited to their public benefits. Patents, remember, were considerably more controversial than post offices. Patents began in England as monopoly privileges granted by the Crown to merchants who garnered royal favor. The drafters of the Constitution wanted to be clear that their reason for protecting the financial interests of authors and inventors was for the public purpose of promoting scientific progress. They were not providing a blanket congressional authorization to set up commercial monopolies or allocate economic privileges, as the Crown had routinely and abusively done in eras past. Indeed, the Constitutional Convention rejected wording that would have granted Congress the power to charter corporations.[12]

There is one other unique feature of the patent clause: It refers to a "right"—the only instance of the word in the Constitution of 1787. This "right"—which we now call an "intellectual property right"—is, however, very different from the rights that would soon be acknowledged in the decalogue of constitutional amendments. The Bill of Rights forbids Congress from abridging or violating the fundamental rights of conscience, speech, and personal security. By contrast, intellectual property rights are left entirely subject to Congress's statutory determination. Benefiting from the commercialization of one's writings and discoveries is not, it seems, a natural right (an inalienable right) but rather a civilly granted privilege.[13]

It's worth thinking about why this is so. Certainly, one has an inviolable right to think one's own thoughts. However, once you publish them, the ideas expressed cease to be yours. They become the shared possession of all who comprehend them. The Pythagorean theorem does not belong to Pythagoras and never did. By nature, the realm of ideas is pure communism. What the copyright clause does is say that in hopes of encouraging more folks to think original thoughts, society will forgo its claim for a certain amount of time and create instead an artificial right in the first thinker who decides to share his thoughts. Kindergarten teachers do the same when they encourage children to share by offering tangible rewards for sharing (candy or gold stars), thereby yoking the self-interest of the child to the public interest. The notion of intellectual property rights is itself a human invention for the encouragement of human invention. But that also means that intellectual property rights can be changed and redefined to fit the needs of the commonwealth.

Although limited in the ways I have outlined, the patent clause is not inconsiderable. As Lincoln so vividly described in his "Lecture on Discoveries and Inventions," what the patent clause does is add "the fuel of *interest* to the *fire* of genius."[14] That is a pretty combustible combination—one that has certainly furthered the Promethean achievements of modern science and technology. The underlying assumptions of the patent provision are that scientific advance will redound to the public good and that the public good can be achieved by rewarding private enterprise.[15]

The Founders

Although the power to establish a national university or to award premiums for discoveries was dropped from the Constitution, some of the Founders continued to press for wider state sponsorship of science, especially applied science. Alexander Hamilton, for instance, concluded his 1791 Report on Manufactures with a plan to establish a board of commissioners whose task would be to incentivize "useful discoveries . . . by proportionate rewards."[16]

Hamilton's boss, George Washington, believed that Congress could go beyond the self-interest-based appeal of patents. "There is nothing which can better deserve your patronage," he told Congress in his first annual message, "than the promotion of science and literature. Knowledge is, in every country, the surest basis of public happiness."[17] Washington put his great moral authority, and substantial financial backing as well, squarely behind the idea of a national university located in the nation's capital.[18] Although endorsed by the next five presidents, the plan was never taken up by Congress.[19] In his farewell to the nation, Washington emphasized the harmony between moral, political, and intellectual progress. Religion and morality, he argued, are the "great Pillars of human happiness," as well as "indispensable supports" for political liberty and prosperity.[20] How can religion and morality be fostered? According to Washington, through education. The first use of the imperative voice in his Farewell Address is a command to "promote then as an object of primary importance, Institutions for the general diffusion of knowledge."[21] Washington anticipates no conflict between religion and reason, between morality and enlightenment.

John Adams, despite his great erudition, was not quite as sanguine about the happy cooperation of the intellectual and moral realms. Listen to his description of what really motivates the men of science and letters.

> Scholars learn the dead languages of antiquity as well as the living tongues of modern nations. . . . They puzzle themselves and others with metaphysics and mathematics. They renounce their pleasures, neglect their exercises, and destroy their health—for what? Is curiosity so strong? . . . If Crusoe on his island had the library of Alexandria and a certainty that he should never again see the face of man, would he ever open a volume? Perhaps he might; but it is very probable he would read but little. A sense of duty, a love of truth . . . may, no doubt, have an influence on some minds. But the universal object and idol of men of letters is *reputation*.[22]

Cynical, perhaps, but hard to gainsay.

The conclusion Adams draws is that the spread of enlightenment will heighten human vanity; "the more knowledge is diffused," he says, "the more the passions are extended, and the more furious they grow."[23] Adams would not be surprised that the technology of social media, which has made everyone and his brother into an author, has also given rise to phenomena such as vengeful trolling and cyberbullying, or even just the vanity-driven obsession with "likes" and "shares" and all the new metrics of reputation-mongering. While Adams was, like Washington, a proponent of public schooling, he put the greatest weight on constitutional structure. Since rivalries were bound to increase with the increase of knowledge, "the essence of a free government," Adams claimed, "consists in an effectual control of rivalries."[24] What he had in mind, of course, were mechanisms such as the separation of powers and an ingenious system of checks and balances.

One final note about Adams: He saw with prophetic clarity how science could turn into "scientism." An ideologized science might become the purveyor of what Adams called "the most disconsolate of all creeds, that men are but fireflies and that this *all* is without a father."[25] He predicted that thoroughgoing materialism would be antihuman in its effects, justifying even genocide. If "man, as man," is not "an object of respect," then, he said, "the extermination of . . . [a] nation" would be "as innocent as the swallowing of mites on a morsel of cheese."[26] The murderous rationalizations of Marxism and Fascism were already glimpsed by Adams. He had a further worry that the natural human response to such atheistic doctrines would be a longing to return to religious belief, but of the worst, most superstitious, fanatical, and modernity-hating kind (a prediction that we perhaps see borne out in the rise of radical Islam).

John Adams and Thomas Jefferson disagreed on many things: the promise and peril of science among them. Of all the Founders, Jefferson came closest to succumbing to what Adams might have called "the French Temptation," expecting too much of reason and underestimating its all-too-human character. Jefferson was radically pro-science, to the extent of asserting that "the general spread of the light of science" would demonstrate the truth of human rights.[27] Despite his faith in the "unbounded exercise of reason," at other times Jefferson insisted that the "only firm basis" for "the liberties of a nation" was "a conviction in the minds of the people that these liberties are of the gift of God."[28] More troubling than his waffling on the foundation of rights is the fact that Jefferson dabbled in the pseudoscience of his day. His speculations on the supposedly natural qualities (and inequalities) of the various races testify to the all-too-human character of his own self-exculpatory reasoning.[29]

And yet, as Lincoln said, "all honor to Jefferson," not only for writing the Declaration but also for his impressive promotion of education.[30]

While Washington pushed for a national university, Jefferson acted locally and with greater success, founding the University of Virginia and setting its curriculum, while also sketching plans for a taxpayer-funded system of primary and secondary schools. Jefferson's writings on the purposes of education, and the place of science within education, are still well worth reading. So too his fascinating letter to Isaac McPherson on the question of whether property in ideas is natural or conventional. Although himself the designer of patentable devices, Jefferson declined to seek what he called "monopolies of invention," in accord with his belief that "ideas should freely spread from one to another over the globe."[31]

Benjamin Franklin agreed, and he was a veritable Vesuvius of discoveries and inventions. An internationally renowned scientist, with an imagination both visionary and eminently practical, Franklin was a disciple of Francis Bacon, looking to science for the relief of man's estate and fully expecting stunning advances in "the Power of Men over Matter."[32] In a letter to fellow scientist Joseph Priestley, Franklin predicts victory over "all Diseases . . . not excepting even that of Old Age."[33] The 74-year-old Franklin fantasizes about conquering gravity so that men might attain "absolute Levity, for the sake," he says, "of easy Transport."[34] One of his own unsuccessful inventions involved a balloon that was to hoist him a few inches off the ground, while a friend walked along with the gout-ridden Franklin blimp in tow. This image of Franklin floating just above the human scene is an apt one, since the levity Franklin aimed at was more than physical; it was philosophic. He had a kind of lightness of spirit or equanimity about the human situation. Although he signed on to the Baconian project, he remained alert to the dangers of scientific hubris. Thus, in that same letter to Priestley, he makes clear that he doesn't expect improvements in "moral Science," since it is unrealistic to think "that Men would cease to be Wolves to one another."[35] Franklin, like that other American original, Mark Twain, turned to humor to deflate the pretensions of believers of all sorts. He skewered the pro-science fanatics as readily as he did the religious enthusiasts.[36] The spoofs and satires Franklin wrote, almost always under one pseudonym or another, were designed to make us a little more modest, a little more charitable, and a lot more cheerful.

Lincoln

That's my quick survey of the Constitution's take on science, supplemented with a few reflections by some of the leading Founders. What I'd like to do in the time remaining is focus on Lincoln's "Lecture on Discoveries and Inventions," which I believe is the most sustained treatment by any American statesmen of the meaning and dilemma of science.[37]

Before hazarding an interpretation, it must be pointed out that we unfortunately don't have the speech in its final form. What we have are two substantial portions (eight to 10 pages each), which were long thought to be separate efforts—the "First Lecture on Discoveries and Inventions" and the "Second Lecture on Discoveries and Inventions"—but which may, in fact, be parts of a larger whole.[38] We do know that versions of the speech were delivered multiple times over the two-year period from early 1858 to early 1860, during a period of extremely heightened public passions. It was first presented a couple of months before Lincoln's House Divided speech: the speech in which he accepted the Republican nomination for the Senate and sketched the contours of the looming crisis. It was presented again, a handful of times, after his electoral loss to Stephen Douglas in that Senate race. The other activity that kept Lincoln occupied during this time was the preparation of a book-length version of his already famous debates with Douglas. As we'll see, the very heart of the "Lecture on Discoveries and Inventions" is a claim about the effect of the invention of the printing press on the affairs of mankind. The medium of print allows one, Lincoln says, to "converse with the . . . unborn, at all distances of time and of space."[39] Getting the Lincoln-Douglas debates into print meant that Lincoln's forensic victory over Douglas stood, in his words, "a better chance of never [being] forgotten," whatever might befall the country—even if what happened was the continuation of the Democratic Party's dominance and the nationaliza-tion of slavery.[40] Finally, Lincoln delivered the lecture one last time after his tremendous Cooper Union address, the speech that fortified his status as a presidential contender in 1860. So, it was during this time of intense partisan involvement that Lincoln saw fit to work on what he thought of as his "Lecture on Man." Apparently, this was material that Americans needed to ponder—in a wisdom-seeking spirit—as "the crisis of the house divided" gathered steam.

* * * *

All right, enough preliminaries. The "First Lecture," which I take to be the opening section of the speech, presents a survey of technological advances as gleaned from the Bible.[41] This is no ordinary account of human ingenu-ity. Let me quote from the opening:

> All creation is a mine, and every man, a miner.

> The whole earth, and all *within* it, *upon* it, and *round* about it, including *himself,* . . . are the infinitely various "leads" from which, man, from the first, was to dig out his destiny.

> In the beginning, the mine was unopened, and the miner stood *naked,* and *knowledgeless,* upon it.[42]

Lincoln rewrites Genesis—presenting man not in the Garden of Eden or even tossed out of the Garden to be a tiller of the soil, but instead as a miner, a deep-digger, engaged in an extractive, industrial process. The mining metaphor, which coincidentally was much used by Bacon, sug-gests that truth is hidden and that nature, even our own nature, does not reveal itself without the application of labor.[43] Lincoln admits that other animals labor too, since they provide themselves with homes and food, but human labor is unique since man is the only animal "who *improves* his workmanship."[44] Human labor, we might say, is scientific. Lincoln, however, doesn't use an abstract word like "science" or "scientific." His language is more explanatory. He says that "this improvement" is accomplished "by *Discoveries*, and *Inventions*."[45] And he gives a memorable illustration of those two operations: Man's "first important discovery was the fact that he was naked; and his first invention was the fig-leaf-apron."[46]

From that beginning point, Lincoln traces the scriptural evidence of human industry and its results. He moves from clothing to iron to forms of transport, then agriculture, and finally various forces that can replace "man's own muscular power"—namely, animal power, wind power, water-power, and steam power.[47] Lincoln quotes from and cites 23 Bible verses, tracking such things as the first mention of "thread" or "*instruments* made of iron" or "chariots."[48]

He also references another dozen or so Bible passages, sometimes quoting but not citing, sometimes citing but not quoting, sometimes merely alluding to particular books of the Bible.[49] His account draws exclusively from the Old Testament, other than a single closing passage from the New Testament. The only New Testament verse, "Two women shall be grinding at the mill," said to be "the language of the Saviour," is offered to prove that the water wheel was unknown in Bible times.[50] The verse, found in both Matthew and Luke, refers to the Rapture at the Second Coming of Christ, while the surrounding verses detail the time of tribulation at the end of days.[51] Thus, the horizon of the "First Lecture" stretches from the creation of the earth to its destruction.

As this last instance more than indicates, this is an unorthodox way to employ the Bible. Now perhaps a pious man turns to the Good Book on all occasions (just as a good American turns to Lincoln), but still, this is making the Bible serve a purpose that seems altogether alien to the text.[52] Matthew 24 is about the "weeping and gnashing of teeth" and Christ's prophecy of his return in power and glory; it is not about when the knowledge of hydropower was acquired.[53] I think the natural question must be "What the heck is Lincoln doing?" I want to suggest that Lincoln is quite aware of what he is doing and that he has carefully selected these Bible references in order to tell two stories simultaneously. The first is a story of technological progress—slow but perceptible. The other is a story of sin, slavery, and divine punishment. Each human invention that is mentioned, beginning with that fig-leaf apron, is linked to a tale of disobedience and suffering.[54]

Let me give another example. After telling of the invention of clothing in response to the discovery of nakedness, Lincoln says, "The Bible makes no other alusion to clothing, *before* the flood. Soon *after* the deluge Noah's two sons covered him with a *garment*; but of what *material* the garment was made is not mentioned."[55] This, of course, is another story of nakedness and shame. Lincoln doesn't mention the third son of Noah, Ham, who both saw and spoke of "the nakedness of his father" and whose descendants were cursed with enslavement as a result. Well-known to Lincoln and his audience was that this Bible story was a staple of proslavery apologetics, providing a supposed theological justification for African slavery.

This is not the only allusion to slavery. Indeed, the entire assemblage of verses that Lincoln cites could be said to revolve around the sojourn of the Jews in Egypt. The two centuries of Hebrew enslavement—with obvious parallels to American slavery—form the subtext of Lincoln's speech. I don't know whether to call Lincoln's method of two-tiered composition "esoteric" or not. It seems to me that Lincoln very much wants his audience to perceive his double inquiry into technological progress on the one hand and, on the other, moral non-progress, as in the hard-heartedness of Pharaoh. Lincoln can assume, as we today cannot, considerable familiarity with these Bible stories, but he also provides chapter and verse for those who want to be miners of the written word, contrasting his text with his source text.

When you follow his "leads," you discover another dimension of man's destiny, a political dimension. Lincoln makes repeated reference to one nation: Egypt.[56] The very last topic in the "First Lecture" is steam power. Lincoln points out that the Egyptians understood the principle, for they had a steam-powered toy (the aeolipile). However, they never applied the principle of steam power to "*useful* machinery."[57] He doesn't say so, but one wonders whether in their pride and stubborn reliance on slave power, the

Egyptians failed to pursue the liberating potential of technology. Certainly, Lincoln emphasizes that the ancient world relied on manpower and animal power, to the neglect of the *"motive power"* of wind, water, and steam.[58]

Like Egypt, the American South was a slave power, neglectful of technology. Although beholden to the Massachusetts inventor Eli Whitney for the cotton gin (patented in 1794), the South was neither theoretically inclined nor mechanically minded: "The Confederate Patent Office issued only two hundred and sixty-six patents during the whole war, as against more than sixteen thousand granted by the Union."[59] The North surely had a genius for invention, but invention by itself is morally ambiguous, as can be seen in the career of Whitney. His quest for efficiency reinvigorated the moribund plantation economy of the early 1800s, giving us King Cotton. But that same Whitney was a pioneer in developing standardized, interchangeable parts, which revolutionized industrial production in Northern factories, especially armories, thus playing a key role in the Union victory in the Civil War.

If it is the case that Lincoln gives us a history of technology through the Bible so that he can deliberately tell two stories at once, what does he hope to achieve thereby? Americans, who had long believed that they were the new Israel, might not welcome being told that they are really the new Egypt, with their black slaves in the role of the chosen people of God.[60] Now, the radical abolitionists frequently invoked this unflattering Biblical parallel, but Lincoln had done so explicitly only once, at the close of his *Dred Scott* speech.[61] In this lecture, he proceeds by indirection, avoiding vituperation and moral fervor but dropping plenty of hints about God's punishment of Egypt ("the horse, and his rider hath he thrown into the sea").[62] The contrast between Lincoln's rhetoric and that of the abolitionists could not be more dramatic. The abolitionists loved to quote Isaiah, the prophet who pronounced judgment upon all the nations with lines of terrifying vividness: "Through the wrath of the Lord of hosts is the land darkened, and the people shall be as the fuel of the fire; no man shall spare his brother."[63] Lincoln mentions Isaiah twice, but only to trace the first mention of "oar" and "sails." His mode is the opposite of the moral harangue; it is oblique and evocative—inviting thoughtfulness and further examination.

Again, for those who follow Lincoln's leads, the verses in Matthew 24 that immediately follow Lincoln's only New Testament quotation refer to a house divided.

> Two women shall be grinding at the mill; the one shall be taken, and the other left. Watch therefore; for ye know not what hour your Lord doth come. But know this, that if the goodman of the house had known in what watch the thief would come, he would have watched, and would not have suffered his house to be broken up.[64]

It is with that implied warning that Lincoln shifts to the second part of the lecture, in which he focuses directly and unmetaphorically on the United States.

"We have all heard of Young America," he begins. He details how this personage, this "most *current* youth," fares with respect to the specific arts—clothing, agriculture, and transportation—that he had examined through scripture in the first part.[65] Young America is a figure of consumerist luxury, wearing fabrics and enjoying delicacies brought from all over the globe. The Egyptian horses drowned in the Red Sea during the Exodus have been replaced by the "iron horse"—the railroad—"panting, and impatient, to carry him everywhere, in no time."[66] Lincoln's tone has a satiric bite. "Young America," it turns out, was a campaign slogan associated with his political rival Stephen Douglas. Lincoln's riff on "Young America" and "Manifest Destiny," another slogan belonging to the Democratic Party, becomes especially pointed when he alludes first to the Mexican War and then to American slavery. Here's what he says:

> [Young America] owns a large part of the world, by right of possessing it; and all the rest by right of *wanting* it, and *intending* to have it. As Plato had for the immortality of the soul, so

Young America has "a pleasing hope—a fond desire—a longing after" territory. He has a great passion—a perfect rage—
for the "*new*"; . . . He is very anxious to fight for the liberation
of enslaved nations and colonies, provided, always, they *have*
land, and have *not* any liking for his interference. As to those
who have no land, and would be glad of help from any quarter, he considers *they* can afford to wait a few hundred years
longer. In knowledge he is particularly rich. He knows all that
can possibly be known . . . and is the unquestioned inventor of
"*Manifest Destiny*." His horror is for all that is old, particularly
"Old Fogy"; and if there be any thing old which he can endure,
it is only old whiskey and old tobacco.[67]

After taking this partisan swipe at Young America's hubris and hypoc-
risy, Lincoln immediately moves to higher ground, inquiring whether
Young America does indeed have the advantage over Old Fogy and, if so,
what the "great difference" really is. Lincoln conducts his own version of
the quarrel of the ancients and the moderns. He starts by returning to the
mode of biblical exegesis, calling to the bar "the first of all fogies, father
Adam." Examining that "first of all inventions . . . *the fig-leaf apron*," Lincoln shows that Adam "had first to invent the art of invention," an art that
depends on the prior habits of observation and reflection, habits which
themselves depend on the human faculty of speech.[68] And speech, says
Lincoln, does not appear to be "an invention of man, but rather the direct
gift of his Creator." Even if it is a human invention, speech is only possible, says Lincoln, because of fixed biological features such as "the capacities of the tongue, in the utterance of articulate sounds"—capacities that
Lincoln declares "absolutely wonderful."[69] Illustrating his meaning about
human communicativeness, Lincoln mischievously adds:

And this reminds me of what I passed unnoticed before, that
the very first invention was a joint operation, Eve having shared
with Adam in the getting up of the apron. And, indeed, judging

from the fact that sewing has come down to our times as "woman's work" it is very probable she took the leading part; he, perhaps, doing no more than to stand by and thread the needle.[70]

Lincoln repeatedly reminds his audience—an audience inclined toward chauvinism of both the male and national varieties—of the humbling things they might prefer to forget.[71]

Not only are human beings beholden to their natural endowment and their immediate fellows (including female fellows), but there are intergenerational debts as well. The current generation is the beneficiary of the advances made by those "very old fogies" of earlier times. Lincoln suggests a humility-inducing thought experiment: "Suppose the art [of writing], with all conception of it, were this day lost to the world, how long, think you, would it be, before even Young America could get up the letter A. with any adequate notion of using it to advantage."[72] It's Lincoln's Obama-esque "you didn't build that" moment.[73] While he doesn't reduce the current generation to pygmies standing on the shoulders of giants, he does stress our position as privileged and rather complacent inheritors.

Still, there is a modern difference. Improvements were achingly slow until the invention of printing, which Lincoln calls the "the *other* half— and in real utility, the *better* half—of writing."[74] Printing expands the field for invention—including political inventions such as our Constitution— because printing awakens in human beings the thought of "rising to equality." Printing is the emancipation proclamation of the mind.[75]

The final section of the speech pursues this question of modern superiority. Lincoln adds two more modern achievements—"the discovery of America, and the introduction of Patent laws"—both of which have played a role in vastly accelerating the rate of discovery and invention.[76] In the midst of his genuinely appreciative account, Lincoln stops suddenly and says:

> Though not apposite to my present purpose, it is but justice to
> the fruitfulness of that period, to mention two other important
> events—the Lutheran Reformation in 1517, and, still earlier, the

invention of negroes, or, of the present mode of using them, in 1434.[77]

Once again, the oddity of Lincoln's procedure is striking. He just drops in that ironical phrase "the invention of negroes" and then resumes his appreciative consideration of printing. What are we to think now of the contrast between ancients and moderns? In the first lecture, we learned of the slaveholding Egyptians who never realized the power of steam; in the second lecture, we get the full-steam-ahead Americans who really have unleashed "the intellects and energies of man" and yet have also contrived to turn other men into inventions.[78]

Lincoln has mentioned five modern events. Together, these five events provide a genealogy of "the crisis of the house divided." The two seminal inventions of modernity presage the conflict: The invention of printing in 1436 pointed humanity toward freedom; "the invention of negroes" in 1434 created a new, more virulent form of slavery. The discovery of America in 1492 provided the ground on which both forces (slavery and freedom) eventually converged. The Reformation in 1517 added religious support for the cause of political liberty. Patent law in 1624, like the discovery of America, is ambiguous or double-edged.

If the Negro is an invention, then that invention can presumably be patented, which is essentially what happened when the Royal African Company was granted exclusive rights to the slave trade in the 17th century or when the cotton gin was invented and the Southern states were refounded on what Lincoln in his sixth debate with Douglas called "the cotton-gin basis."[79] We might with justice say that Lincoln's entire public career was devoted to dis-inventing the Negro, or dis-inventing the present mode of using him. He sought to move the Negro from his status as an invention to his rightful status as a human being.[80]

Clearly, not every invention advances civilization. Lincoln concludes his speech by returning to the one invention he considers most efficacious for good: namely, the printing press. He credits a technological advance with breaking the "slavery of the mind." Slavery has been present throughout the speech, first by implication through the references to Pharaoh and Egypt, Moses and the children of Israel, then through the reference to "enslaved nations and colonies" in his denunciation of American expansionism, and finally in that mordant line about the invention of Negroes.[81] Now, at the very end of the speech, Lincoln shows that there is another aspect of slavery, an internal or spiritual aspect. He unearths the deepest cause of slavery, which turns out not to be political oppression but rather ignorance—ignorance of one's human nature. Before the print revolution,

> the great mass of men . . . were utterly unconscious, that their *conditions*, or their *minds* were capable of improvement. They not only looked upon the educated few as superior beings; but they supposed themselves to be naturally incapable of rising to equality. To immancipate the mind from this false and under estimate of itself, is the great task which printing came into the world to perform.[82]

And yet, Lincoln indicates, technology by itself is insufficient, since it only supplies the *"means* of reading."[83] The existence of printed matter doesn't guarantee literacy. For that you need teachers—and teachers, Lincoln laments, have not been "very numerous, or very competent."[84] We are back at the one piece of advice that the Founders and Lincoln agreed on: America is dedicated to the proposition that "all men are created equal," but it is only through education, and a certain kind of education, that individuals actually become capable of "rising to equality."[85] Of course we need training in the STEM fields, and yes, our regime is uniquely open to science, but we should not forget that applied science can underwrite slavery as easily as liberty. We need civic education and liberal education—education that reminds Americans of the great difference between self-aggrandizement and self-government, between mastery of self and mastery over others—education that promotes not only science and useful arts but wisdom, Lincolnian wisdom.

Notes

1. US Const. art. I, § 8, cl. 8.

2. The Spartan way of life was designed to be the unexamined life. As described by Plutarch, Spartan habituation was singularly harsh, even inhumane. The collective was all; the individual nothing. Love of country was achieved by repressing all other loves, whether love of others or love of self. This was a hypertrophic patriotism that left no room for private life, private property, or the private pursuit of fame, fortune, or learning. No self-interest, no self-preservation, certainly no self-promotion—no self at all, really.

3. US Const. pmbl. (emphasis added).

4. US Const. art. V; and US Const. art. IV, § 3, cl. 1.

5. Declaration of Independence para. 2 (US 1776).

6. *Federalist*, no. 9 (Alexander Hamilton), https://avalon.law.yale.edu/18th_century/fedo9.asp; and *Federalist*, no. 14 (James Madison), https://press-pubs.uchicago.edu/founders/documents/v1ch4s22.html.

7. US Const. art. I, § 8, cl. 8.

8. US Const. art. I, § 8, cl. 2; and US Const. art. I, § 8, cl. 7.

9. US Const. art. I, § 8, cl. 18.

10. Many types of institutions were recommended, from seminaries (a term that often referred to educational academies for women) and trade schools to universities. James Madison, *Notes of Debates in the Federal Convention of 1787 Reported by James Madison* (1787), notes for August 18, 1787.

11. Madison, *Notes of Debates in the Federal Convention of 1787 Reported by James Madison*, September 5, 1787.

12. Madison, *Notes of Debates in the Federal Convention of 1787 Reported by James Madison*, August 18, 1787.

13. In saying that the right is to be secured "for limited Times," it is strongly implied that the right is not to be lifelong. It is alienable, not inalienable. Moreover, Congress is not *required* by the Constitution to grant authors and inventors copyrights and patents. Congress could have allowed this power to lie fallow, without violating anyone's rights.

14. Abraham Lincoln, "Lecture on Discoveries and Inventions," in *The Writings of Abraham Lincoln*, ed. Steven B. Smith (Yale University Press, 2012), 238. Lincoln regularly employed italics to feature key words.

15. James Madison discusses the patent clause in *Federalist* 43, in which he declares that in this matter of extending copyrights and patents to authors and inventors, "the public good fully coincides . . . with the claims of individuals." *Federalist*, no. 43 (James Madison), https://avalon.law.yale.edu/18th_century/fed43.asp.

16. Alexander Hamilton, "Report on Manufactures," December 5, 1791, in *The Founders' Constitution*, ed. Philip B. Kurland and Ralph Lerner (University of Chicago Press, 1986; 2000), art. 1, § 8, cl. 8, document 9, http://press-pubs.uchicago.edu/founders/documents/a1_8_8s9.html.

17. George Washington, "First Annual Message," in *George Washington: A Collection*, ed. W. B. Allen (Liberty Classics, 1988), 469.

18. George Washington hoped a national university would do the additional good work of lessening the North-South divide through the power of youthful friendship and a common curriculum.

19. John Quincy Adams was the last to call for it. Andrew Jackson did not follow suit.

20. George Washington, "Farewell Address," in Allen, *George Washington*, 521.

21. Washington, "Farewell Address," in Allen, *George Washington*, 522.

22. John Adams, *Discourses on Davila: A Series of Papers on Political History*, in *The Works of John Adams*, ed. Charles Francis Adams (Little, Brown and Co., 1856), 6:240, http://oll.libertyfund.org/titles/adams-the-works-of-john-adams-vol-6. (Emphasis in original).

23. Adams, *Discourses on Davila*, 6:275.

24. Adams, *Discourses on Davila*, 6:280.

25. Adams, *Discourses on Davila*, 6:281 (emphasis in original).

26. Adams, *Discourses on Davila*.

27. Thomas Jefferson, "To Roger C Weightman," in Merrill D. Peterson, ed., *The Portable Thomas Jefferson* (Viking Penguin, 1975), 585.

28. Thomas Jefferson, "Query XVIII Manners," in Peterson, *The Portable Thomas Jefferson*, 215.

29. Thomas Jefferson, "Query XIV Laws," in Peterson, *The Portable Thomas Jefferson*, 186–93.

30. Abraham Lincoln, "Letter to H. L. Pierce and Others April 6, 1859," in *Abraham Lincoln: His Speeches and Writings*, ed. Roy P. Basler (Da Capo Press, 2001), 489.

31. Thomas Jefferson, "To Isaac McPherson," in Peterson, *The Portable Thomas Jefferson*, 530. Jefferson also spoke of "the embarrassment of an exclusive patent." Jefferson, "To Isaac McPherson," 531.

32. Benjamin Franklin, "To Joseph Priestley," in *Benjamin Franklin: Writings*, ed. J. A. Leo Lemay (Library of America, 1987), 1017.

33. Franklin, "To Joseph Priestley."

34. Franklin, "To Joseph Priestley."

35. Franklin, "To Joseph Priestley."

36. See especially Benjamin Franklin, "To the Royal Academy of *****," in Lemay, *Benjamin Franklin*, 952–55.

37. Abraham Lincoln combines elements of the four Founders I've mentioned. He was a mechanically minded inventor like Benjamin Franklin and Thomas Jefferson, but unlike them the holder of a patent (for a device to lift boats over shoals). Devoted to Jefferson's Declaration, he had a deeper understanding of the document than did its author. Like John Adams, he was by temperament a conservative, acutely aware of the limits of human nature and political action. Like Franklin, he was the discoverer of new modes of reaching a democratic audience through the written word. Finally, and most importantly, he was a statesman to rival Washington.

38. The first lecture is available here: Abraham Lincoln, "First Lecture on Discoveries and Inventions," lecture, Young Men's Association of Bloomington, Bloomington, IL, April 6, 1858, https://quod.lib.umich.edu/l/lincoln/lincoln2/1:483. The second lecture is more frequently included in volumes of Lincoln's speeches. Both the Library of America collection and the Steven B. Smith collection (see endnote 14) include it, although it is not present in the one-volume Roy P. Basler edition. There is both internal textual evidence and journalistic accounts that suggest these two parts belong to a larger whole. Moreover, upon heading to Washington to assume the presidency, Lincoln taped the two manuscripts together and entrusted them to a Springfield, Illinois, acquaintance for safekeeping. In early 1865, he expressed an intention to put the lecture into final form, post-presidency or, as he put it, "when I get out of this place." See Wayne C. Temple, "Lincoln as a Lecturer on 'Discoveries, Inventions, and Improvements,'" *Jacksonville Journal Courier*, May 23, 1982, 1–12; and John Channing Briggs, *Lincoln's Speeches Reconsidered* (Johns Hopkins University Press, 2005), 190–92.

39. Lincoln, "Lecture on Discoveries and Inventions."

40. Lincoln, "Lecture on Discoveries and Inventions."

41. Lincoln biographer Michael Burlingame reports Mrs. Norman B. Judd's version of the lecture's origin: "In 1856, Lincoln told her that one evening he and fellow lawyers on the circuit were discussing the date at which the brass age began. He recalled that Tubal Cain the son of Lamech, worked in brass and that his brother Jubal made harps and organs. Checking his recollection in the Bible, he ransacked the Old Testament and compiled a list of the discoveries and inventions mentioned there. Shortly afterward, he accepted an invitation to address the Young Men's Literary Society in Bloomington; he used those Old Testament notes, as well as some research in an encyclopedia, to create his lecture." Michael Burlingame, *Abraham Lincoln: A Life*, vol. 1 (Johns Hopkins Press, 2013), 443. Scholars have been generally dismissive of his effort: "Unharnessed from the great issues with which he had been engaged, Lincoln's humor unraveled into whimsy; his interest in history shrank to a harvest of trivia." Richard Brookhiser, *Founders' Son: A Life of Abraham Lincoln* (Basic Books, 2014), 140. An exception is John Channing Briggs, who in *Lincoln's Speeches Reconsidered* gives a well-considered reading of the address, from which I have learned much. Briggs situates Lincoln's lecture as a critical response to two well-known pieces of the day: George Bancroft's "The Necessity, the Reality and the Promise of the Progress of the Human Race" (1854) and Wendell Phillips's 1853 lecture "The Lost Arts."

42. Lincoln, "First Lecture on Discoveries and Inventions" (emphasis in original).

43. Francis Bacon, in *The Advancement of Learning*, compares natural philosophy to mining: "If then it be true that Democritus said, 'That the truth of nature lieth hid in certain deep mines and caves;' and if it be true likewise that the alchemists do so much inculcate, that Vulcan is a second nature, and imitateth that dexterously and compendiously, which nature worketh by ambages and length of time, it were good to divide natural philosophy into the mine and the furnace, and to make two professions or occupations of natural philosophers—some to be pioneers and some smiths; some

to dig, and some to refine and hammer. And surely I do best allow of a division of that kind, though in more familiar and scholastical terms: namely, that these be the two parts of natural philosophy—the inquisition of causes, and the production of effects; speculative and operative; natural science, and natural prudence." Francis Bacon, *The Advancement of Learning* (1605), book 2, § VII, para. 1, https://classic-literature.co.uk/francis-bacon-the-advancement-of-learning-the-second-book-of-francis-bacon/. See also Cesare Pastorino, "The Mine and the Furnace: Francis Bacon, Thomas Russell, and Early Stuart Mining Culture," *Early Science and Medicine* 14, no. 5 (2009): 630–60, http://www.academia.edu/1040095/The_Mine_and_the_Furnace_Francis_Bacon_Thomas_Russell_and_Early_Stuart_Mining_Culture.

44. Lincoln, "First Lecture on Discoveries and Inventions" (emphasis in original).

45. Lincoln, "First Lecture on Discoveries and Inventions" (emphasis in original).

46. Lincoln, "First Lecture on Discoveries and Inventions."

47. Interestingly, Lincoln does not mention the making of bricks for the building of the city and tower of Babel. His focus is more on "motive" power, the power to make things move. Still, the oversight is intriguing. He may not want to highlight God's clearly expressed opposition to human technological aspirations. And given his praise for speech, writing, and printing, he may not want to feature God's confounding of mankind's quest for one universal tongue. Lincoln, "First Lecture on Discoveries and Inventions."

48. Lincoln, "First Lecture on Discoveries and Inventions" (emphasis in original).

49. The account in the first lecture draws very heavily from Genesis, Exodus, and Deuteronomy. These are the verses either alluded to, quoted, or cited by Lincoln, in the order he gives them, following his ordering of the topics. Provision of food: Lincoln alludes to Solomon's advice to imitate the animals, though without either quoting from or citing Prov. 6:6. Clothing: Gen. 3:21, 9:23, 14:23; and Exod. 28:42, 35:25, 35:26, 35:35. In addition, Job is quoted but not cited. The quote is from Job 7:6. Tools of iron: Gen. 4:22; Num. 35:16; and Deut. 3:11, 4:20, 27:5, 19:5, 8:9. The need for an axe "or a miracle" to hew the "'gopher wood' for the Ark" is mentioned but not cited. The reference is to Gen. 6:14. Transportation: Gen. 41:43; and Exod. 14:25, 14:9, 14:23, 49:13. In addition, Isaiah is quoted but not cited; the reference is to Isa. 33:21–23. Note: Lincoln decides to "pass by the Ark" as "belonging rather to the *miraculous*, than to *human* invention." (Emphasis in original.) Lincoln, "Lecture on Discoveries and Inventions." Agriculture: Two verses are quoted but are not cited: Gen. 2:15, 3:23. Animal power: Gen. 22:3, 24:61; Exod. 15:1; and Gen. 42:26. Four additional verses are cited as evidence of plows and chariots, without quotation: Deut. 22:10; Gen. 41:43 (second reference), 46:29; and Exod. 14:25 (second reference). Wind power: Isaiah is mentioned but not quoted. For waterpower, Lincoln quoted one verse but did not cite it. The verse is found in Matt. 24:41; and Luke 17:35. Lincoln did not include a biblical reference for steam power. In the second lecture, one final biblical reference is made to "the new earth mentioned in the revelations." The reference is to Rev. 21:1. (All these biblical references are from the King James Version.)

50. Lincoln, "First Lecture on Discoveries and Inventions."

51. See Matt. 24:41 (KJV); and Luke 17:35 (KJV).

52. The Bible is, of course, interested in man's desire for knowledge and the meaning of human artfulness. However, Lincoln is—on the surface at least—looking simply for the facts of the history of technology. His official purpose is oddly disconnected from any moral inquiry. In *The Advancement of Learning*, Bacon had noted that the Bible preserved the memory of the earliest inventors: "So in the age before the flood, the holy records within those few memorials which are there entered and registered have vouchsafed to mention and honour the name of the inventors and authors of music and works in metal." Bacon, *The Advancement of Learning*, book 1, § VI, para. 8.

53. Matt. 24:51 (KJV).

54. The Bible has its own view of artificers, beginning with Cain, whose name comes from a stem meaning "to fashion, shape, give form to." See Umberto Cassuto, *A Commentary on the Book of Genesis Part 1: From Adam to Noah*, trans. Israel Abrahams (Magnes Press, 1961), 197. The Bible suggests a connection between the arts and the murderers Cain and Lamech. Cain's descendant Tubal-Cain (whom Lincoln mentions) was the inventor of the first tools.

55. Lincoln, "First Lecture on Discoveries and Inventions" (emphasis in original).

56. While he mentions Abraham, Isaac, Jacob, Joseph, and Moses by name and refers to the "promised land," only once does he mention "the children of Israel." Lincoln, "First Lecture on Discoveries and Inventions."

57. Lincoln, "First Lecture on Discoveries and Inventions" (emphasis in original).

58. Lincoln, "First Lecture on Discoveries and Inventions."

59. Robert V. Bruce, *Lincoln and the Tools of War* (University of Illinois Press, 1989), 68. For more on Lincoln's interest in technology, see "Lincoln: First Technology President," in Lewis E. Lehrman, *Lincoln "by littles"* (Lehrman Institute, 2013), 165–68.

60. See the first attempt at a design for the Great Seal: "Pharaoh sitting in an open Chariot, a Crown on his head and a Sword in his hand, passing through the divided Waters of the Red Sea in Pursuit of the Israelites: Rays from a Pillar of Fire in the Cloud, expressive of the divine Presence and Command, beaming on Moses who stands on the shore and extending his hand over the Sea causes it to overwhelm Pharaoh. Motto: 'Rebellion to Tyrants is Obedience to God.'" John D. MacArthur, "First Great Seal Committee—July/August 1776," GreatSeal.com, http://www.greatseal.com/committees/firstcomm/index.html.

61. For an abolitionist example from this same time, see M. H. Freeman, "One of the Elements of Reform," *Anglo-African Magazine*, January 1860. In his discussion of colonization at the close of the *Dred Scott* speech, Lincoln compares America's enslaved population to the "children of Israel," who "went out of Egyptian bondage in a body," Abraham Lincoln, "The Dred Scott Decision," in Basler, *Abraham Lincoln*, 365.

62. Lincoln, "The Dred Scott Decision."

63. Isa. 9:19 (KJV).

64. Matt. 24:41–43 (KJV).

65. Lincoln, "Lecture on Discoveries and Inventions" (emphasis in original).

66. Lincoln, "Lecture on Discoveries and Inventions."

67. Lincoln, "Lecture on Discoveries and Inventions" (emphasis in original).

68. Lincoln, "Lecture on Discoveries and Inventions" (emphasis in original).

69. Lincoln's "Lecture on Discoveries and Inventions" confirms the wonder. Based perhaps on a trial of his own, he provides the following statistics: "You can count from one to one hundred, quite distinctly in about forty seconds. In doing this two hundred and eighty three distinct sounds or syllables are uttered, being seven to each second; and yet there shall be enough difference between every two, to be easily recognized by the ear of the hearer." Lincoln, "Lecture on Discoveries and Inventions."

70. The speech is remarkable for the respectful attention Lincoln gives to women and women's work. Of clothing, Lincoln declares it "the one thing for which nearly half of the toil and care of the human race has ever since been expended." Lincoln, "Lecture on Discoveries and Inventions." Lincoln gives two passages about women's spinning—verses that emphasize women's wisdom: "All the women that were wise hearted, did *spin* with their hands" and "all the women whose hearts stirred them up in wisdom, *spun* goat's hair." (Emphasis in original.) Lincoln, "Lecture on Discoveries and Inventions." In addition to Eve, Lincoln names Rebecca, and Miriam is specially praised. In a version of the speech now lost to us but reported in detail in a newspaper account, Lincoln was said to have "paid a feeling tribute" to "plaintive songs." He singled out "the triumphal exultation" of Miriam. Briggs cites the coverage in the *Bloomington Pantagraph* of April 9, 1859. He speculates that Miriam may have been a reference to Mary and the "Magnificat" of Luke 1:46–55, although I think it much more likely that Lincoln had in mind the Miriam of the Old Testament, who was the sister of Moses and Aaron and who led the women of Israel in songful celebration of their deliverance from Egyptian bondage. See Exod. 15:20–21 (KJV); and Briggs, *Lincoln's Speeches Reconsidered*, 213.

71. Just as he had with speech, Lincoln indicates that writing, which he calls "the great invention of the world," is only possible because of "the wonderful powers of the *eye*," which are not of human making. (Emphasis in original.) Lincoln, "Lecture on Discoveries and Inventions."

72. Lincoln, "Lecture on Discoveries and Inventions."

73. This is similar to the Lyceum Address's claim about political goods: "We find ourselves under the government of a system of political institutions, conducing more essentially to the ends of civil and religious liberty, than any of which the history of former times tells us. We, when mounting the stage of existence, found ourselves the legal inheritors of these fundamental blessings. We toiled not in the acquirement or establishment of them." Abraham Lincoln, "The Perpetuation of Our Political Institutions," in Basler, *Abraham Lincoln*, 76–77.

74. Lincoln, "Lecture on Discoveries and Inventions" (emphasis in original).

75. Bacon agreed. He credits three inventions—printing, gunpowder, and the compass: "No empire, no sect, no star has been seen to exert more power and influence

over the affairs of men than have these mechanical discoveries." Francis Bacon, "Aphorisms—Book I: On the Interpretation of Nature and the Empire of Man," in *Novum Organum*, ed. Joseph Devey (PF Collier, 1902), https://oll.libertyfund.org/titles/bacon-novum-organum.

76. Lincoln, "Lecture on Discoveries and Inventions."

77. The date Lincoln gives for "the invention of negroes" is the date when Portuguese explorers first rounded the treacherous Cape Bojador on the western coast of Africa, a feat of navigational expertise and daring that led almost immediately to the start of the African slave trade. Not all discoveries advance the cause of civilization.

78. Lincoln, "Lecture on Discoveries and Inventions."

79. From Lincoln's rejoinder at the Sixth Joint Debate: "It is precisely all I ask of him in relation to the institution of slavery, that it shall be placed upon the basis that our fathers placed it upon. Mr. Brooks, of South Carolina once said, and truly said, that when this Government was established, no one expected the institution of slavery to last until this day; and that the men who formed this Government were wiser and better than the men of these days; but the men of these days had experience which the fathers had not, and that experience had taught them the invention of the cotton gin, and this had made the perpetuation of the institution of slavery a necessity in this country. Judge Douglas could not let it stand upon the basis which our fathers placed it, but removed it, and *put it upon the cotton-gin basis*. It is a question, therefore, for him and his friends to answer—why they could not let it remain where the fathers of the Government originally placed it." (Emphasis in original.) Robert W. Johannsen, ed., *The Lincoln-Douglas Debates* (Oxford University Press, 1965), 278.

80. Lincoln's phrase "the invention of negroes, or, of the present mode of using them" should be read in conjunction with Lincoln's speech at Edwardsville, Illinois, on September 11, 1858, where he inquires into "what Douglas really invented, when he introduced, and drove through Congress, the Nebraska bill." He concludes that Stephen Douglas did not invent "popular sovereignty"—an idea that predated Columbus and was given "tangible form" in 1776. What then did Douglas invent? Lincoln spells it out with brutal frankness, giving the violent specifics of the "present mode" of "dehumanizing the negro":

> Then, if Mr. Douglas did not invent *this* kind of sovereignty [the 1776 kind], let us pursue the inquiry and find out what the invention really was. Was it the right of emigrants in Kansas and Nebraska to govern themselves and a gang of niggers too, if they wanted them? Clearly this was no invention of his, because Gen. Cass put forth the same doctrine in 1848, in his so-called Nicholson letter—six whole years before Douglas thought of such a thing. Gen. Cass could have taken out a patent for the idea, if he had chosen to do so, and have prevented his Illinois rival from reaping a particle of benefit from it. Then what was it, I ask again, that this "Little Giant" invented? It never occurred to Gen. Cass to call his discovery by the odd name of "Popular Sovereignty." He had not the *impudence* to say that the *right of people to*

govern niggers was the *right of people to govern themselves*. His notions of the fitness of things were not moulded to the brazen degree of calling the right to put a hundred niggers through under the lash in Nebraska, a *"sacred right of self-government."* And here, I submit to this intelligent audience and the whole world, was Judge Douglas' discovery, and the whole of it. He invented a *name* for Gen. Cass' old Nicholson letter dogma. He discovered that the right of the white man to breed and flog niggers in Nebraska was POPULAR SOVEREIGNTY!

Abraham Lincoln, "Portion of Speech at Edwardsville, Illinois," in *The Writings of Abraham Lincoln*, 188–89.

81. Lincoln, "Lecture on Discoveries and Inventions."

82. Lincoln, "Lecture on Discoveries and Inventions."

83. Lincoln, "Lecture on Discoveries and Inventions" (emphasis in original).

84. Today, we have plenty of teachers and plenty of classroom technology, but we still have problems with competence.

85. US Const. pmbl; and Lincoln, "Lecture on Discoveries and Inventions."

8

Common-Law Originalism

JAMES R. STONER JR.
September 17, 2019

It will not have escaped the notice of my learned listeners this evening that the title of my lecture, "Common-Law Originalism," seems to encase a contradiction or at least present a paradox. I'll begin by discussing why this is so and then hope to persuade you that if both terms, originalism and common law, are properly understood, the paradox is resolved. I mean to argue not only that taking common law seriously should make one attentive to originalism but also that originalism, if it is to be complete, needs to attend to the fact that the Constitution we celebrate this evening was written in a legal environment formed by common law, that our written Constitution emerged from a tradition of unwritten law.

So much, at least, I planned when I chose my title last spring. But reviewing the major decisions of the Supreme Court last term, thinking I would find a few illustrations to buttress my thesis, I discovered that in fact common law was subject to extended treatment in a number of the justices' opinions, and I have become convinced that this is indeed no accident: As the new majority on the Court brings originalist argumentation to the forefront, the justices have noticed that to understand the meaning of constitutional language, recourse must be had to preexisting law, and that often means common law. Besides, the question of the authority of precedent, over against original intent, has naturally come to the forefront, as feebly grounded case law feels its frailty.

All this gives a certain timeliness to what I have to say, or at least I'll see whether I can persuade you of that, too, when I discuss several cases— which, being a political scientist and not a lawyer, I will attempt to do in a manner that avoids tedious detail at the risk of technical error. Finally, since I think ours is still a republican form of government, I will conclude with a few words about what the common-law way of thinking means for legislation, in which those of us whose office is merely "citizen" might be thought, through our representatives, to have some say.

In our politically polarized era—perhaps I should say, in this notoriously polarized era, for American politics have always been characterized by partisan division—the Constitution of the United States might seem to serve as a common point of reference. Whether Democrat or Republican, the overwhelming majority of Americans concede that the Constitution is something we have in common, the written rules that govern political competition and perhaps a few principles, especially concerning basic rights, that we all share. But a moment's reflection or a little experience teaches that, whatever our unity regarding the Constitution as a symbol, in practice, partisanship reemerges when it comes to interpreting what the Constitution means in our world today.

In one corner, we find the originalists, those who claim or at least aspire to interpret the Constitution according to the meaning given to its clauses at the time they were enacted: for Articles I–VII, in 1787–88, at the time of ratification; for the Bill of Rights, a few years later; for Amendments 13 through 15, at the close of the Civil War and the beginning of Reconstruction; and so forth.[1] Originalists recognize that the courts and the Supreme Court have not always been faithful to the original meaning or have been mistaken when they have tried, but originalists insist that fidelity to the text is essential to vindicate the popular character of the Constitution, its source in "we the people" whenever we have chosen to engage in the "solemn and authoritative act" of constitution making.[2]

In the other corner, we find the living constitutionalists, who see in the imposition of the dry meaning of old texts either the dead hand of the past or a glove that conceals a political fist in the present.[3] The "people" who wrote the Constitution long ago are emphatically not the people today, they remind us, or, given demographic change, even their ancestors, or at least not the ancestors of today's majority. There is much in the Constitution that living constitutionalists can live with—particularly the procedural rules, although they find some of these, like the electoral college, chafe—and there are several principles they genuinely admire (for example, concerning civil liberties [or some of them], majority rule, and equal protection). But they would interpret these expansively and treat them aspirationally, as goals for the future rather than confined by the specific meanings they had in the 18th or 19th centuries.

It's hard to say who is winning the debate. On the one hand, the originalists have had a couple of staunch advocates on the Supreme Court, including the late Justice Antonin Scalia and even more consistently Justice Clarence Thomas. Their approach is openly endorsed by one of the major political parties, and they have successfully developed a cottage industry of publication and debate in law schools, even though law school faculty trend overwhelmingly left—with liberal faculty now proclaiming their adherence to "living originalism," a half concession. Although the original originalists did not reverse any of the major constitutional developments they arose to combat, they stanched the expansion of some—especially in the field of criminal law but also, hesitatingly, on the question of Congress's commerce power—and they succeeded in gaining constitutional recognition for the Second Amendment right to bear arms.

On the other hand, while the living constitutionalists have had some trouble developing a catchy name or jurisprudential theory, they have not only held on to the gains of the post–New Deal and Warren Courts but have even succeeded in expanding non-textual rights on questions of sex discrimination and especially sexual autonomy and its encumbrances. Theirs, they might say, is the vector of change, the only question being how quick the progress. Besides, they point out to the party of originalism, there is nothing conservative about upsetting long-established precedents. The Warren Court, after all, is as far away from us as the War of 1812 was from the Civil War, and its decisions and even its way of deciding are now deeply woven into American law.

The best explanation and defense of what I have been calling the "living Constitution" mode of jurisprudence is a 1996 *Chicago Law Review* article by Chicago Law Professor David Strauss called "Common Law Constitutional Interpretation," developed in a series of subsequent articles.[4] Strauss explicitly takes on originalism and articulates its alternative, which he anchors in what he calls the common-law method. American courts, even when referring to the text of the Constitution, in fact proceed by this method, not only in areas of law such as torts and contracts in which unwritten common law is known to govern (as "big pharma" is discovering) but really in everything they do, including the interpretation of statutes and even more so the interpretation of constitutional clauses. Judges in a common-law system generally follow precedent, and when they depart from it, it is only in circumstances that Strauss thinks are pretty clearly defined. Their general attitude is conservative—stick to the tried and true—and although Strauss is clearly liberal in his sentiments, he sees value in the gradualness of change the system encourages, if only because it is less easily reversed. Besides, he notes, even the father of modern conservatism, Edmund Burke, not to mention good old Aristotle, acknowledged the need for law to be flexible and accommodate social change.

Strauss's argument is partly analytical or even descriptive; his claim is that judges decide cases of constitutional law in ways better explained by the common-law method than by the method of originalism, even when they cite the text or historical evidence from the time of its enactment. The common-law method places precedent and adherence to precedent at the center of legal discussion. In a common-law system like our own, judges begin the consideration of any legal question by asking how that question, or one similar to it, has been decided in the past.

To imagine an example, one might cite the First Amendment's guarantee of freedom of speech in a case involving prosecution for obscenity. The text alone does not settle the matter, and evidence of prosecution at the time the First Amendment was ratified is scant and not sufficient either. Instead, the Court will probably look back no further than *Roth v. United States* in the 1950s or *Miller v. California* in the 1970s and then at more recent cases, too, to determine where the law stands.[5] This guides the Court's judgment and limits arbitrariness, and it guides lawyers in advising their clients, ensuring stability and predictability in law.

The mindset is "traditionalist," Strauss says, but not blindly; it is a "rational traditionalism" that presumes that rules have been established for reasons and that when judicial bodies have reasoned a case through, their conclusions deserve respect—at least until better reasons can be found. There need be no mysticism about traditions having been in place, as in the old English common law, so long that "the memory of man runneth not to the contrary."[6] And traditions that come to be seen as irrational—such as race discrimination or sex stereotyping—can be abandoned, but these, he supposes, are the exception, not the rule. Moreover, especially on matters that are morally indifferent—legal formalities, say, or procedural issues—it is more important that the law be settled than that it be perfect, so people can rely on it in their affairs while working around its imperfections. By making law predictable, settled precedent embraces a free society, something judges need to understand, and most do.

I think Strauss is correct as far as he goes, both descriptively and to some extent normatively. American judges in fact work from precedent even in cases of constitutional law, and despite the impatience one naturally feels, especially when young, in the face of the apparent folly of the past, one ought to inquire about the reasons things are done as they are before rejecting them—for there are always reasons, sometimes even good ones. And as for the small stuff, predictability often enough outweighs perfection.

But Strauss himself overlooks something important about common law that makes his account of the common-law method as a competitor to originalism misleading. As he admits but doesn't emphasize, his reference to common law as a method apart from the substantive body of law inherited from England alters the way the term "common law" would have been understood at the time of the American founding, when Americans claimed the common-law heritage as their own.

Detaching common law from its roots was the work of Oliver Wendell Holmes, who redefined common law as judge-made law. He redefined it so successfully that this new definition has now been taken for granted by law professors, law students, lawyers, and judges for several generations.[7] Strauss does not cite Holmes, but he regularly refers to Holmes's protégé, Benjamin Cardozo, whose term "judicial process" is less misleading.[8]

You don't have to read the Constitution twice to know that judge-made law is problematic; legislation or lawmaking powers belong to Congress, so the judicial power must be something else. Holmes meant his definition to be paradoxical, even startling, since his point was to emphasize how common-law precedents changed over time, almost imperceptibly at each step but sometimes decisively over centuries. Even then he did not claim judges made these changes self-consciously, though now that the truth is out, he thought they should—sparingly and artfully was his hope and his practice, but honestly and openly like any other policymaker, looking to the good, as he preferred to think of it. For Holmes also was a relativist, who held not only that the common law evolved but that all human values are susceptible of change.[9]

Strauss can say all rational tradition should be followed, but the question is who decides what traditions have become irrational and how they reach that judgment. His endorsement of not only the reinterpretation of the commerce power and due process liberty during the New Deal and the rejection of racial segregation after World War II but also the line of precedents that issued in and developed from *Roe v. Wade* indicates that something deeply political, not only professional, is at stake.[10] Customs change, to be sure, often unnoticeably, at least at first, but they claim unbroken authority from the past. Even if historical research can show the change, why is the response necessarily to acquiesce in it, rather than to see the change as corruption and seek a return to the tradition as it was followed in a more distant past?

Something like this has happened more than once in the history of common law: Sir Edward Coke, in the 17th-century heyday of the common lawyers, looked back to the age before Tudor absolutism. And it happens even in our constitutional law—for example, when the criminal protections in our Bill of Rights were revitalized in the mid-20th century after Progressive Era modification.[11] In other words, even if customs alter, there is no reason to suppose that judges have the power to alter them at will or to declare them altered according to their own perception of change in public opinion, even if at each step in the development of a line of precedent they have the duty to draw the best analogy they can.[12] The law seeks, after all, not merely the customary but the good.

According, then, to what I would call the authentic tradition of common law, that law, though inclusive of ancient customs, some of whose reasons may have been lost to time, is actually anchored in natural law—that is, in what human beings can know about the human good, itself defined by human nature. In common law, this was typically expressed negatively: Nothing that was against natural law could be incorporated in common law, even though many of the specific rules or determinations of common law were not settled by natural law one way or another. Common law can indeed change—first of all by statute, for it was a rule of common law that statutory provisions superseded anything contrary in common law. Moreover, a rule of common law might be altered by judges if circumstances altered, so that the old rule was no longer really the same rule at all—or if new knowledge superseded the reason behind the older rule of law.

To take a clear if controversial example of the latter, the common law forbade abortion after quickening, but the modern science of embryology has established that there is not a discrete moment after conception when a developing embryo becomes human; its species character is established when its genetic makeup is complete, and fetal development after that is continuous and largely self-organizing. It would now be irrational, in the absence of other law, to say the common law insists on quickening as a division line between permissible and impermissible abortions; a judge would have to inquire into the reason for the established rule, and if it were that quickening indicated ensoulment and so the moment of humanization, the underlying rule being no taking of an innocent human life, then the common law would protect life from the moment of conception.[13] Even if the old common-law rule were evidentiary rather than biological, it might need to be replaced given modern pregnancy tests.

As for changes in circumstances, I would give an example from constitutional law: Chief Justice Charles Evans Hughes's determination that the modern economy has so changed the circumstances of economic life by subjecting all monetary value to an interlocking whole that rigid interpretation of the Contract Clause, and of distinctions between manufacturing and commerce in interpreting the Commerce Clause, must adjust to the new economic reality.[14]

So it seems to me that appealing to common law against originalism, as Strauss attempted to do, is persuasive only if one detaches common law from its original meaning, turning it into a relativistic method of managing legal flux by ignoring its anchor in a claim of intrinsic justice. What about looking at the purported opposition between originalism and common law from the alternative perspective, that of constitutional originalism? Here, it seems to me, an honest originalism would pay more attention to common law than most originalists seem to do.[15]

In the first place, even the most textually precise originalist will notice that there are technical phrases in the Constitution that can be explained only by reference to common law. During the Philadelphia Convention in 1787, the question was raised whether the term "ex post facto" applied to only criminal law or also laws related to the definition of property rights. John Dickinson went home and looked it up in William Blackstone's *Commentaries on the Laws of England*, reporting that it only applied to criminal law—thus prompting the drafting of the Contract Clause to protect property rights from unjust alteration.[16] What does it mean that the president must be a natural-born citizen? The common law is the usual referent here: one born in the country, owing allegiance to its government and law, as one born in England would have owed allegiance to the king.[17]

But I want to suggest that the common law imbues the Constitution in more than just the technical language. The very term "judicial power" was meant to refer to courts established like common-law courts, where pleading was adversarial rather than inquisitorial, where precedent would be followed, where juries would be empaneled to find facts even as judges reserved for themselves the law, and where judges would ordinarily be drawn from the bar rather than separately trained. One sees all this taken for granted in Alexander Hamilton's papers on the courts in the Federalist Papers, or all but the jury, which is of course separately named in the Constitution's text. And just to be sure, the Bill of Rights was quickly added to the Constitution as part of the compromise that ensured its ratification, and many of these amendments put in writing the rights of due process anchored in common law since as far back as the Magna Carta.

Moreover, the very practice of judicial review, the power of courts to declare statutes unconstitutional and refuse to enforce them, makes no sense outside of the common-law context in which the Constitution was formed. It is, after all, a paradoxically unwritten power to enforce a written constitution. That Americans put our Constitution in writing, unlike the unwritten constitution of England, was seen as a statute-like improvement on the old common-law way.

But the defense of the unwritten power of judges to enforce it depends, like much of the way courts decide on common law, on the "nature and the reason of the thing," to use Hamilton's words. In both *Federalist* 78 and John Marshall's decision in *Marbury v. Madison*, the power is defended on analogy to the way common-law judges deal with contradictory statutes: If two statutes are at odds, the more recent one is taken as indicating the will of the legislator, but if a constitution and a statute are at odds, the superior authority supersedes, whether it is older or newer.[18] Moreover, the power to decide such things is asserted and defended only in the context of a legal case or controversy—the judicial power being the power to decide according to law particular cases brought within the court's jurisdiction, not the power to range freely as a censor of legislation, the proposal of a council of revision having been rejected at Philadelphia. Reflecting on this, by the way, would help guide those on the bench and off who would limit judicial supremacy and return ownership of the Constitution to those who first gave it authority, named in the document's first three words.

In short, the supposed polarities of constitutional originalism and common-law judging are not opposites if properly understood, but integral to one another. If this were accepted, how might it change the way judges go about interpreting the Constitution and even the way citizens see the law? I don't have a Herculean theory to offer or a method to propose—that would contradict my whole argument—but let me discuss five cases from the Supreme Court's recently concluded term and a sixth matter now in controversy and suggest how remembering the common-law dimension of the Constitution might make a difference in how lawyers go about arguing them and how judges go about deciding.

The first case I will discuss is *Franchise Tax Board of California v. Hyatt*, in which the justices split according to the party of the president who appointed them, but not in the way a purely results-oriented analysis might have predicted: The five Republican-appointed judges took the side of California tax collectors and the four Democrat-appointed judges favored the entrepreneur who moved to Nevada apparently to escape the California income tax.[19] The case has involved 25 years of legal wrangling, this being its third trip to the supreme bench. At issue this time was whether the Court should overrule its 1979 decision in *Nevada v. Hall*.[20] The majority decided it should, finding that the original meaning of the Constitution was to accord the states absolute sovereign immunity in one another's courts.

The question of sovereign immunity has regularly caused such a split over the past quarter century, but in other cases at issue has been the immunity of states from suits in federal court, while here the question is the immunity of one state in the courts of another. Since *Hall*, the Court has held that under the Full Faith and Credit Clause, state entities were entitled to comity—that is, to be treated in the courts of a sister state as the analogous entity would be treated by its own courts. In an earlier phase of this case, that led the Supremes to reduce a judgment against the California board for harassment from $1 million to $50,000, but now the Court held that the principle of sovereign immunity vacated the judgment altogether.

Of course, the term "sovereign immunity" does not appear in the Constitution's text, either in its absolute form as in common law or its permissive form as in the contemporary law of nations. But Justice

Thomas dismissed what he called "ahistorical textualism," which would ignore the principle's implicit presence in the Constitution's structure—states' consent to be sued in federal court only by one another, otherwise maintaining their common-law right—as well as the stunning rebuke to the Court upon its maiden voyage in constitutional interpretation, *Chisholm v. Georgia*, by the 11th Amendment, which again is silent about the common-law principle but makes explicit that Article III had been misconstrued.[21]

Justice Stephen Breyer in dissent reads the Constitution's structure differently, eschewing common law and citing rather the law of nations, which encouraged but did not command comity. Moreover, he chastises the majority for overruling a settled precedent, none of the usual reasons for upsetting precedent—unworkability, a change in the legal environment, a change in circumstances, and the absence of reliance interests—being present in this case. "Today's decision can only cause one to wonder which cases the Court will overrule next," he concludes, a sentence immediately echoed in the press.[22]

My second case is *Gamble v. United States*, decided by a vote of 7–2, with Justice Samuel Alito writing for the majority and Justices Ruth Bader Ginsberg and Neil Gorsuch in dissent.[23] Once again the justices take up the matter of common law, for the issue is double jeopardy, and the question is whether it is violated when a man is convicted for offenses—in this case, an ex-felon possessing a handgun—violating both state and federal law.

Justice Alito holds that as the offenses are defined by separate statutes, they are by definition not the same offense. He reviews a series of English cases from the 18th century, finding that none of them clearly eschews the power of English courts to try offenses alleged to have been tried in foreign courts. To his mind—and to the satisfaction of Justice Thomas, who in a previous case signaled his willingness to reconsider the so-called dual sovereignty doctrine—the Fifth Amendment's prohibition against subjecting any person "for the same offense to be twice put in jeopardy of life or limb" applies only to the actions of the same sovereign under its own laws.[24]

Justice Thomas takes the occasion, perhaps because he is sticking to the precedent, to explain when a precedent should be overturned—not by taking into account mere matters of policy, nor even following the practices of common law, which he concedes is the source of according legal force to precedent, and which he helpfully and I think correctly describes as "identifying and applying objective principles of law—discerned from natural reason, custom, and other external sources—to particular cases."[25] But since federal judges consult only positive law—the Constitution, federal statutes, rules and regulations, and treaties—the rule of reversal should be "demonstrably erroneous precedent," or rather, when there is one, writes Thomas, "my rule is simple: We should not follow it."[26]

Although Justice Thomas was not convinced the precedent here is demonstrably erroneous, Justices Ginsberg and Gorsuch think it is, the first because she rejects the notion of dual sovereignty, the people being sovereign behind both governments, the latter because he differs with the Court's narrow reading of the English precedents, which ignores the larger principle that common law—and ancient Athens, Rome, the Old Testament, and the Church—considered deeply unjust and the problematic character of the American precedents, the first of which involved punishment under state law for harboring a fugitive slave, the later ones stemming from the era before the double jeopardy prohibition was applied by incorporation to the states. For Justice Gorsuch, the precedent deserves no standing even under Justice Breyer's test: "The only people who have relied on the separate sovereigns exception are prosecutors who have sought to double-prosecute and double-punish."[27]

Common law makes a brief appearance in *Kisor v. Wilkie*, in which the Court by a split vote declined the invitation to abandon so-called *Auer* deference—that is, the courts' duty to defer to agencies' interpretations of their own regulations, at least if the regulation is genuinely ambiguous in the first place and the agency's interpretation is reasonable, authoritative, within its expertise, and reflects "fair and considered judgment."[28] Justice Elena Kagan finds the *Auer* regime consistent with the Administrative Procedure Act (APA), quoting one of her successors as Harvard

Law dean to show that before the APA, courts used "flexible common law methods to review administrative action."[29]

In his concurrence in the judgment, joined by Justice Thomas and in part by Justices Alito and Brett M. Kavanaugh, Justice Gorsuch emphatically disagrees. *Auer* should be overruled, he thinks, since what the Court is deferring to may in some cases be unsupported opinions, as the Court itself recognizes in developing its five-part test; far simpler for judges to return to making their own judgments as to the meaning of regulations, as Justice Robert Jackson had insisted in his *Skidmore* opinion in 1944, a position that Gorsuch thinks is actually mandated by the APA—and mandated by the role of the judicial power supposed by the Constitution, which is intended to check, not merely ratify, executive action.[30] His opinion concludes, as by now you should expect, with a section on stare decisis, doubting it even applies in a case like this, where at issue is not a rule for the world but a rule about how judges arrive at their own conclusions—about judicial reasoning, in other words, or about its restraint.

The next case I'll mention, *American Legion v. American Humanist Association*, the Bladensburg cross case, does not involve common law in any technical sense.[31] In England, of course, common law coexisted alongside a religious establishment and in fact incorporated Christian morals, though not canon law, which belonged to separate courts. The American situation was different, at least in some states; in these and of course at the federal level, official recognition of a church and financial support was forbidden, though this change from common law seems not to have touched the moral order basically agreed to by the different denominations.

The key precedent in the constitutional law of the Establishment Clause is *Lemon v. Kurtzman*, which seems unable now for 30 years to command a majority to either affirm it or overturn it; Justice Alito's opinion here gains a majority except for his discussion of that case.[32] Nevertheless, the Court seems pleased to set the precedent aside and begin instead simply with an assertion of "a presumption of constitutionality for longstanding monuments, symbols, and practices," an approach that goes back to the legislative chaplain case in the 1980s, *Marsh v. Chambers*, and explains as well *Van Orden v. Perry*, in which the Court left in place a Ten Commandments marker on the Texas State Capitol grounds.[33]

There is a certain traditionalism at work in Alito's opinion, with its presumption for the long-standing—monuments themselves of course not changing as customs do, though perhaps their human perception does—and his sense that, whatever the original intention was of those who planted the stone, monuments "can become embedded features of a community's landscape and identity," secularizing the sacred or sacralizing the secular; the justice doesn't quite say.[34] The discussion of the commonness of the cross as a symbol of World War I—without mention of the symbol of crusade widely added among Americans or the way in which the war signaled the denouement of Christianity on the continent where it was principally fought—seems to assure the majority that it was meant to be inclusive, as more particularly do the non-Christian names.

Justice Thomas meanwhile swings for the originalist fences, so to speak: The Establishment Clause was written to protect state arrangements, local establishment or no establishment, from federal preemption, so it is illogical to incorporate it and apply it to the states; moreover, its terms forbid making laws, not placing monuments. He also joins Justice Gorsuch's opinion that would simply dismiss the case for lack of standing, doing away with the special exception from usual principles of standing created years ago for establishment challenges. Justices Ginsburg and Sonia Sotomayor dissent, on grounds that a generation ago probably would have commanded a majority on the Court.

The final case from last term I will mention is *Iancu v. Brunetti*, in which, on free speech grounds, the Court struck down more of the Lanham Act that was written to limit the kinds of trademarks that the Patent and Trademark Office (PTO) can grant.[35] Common law is conspicuous here only by its utter absence, as I suppose is originalism too. The PTO had denied a trademark to a clothing designer who boldly prints on his T-shirts the letters F, U, C, and T, the Lanham Act forbidding trademarks that are "immoral" or "scandalous." Justice Kagan fires a big cannon of First Amendment doctrine here, the principle of "viewpoint neutrality," noting how trademarks have been given to drug-enforcement programs like "D.A.R.E." but denied to "Bong Hits 4 Jesus," or given for slogans against terrorism but denied for "Baby Al-Qaeda."

Now I think James Madison got it right in his *Report on the Virginia Resolutions* when he said that republican government requires greater liberty for animadversion—spirited critique—than the common law of seditious libel had permitted.[36] But it seems to me nothing short of nihilism to say a public body can exercise no judgment about what is moral and immoral or decent and indecent—where at issue is not even a question of suppressing speech but the granting of a special privilege thought to yield commercial advantage, and even then when the purpose of the act was probably to prevent fraud and ensure quality and responsibility in commercial exchange.

The common law, whatever else might be said of it, was not nihilistic; it allowed liberty to individuals but allowed communities to sustain a common morality, originally embodied in a moral code that owed much to a common faith, but later in its successor in the states, the police power, to regulate society for the sake of protecting health, safety, and morals, with the promotion of education sometimes added to the enumeration. A jurisprudence that turns a blind eye to the question of morals seems hardly originalist to me—but whether public attention to the moral atmosphere of society is still secured by common law seems to me an open question. Insofar as moral change is customary, perhaps this happens with barely our notice.

In the *Brunetti* case, three justices dissent in part—Chief Justice John Roberts and Justices Breyer and Sotomayor, who in slightly separate ways would read the statute to strike the "immoral" clause but save the "scandalous" clause by interpreting it to mean obscene or indecent, which these T-shirts obviously were meant to be. Justice Sotomayor, in fact, proves she means what she says by altering the passage in *Cohen v. California* where Justice John Marshall Harlan II showed himself hip in a way reminiscent of the late '60s by quoting verbatim in the *US Reports* the nasty slogan about the draft sewn into the protestor's jacket—putting asterisks after the first letter as decorum demands. I thought it a fine gesture on her part, and I think Walter Berns would have too.[37]

Now, I promised a sixth topic after five cases, and that would be the question of birthright citizenship, in which a common-law perspective explains what social contract theory cannot. The extension of citizenship in the 14th Amendment by right of birth restored, I think, the English common-law understanding that citizenship is established by jus soli, right of the soil or birthplace, rather than by one's parentage, as on the continent. The Framers would have known this from Coke's report of *Calvin's Case* and from Blackstone's discussion of the term "natural born" in the *Commentaries*.[38] They certainly knew *Somerset's Case*, decided in 1772, in which Lord Chief Justice Mansfield declared an African held in slavery became free the moment his foot touched English soil, and that was one part of common law some of our Founding Fathers openly repudiated.[39] But when slavery was abolished, as when a statute against common law was repealed, the natural consequence was to restore common law, hence citizenship by birthright, an understanding that James Ho and John Yoo have shown was articulated by the congressional framers of the 14th Amendment.[40]

Our social compact friends insist that the first clause extended citizenship, as Thomas Hobbes or John Locke would have said, by arbitrary choice, but I think the spirit of that clause is rather to right a wrong than to convey a gift. What this means for the current immigration debate is unclear— unless it is that everyone has a right to some country, and if not ours, at least their birthplace—and I concede that the common-law doctrine of allegiance to the king by place of birth cannot be exactly the same when one is born in a republic.[41] But I have meant in these examples to make the case that the common law needs to be considered as an important voice in our legal conversation, not that it is the voice that always deserves to win.

As this last discussion indicates, I think that common law can guide not only adjudication but the way we think about legislation. Seen from a common-law perspective, new legislation is never created out of nothing; rather, the legislative power is the power either to declare the law—to put in writing what is already done or what ought to be done given the logic of existing law—or the power to change the law, in the words of Blackstone, to remedy some mischief that has arisen. Sometimes the change is big—for example, when the old common law of master and servant had become so tangled in allotting liability for industrial accidents in the manufacturing age that it was replaced by workers' compensation legislation. Sometimes the change can be less, at least in words if not in effect, as when a new category is added to antidiscrimination law. In considering legislation, Congress or the state legislature ought to and often does identify the mischiefs—but they ought also to be sure to identify the reasons behind the existing legal order, not take for granted its need to be altered or replaced.

The presumption of common law is for the tried and true, a presumption worth restoring, I think, not treated as mere prejudice, but of course a rebuttable presumption. To recover respect for common law and the way it still structures our lives—at least when we think about guilt or innocence, freedom of speech, the rights of property, or our responsibilities as jurors—might help restore a sense of gratitude for our legacy of liberty and even point us back toward an appreciation of, and an inquiry into, not just immemorial custom but the even more permanent things.

Notes

1. The literature on originalism has grown enormously in recent years. For a history of its emergence in response to the Warren Court, see Johnathan O'Neill, *Originalism in American Law and Politics: A Constitutional History* (Johns Hopkins University Press, 2003). O'Neill, however, overlooks the contribution of Walter Berns. For example, see Walter Berns, *In Defense of Liberal Democracy* (Gateway Editions, 1984); and Walter Berns, *Taking the Constitution Seriously* (Simon and Schuster, 1987). See also Keith E. Whittington, *Constitutional Interpretation: Textual Meaning, Original Intent, and Judicial Review* (University Press of Kansas, 1999); and Gary L. McDowell, *The Language of Law and the Foundations of American Constitutionalism* (Cambridge University Press, 2010).

2. The phrase is from George W. Carey and James McClellan, eds., *The Federalist* (Liberty Fund, 2001), 406.

3. Perhaps the best introduction to the vast literature in this camp is Jack M. Balkin, *Living Originalism* (Harvard University Press, 2011).

4. David A. Strauss, "Common Law Constitutional Interpretation," *University of Chicago Law Review* 63 (1996): 877. See also David A. Strauss, "Does the Constitution Mean What It Says?," *Harvard Law Review* 129, no. 1 (2015): 2, https://harvardlawreview.org/print/vol-129/does-the-constitution-mean-what-it-says/; and David A. Strauss, "Book Review," *Law and Philosophy* 32 (2013): 369, https://chicagounbound.uchicago.edu/cgi/viewcontent.cgi?article=7882&context=journal_articles.

5. Roth v. United States, 354 US 476 (1957); and Miller v. California, 413 US 15 (1973).

6. See William Blackstone, *Commentaries on the Laws of England* (1765; University of Chicago Press, 1979), 67.

7. See Oliver Wendell Holmes, "The Path of the Law," in *Collected Legal Papers* (Harcourt, Brace, and Howe, 1920); and Oliver Wendell Holmes, *The Common Law* (Little, Brown, 1881).

8. Benjamin Cardozo, *The Nature of the Judicial Process* (Yale University Press, 1921).

9. See, for example, Oliver Wendell Holmes, "Natural Law," in *Collected Legal Papers*.

10. Roe v. Wade, 410 US 113 (1973); and Planned Parenthood v. Casey, 505 US 833 (1992).

11. I discuss these instances at greater length in, respectively, James R. Stoner Jr., *Common Law and Liberal Theory: Coke, Hobbes, and the Origins of American Constitutionalism* (University Press of Kansas, 1992); and James R. Stoner Jr., *Common-Law Liberty: Rethinking American Constitutionalism* (University Press of Kansas, 2003).

12. On common-law reasoning as reasoning by analogy, see Edward Levi, *An Introduction to Legal Reasoning* (University of Chicago Press, 1962).

13. See Joseph Dellapenna, "The History of Abortion: Technology, Morality, Law," *University of Pittsburgh Law Review* 40 (1979): 359–428.

14. See James R. Stoner Jr., "Rational Compromise: Charles Evans Hughes as a Progressive Originalist," in *Toward an American Conservatism: Constitutional Conservatism During the Progressive Era*, ed. Joseph Postell and Johnathan O'Neill (Palgrave Macmillan, 2013).

15. Diarmuid F. O'Scannlain, "Rediscovering the Common Law," *Notre Dame Law Review* 79, no. 2 (2004): 755, https://scholarship.law.nd.edu/ndlr/vol79/iss2/6/.

16. James Madison, *Notes of Debates in the Federal Convention of 1787*, ed. Adrienne Koch (Ohio University Press, 2009).

17. Paul Clement and Neal Katyal, "On the Meaning of 'Natural Born Citizen,'" *Harvard Law Review Forum* 128, no. 5 (2015): 161, https://harvardlawreview.org/forum/vol-128/on-the-meaning-of-natural-born-citizen/.

18. Carey and McClellan, eds., *The Federalist*, 404–5; and Marbury v. Madison, 5 US 137 (1803), 177–78.

19. Franchise Tax Board of California v. Hyatt, No. 17-1299, 587 US 230 (2019).

20. Nevada v. Hall, 440 US 410 (1979).

21. *Franchise Tax Board of California v. Hyatt*, slip op. at 15–16; and Chisholm v. Georgia, 2 US 419 (1793).

22. *Franchise Tax Board of California v. Hyatt*, slip op. at 13.

23. Gamble v. United States, No. 17-646, 587 US 678 (2019).

24. US Const. amend. V.

25. *Gamble v. United States*, slip op. at 7.

26. *Gamble v. United States*, slip op. at 9.

27. *Gamble v. United States*, slip op. at 23–24.

28. Kisor v. Wilkie, No. 18-15, 588 US 588 (2019); Auer v. Robbins, 519 US 452 (1997); and *Kisor v. Wilkie*, slip op. at 18 n.6.

29. *Kisor v. Wilkie*, slip op. at 22.

30. Skidmore v. Swift & Co., 323 US 134 (1944).

31. American Legion v. American Humanist Association, No. 17-1717, 588 US 29 (2019).

32. Lemon v. Kurtzman, 403 US 602 (1971).

33. *American Legion v. American Humanist Association*, slip op. at 16; Marsh v. Chambers, 463 US 783 (1983); and Van Orden v. Perry, 545 US 677 (2005).

34. *American Legion v. American Humanist Association*, slip op. at 19.

35. Iancu v. Brunetti, No. 18-302, 588 US 388 (2019).

36. James Madison, "The Report of 1800," https://founders.archives.gov/documents/Madison/01-17-02-0202.

37. Cohen v. California, 403 US 15 (1971). See Walter Berns, "Beyond the (Garbage) Pale, or, Democracy, Censorship, and the Arts," in *In Defense of Liberal Democracy* (Gateway Editions, 1984).

38. See Clement and Katyal, "On the Meaning of 'Natural Born Citizen.'"

39. Somerset v. Stewart, 98 E.R. 499 (1772).

40. See James Ho, "Defining 'American': Birthright Citizenship and the Original Understanding of the Fourteenth Amendment," *The Federalist*, August 25, 2015, https://thefederalist.com/2015/08/25/defining-american-birthright-citizenship-and-the-original-understanding-of-the-14th-amendment/; and John Yoo, "Settled Law: Birthright Citizenship and the Fourteenth Amendment," *The American Mind*, March 19, 2019, https://americanmind.org/features/the-case-against-birthright-citizenship/settled-law-birthright-citizenship-and-the-14th-amendment/.

41. John C. Eastman, "From Feudalism to Consent: Rethinking Birthright Citizenship," Heritage Foundation, March 30, 2006, https://www.heritage.org/the-constitution/report/feudalism-consent-rethinking-birthright-citizenship.

9

"Remember the Ladies": Reflections on a Centennial of Women's Suffrage

CATHERINE H. ZUCKERT
September 17, 2020

August 26, 2020, marked the 100th anniversary of the official addition of the 19th Amendment to the Constitution. It states: "The right of citizens of the United States to vote shall not be denied by the United States or any state on account of sex."[1] In celebrating Constitution Day this fall, it thus seems particularly appropriate to look back at the history of this amendment, to see how and why it was adopted, and to see why its adoption has not satisfied many of the demands and hopes of its proponents.

First, I will present a brief account of the history. Then, I will look to a rather unconventional source of wisdom about the significance of the amendment in Henry James's novel, *The Bostonians*.[2] James's novel not only shows that the women's movement has been frustrated by many of the same sources of opposition and division for more than a century. It also shows that the problems encountered in the attempt to secure women's rights are by no means limited to women. The problems are inherent in American democracy more generally, and they are, therefore, more difficult for Americans to recognize, much less address.

I have taken the title of this talk from a letter Abigail Adams wrote to her husband shortly before the American Revolution. In it, she famously urged:

> In the new Code of Laws which I suppose it will be necessary for you to make, I desire you would Remember the Ladies, and be more generous . . . to them than your ancestors. Do not put such unlimited power into the hands of the Husbands. Remember all Men would be tyrants if they could.[3]

Neither John Adams nor his fellow revolutionaries heeded her entreaty. Although women had been able to vote in some of the colonies before the revolution, they were denied the franchise in all the new states except New Jersey, which allowed women with property to vote until 1807. What became known as the woman's suffrage movement grew out of societies formed after the revolution to further moral and political reforms, such as the abolition of slavery and the temperance movement.

The emergence of the women's suffrage movement in the United States is usually dated from a conference on women's rights held in 1848 in Seneca Falls, New York. The conference was organized by Lucretia Mott and Elizabeth Cady Stanton. They had both attended a world conference of antislavery societies held in London in 1840. They were shocked to discover that women were not allowed to take part in the proceedings but were confined to a room upstairs where, hidden behind curtains, they could listen—even if the women had been elected and sent as official delegates. After they returned to the United States, Mott and Stanton organized a convention to discuss women's rights. At that convention, some of the participants voted to adopt a "Declaration of Sentiments" stating the reformers' goals and rationale.

The Declaration of Sentiments is obviously based on the Declaration of Independence, replicating most of its language and organization but modifying the content to address women's specific concerns. The point of the replication is, obviously, to show that extending voting rights to women constitutes an application of the principles on which the United States was founded.

The Declaration of Sentiments begins with the familiar "when in the course of human events" and goes on to affirm:

> We hold these truths to be self-evident: that all men *and women* are created equal; that they are endowed by their Creator with certain inalienable rights; that among these are life, liberty, and the pursuit of happiness; that to secure these rights governments are instituted, deriving their just powers from the

consent of the governed. Whenever any form of Government becomes destructive of these ends [and here comes another slight change], it is the right of those who suffer from it *to refuse allegiance to it, and to insist upon the institution of a new government.*[4]

The suffragists were not revolutionaries, so they explain:

Such has been the patient sufferance of the women under this government, and such is now the necessity which constrains them to demand the equal station to which they are entitled. The history of mankind is a history of repeated injuries and usurpations on the part of man toward woman, having in direct object the establishment of an absolute tyranny over her.[5]

Unlike the American Revolution, the rebellion of women against the tyranny of men will be peaceful—a matter of demands rather than arms—even though the wrongs that need to be righted are equally egregious.

Like the Declaration of Independence, the Declaration of Sentiments concludes with a list of the tyrannical acts that justify the rebellion. The first and most important has been denying women the right to vote. Like the American colonists who insisted that there should be no taxation without representation, the signers of the Declaration of Sentiments maintain that lacking the electoral franchise, women have no voice in the formation or execution of laws to which they are subjected without their consent.

Frederick Douglass spoke passionately in favor of the Declaration of Sentiments at the convention in Seneca Falls, and the suffragists worked hand in hand with antislavery forces until the end of the Civil War. However, when Douglass and other antislavery activists supported adoption of the 15th Amendment, which prohibited the denial of voting rights based on race, but not sex, Stanton and Susan B. Anthony broke with their former abolitionist allies and formed a new National Woman Suffrage Association dedicated to obtaining the vote for women.

The break with activists who insisted that securing the rights of black citizens was the most urgent need also produced two fissures in the women's movement itself. With the support of such Civil War luminaries as Julia Howe and Harriet Beecher Stowe, Lucy Stone organized the American Woman Suffrage Association (AWSA), which supported suffrage for women and black men. Instead of seeking to amend the federal Constitution, AWSA pursued a more moderate, incremental strategy of obtaining partial voting rights for women state by state. But neither organization had much success. In 1890, the two associations merged, but in the two decades that followed, only one state, Idaho, followed Wyoming's example by granting the franchise to women.

Some white suffragists had alienated their African American allies in the 19th century by not supporting the adoption of the 15th Amendment, and they did so again in the 20th century by adopting strategies intended to mute Southern opposition—by refusing to condemn white supremacy outright and requiring black women to march at the end of the first suffrage parade in Washington, DC, in 1913. However, the most serious problem the suffragists faced was that most Americans, especially women, did not think gaining the vote for women was all that important.

Some proponents of women's suffrage thus changed the basic rationale. Instead of seeking equal status under law to secure their inalienable natural rights, these proponents of woman's suffrage maintained that women should be granted the vote not simply because they are human beings, just like men, but because women are better. Precisely because women are physically weaker by nature and have as a consequence suffered more from the unjust use of force, they would raise the moral tone of American public life by trying to alleviate, if not abolish, sources of widespread pain such as the misuse of alcohol and war. As Jane Addams pointed out, the superior physical strength that had enabled men to claim the right to participate in politics in exchange for their military service was no longer as relevant to solving the problems confronting an industrializing society as the skills and experience women had acquired in managing their households. Yet as more women entered the workforce, it became clear that their lesser physical strength and liability to become pregnant meant they needed special protections to keep and perform their jobs.

Ironically, in light of the pacifist thrust of this early version of what has come to be called "difference feminism," it was America's entry into World War I that created the conditions, if not the impetus, for adopting the 19th Amendment. Under the leadership of Carrie Chapman Catt, the National American Woman Suffrage Association (NAWSA) had sought to gain the franchise for women at both state and federal levels. But by the time the US entered the war in 1914, only eight states had granted women the right to vote.

Impatient with the lack of success of the more moderate NAWSA, in 1913 a new generation of suffragists led by Alice Paul and Lucy Burns formed the Congressional Union for Woman Suffrage, and they adopted some of the more radical forms of protest that had been used in Europe. At President Woodrow Wilson's inauguration, they organized a parade of 5,000 marchers, which drew an audience of 50,000 and, consequently, a good deal of public attention. They then set up protesters dubbed "silent sentinels" outside the White House, and the arrest and mistreatment of these protesters after they were imprisoned and went on a hunger strike aroused a public outcry. But it was only after women had demonstrated their contributions to the general welfare, by serving as nurses in the war and during the Spanish influenza and by taking up the jobs vacated by men who had to leave for the front, that public support for granting women the vote increased.

The amendment was passed by both the House and Senate in 1918 and sent to the states. But it was barely ratified by the requisite three-fourths of the states on August 18, 1920, when, at the request of his mother, one state legislator in Tennessee changed his vote. Three generations of women had worked hard to get the amendment adopted, but from none of the varied perspectives of its proponents did it have its desired effects. Only 36 percent of the newly enfranchised female voters chose to exercise that right in the 1920 presidential election (as opposed to 69 percent of the men). There were multiple causes for the low turnout, but it quickly became clear that there was no "woman's party or lobby" to which elected politicians had to respond.

So, in 1921, a year after the adoption of the 19th Amendment, Paul and her National Woman's Party began agitating for the adoption of a second Equal Rights Amendment (ERA). But in the first half of the 20th century, the ERA was opposed by liberal progressives, such as Eleanor Roosevelt. They argued that legislation including mandated minimum wages, safety regulations, restricted daily and weekly hours, lunch breaks, and maternity provisions would benefit women forced to work out of economic necessity. The prohibition of any legal distinctions based on sex was seen to be the desire of a few upper-middle-class white women who wanted to have more successful careers.

Although an ERA was proposed in every session of Congress after the 19th Amendment was adopted in 1920, it came to a vote and acquired the requisite two-thirds support in both houses only in 1972—after the nation had fought World War II, during which women again took on many of the jobs that had been performed by men who were drafted, and was confronted by the civil rights movement, led by black citizens demanding the effective enforcement of rights they had supposedly been granted because of the 13th, 14th, and 15th Amendments.

It often requires widespread perception of a crisis to induce people to make fundamental changes in their basic law. But in the 1970s, the adoption of the ERA appeared to be an almost foregone conclusion. With the support of three consecutive presidents and both national parties, it was quickly ratified by 30 states. However, after Phyllis Schlafly mobilized conservative women in opposition, the number of states ratifying the proposed amendment dropped precipitously, and the legislatures of four states voted to rescind their previous ratification. President Jimmy Carter signed an extension of the deadline Congress had set for ratification from 1979 to 1982, but no state legislature took advantage of that opportunity.

Nevertheless, renewed agitation for adopting an ERA resulted in the ratification of the amendment by Nevada's state legislature in 2017.

Illinois followed Nevada by ratifying the amendment in 2018, and in 2020, a newly elected Democratic majority made Virginia the last of the 38 states required. It is not clear, however, whether the state legislatures' votes either to rescind ratification or to ratify so many years after the mandated deadline are valid. It does seem clear that an amendment stating that "equality of rights under law shall not be denied or abridged by the United States or by any State on account of sex" will not be officially added to the Constitution any time soon.[6]

Some commentators have suggested that another attempt to get an ERA ratified would not be worth the time and effort, since women have gained most of the rights and protections they desired by means of legislation and court decisions. The status of women in American law has improved, but the rights gained are not as secure as they would be if they were guaranteed by the Constitution. And, as the emergence of what are called the second, third, and fourth "waves" of feminism in the 1970s, 1990s, and the 2010s indicates, many advocates do not think women have achieved the equality under law that the original suffragists sought.

The effective abrogation of the 15th Amendment's grant of voting rights to African American citizens by so-called Jim Crow laws in the South may be the best illustration of the limited power of a constitutional amendment to change long-established public opinions and practices. But, history shows, resistance to granting women equal rights has not taken the same form or had the same causes as those experienced by blacks.

In seeking the particular causes of both the organized attempts to obtain equal rights for women in America and the resistance to them, I thus turn to a rather unconventional source of political wisdom: a novel. To be precise, to Henry James's novel, *The Bostonians*.

Asked why he had uncharacteristically written a novel about a political movement, James explained that he "wished to write a very *American* tale." And having asked himself, "What was the most salient and peculiar point in our social life?," he concluded that it was "the situation of women, the decline of the sentiment of sex, the agitation on their behalf."[7]

James did not think that American social life could be understood apart from American politics. Like Alexis de Tocqueville (whose work he mentions in the novel), James thought that "the more we look at American life, the more we see that any social aspect takes its main sense from its democratic connections."[8] Further, like Tocqueville, James observed that the freedom given young American girls to go into public unsupervised by their families and decide their own future was unprecedented. Unlike Tocqueville, however, James did not think that the freedom of an American woman was or should be limited to choosing a husband and then voluntarily restricting her activity to caring for him and their children in the privacy of their home. When the man said to be representative of his sex in *The Bostonians* articulates such a view, James describes it as too narrow and primitive for the modern age. But the question then arises: What alternative or alternatives did—or do—American women have?

The central plot of *The Bostonians* is easily summarized: A young, single, intelligent, and independently wealthy but plain woman named Olive Chancellor competes with her handsome but poor Southern cousin, Basil Ransom, for the affections of a young beautiful girl, Verena Tarrant. Supported and tutored by Olive, Verena promises to become a successful public speaker on behalf of women. Yet, despite Basil's reactionary views of women as naturally weaker and inferior to men, whose activities should be restricted to the domestic sphere, Verena chooses to marry Basil and retire into obscurity.

At first glance, it might look as if James agrees with Basil in simply condemning the women's movement. However, James forces his readers to reconsider that first impression in the last two sentences of the novel. After Basil drags Verena away from her friends, family, and sponsors in the lecture hall where she was about to address a huge crowd, she says that she is glad he had done so. But, the narrator reports, Basil "presently discovered that, beneath her hood, she was in tears." And, the narrator comments, "It is to be feared that with the union, so far from brilliant, into which she was about to enter, these were not the last she was destined to shed."[9]

James clearly does not think that Verena made a happy choice. But could she have made a better one? Throughout the novel, she is offered fame, wealth, social position, love, and friendship. James shows that there was something lacking in all the opportunities she is offered and that Verena did not have the education or experience needed to choose wisely.

"As a representative of his sex," James declares, Basil Ransom is "the most important personage in my narrative."[10] In making that declaration, James suggests that men are part, if not the sole cause, of the problematic situation of women in America. A Southerner who had fought in the Civil War might appear to be a strange "representative" of the American man in 1886, when the novel was published. But James explains: Basil

> was not of a mercenary spirit, but he had an immense desire for success. . . . He had seen in his younger years one of the biggest failures that history commemorates, . . . and it had implanted in his mind a deep aversion to the ineffectual.[11]

Having tried to manage his family's plantation in Mississippi after the war and acquiring only a pile of debts, Basil had decided to come north to make money by practicing law. His cousin Olive invites him to dinner, because Basil's move north indicates that he acknowledges that the North won the war and that it is one country. However, as Basil's shabby appearance reveals, he has not been much more successful in the big city than he had been back on the farm.

Basil prides himself on his insight, but James shows that Basil's views of other people merely touch the surface. For example, upon meeting Olive, Basil concludes that she is "visibly morbid." But the narrator comments:

> It proved nothing of any importance with regard to Miss Chancellor, to say that she was morbid; any sufficient account of her would lie very much to the rear of that. Why was she morbid, and why was her morbidness typical?[12]

These are the questions James poses for himself and the reader.

Likewise, when Basil has to judge character rather than appearance, he fails abominably, as in his choice of a law partner who absconded with the firm's funds. Basil "wondered whether he were stupid and unskilled, and he was finally obliged to confess to himself that he was unpractical." As the narrator comments, "This confession was in itself a proof of the fact, for nothing could be less fruitful than such a speculation. . . . [Basil] was perfectly aware that he cared a great deal for theory." So visitors to his law office "must have thought when they found him . . . reading a volume of de Tocqueville. This was the kind of reading he liked."[13]

James explicitly does "not attempt to give a complete description of Ransom's ill-starred views." He says merely that Basil

> was by natural disposition a good deal of a stoic, and that, as a result of considerable intellectual experience, he was, in social and political matters, a reactionary . . . with a more primitive conception of manhood than our modern temperament appears to require, and a program of human felicity much less varied.[14]

When Verena talks about the superiority of women as a result of their suffering, Basil thus retorts, "The suffering of woman is the suffering of all humanity. Do you think that any movement is going to stop that—or all the lectures from now to doomsday?" Because men are stronger, Basil thinks, they should attempt to protect weaker women, and women should gratefully "accept the lot which men have made for them."[15]

Not believing any fundamental improvement in the human condition is possible, Basil does not believe in the efficacy of political action. Yet he acknowledges that his highest ambition is to see his "ideas embodied in national conduct."[16] He even ironically admits that he would like to be elected president. But recognizing that his opinions are not popular, he does not expect to succeed immediately. While he waits, he wants the comfort of a wife who seeks only to please him. He does not propose to

Verena at first, because he lacks a visible means of support. Not having succeeded at law, he had turned to writing, but he again became discouraged after his submissions to journals were rejected. However, when an editor of *The Rational Review* accepts his 13th effort for publication two years hence, Basil feels justified in pursuing Verena and pressing her to marry him. He is, indeed, not a practical man.

However, James suggests, the reason for his lack of practical judgment is not his nature, Southern origins, or masculinity, so much as his taste for theory. Basil thinks he has understood a person if he can identify him or her as a type, and he generalizes broadly. His views of the possibilities of human happiness are narrow. Everyone suffers, but women—all women without regard to any differences of intellect, appearance, talent, education, or inclination—should be required to live entirely in the private sphere.

Verena objects to his exclusion of half the human race from society and, in particular, his denying that she has anything special to contribute. She asks what he proposes to do about the millions of women who have no home. "Women marry [or] are given in marriage less and less," she observes. "You can't tell them to go and mind their husband and children, when they have no husband and children to mind."[17] But Basil brushes her observation aside as "a detail" and asserts that

> there are a thousand ways in which any woman . . . may find
> occupation . . . in making society agreeable . . . to men. . . . What
> is most agreeable to women is to be agreeable to men! That is
> a truth as old as the human race.[18]

Basil nevertheless assures her that he thinks she is unique and extraordinary. Everything she says has been imposed on her by unfortunate associations, and she has accepted these views because of the sweetness of her nature. "You always want to please someone," he tells her. "Now you go lecturing about the country, and trying to provoke demonstrations, in order to please Miss Chancellor, just as you did before to please your father and mother. It isn't *you*."[19] But, he suggests, you might greatly "please someone else by jettisoning the inflated public figure [you have] invented and standing forth in [your] freedom as well as in [your] loveliness!"[20]

Although she initially finds Basil's views appalling, Verena accepts his offer of marriage in the end because she gradually comes to believe what he had told her earlier about her true vocation. "And, strange to say," the narrator comments, "she liked herself better."[21] Earlier in the novel, the narrator said he did not know "whether Ransom was aware [that he] attributed to Miss Tarrant a singular hollowness of character."[22] But the narrator later observes that "it was in her nature to be easily submissive, . . . and the struggle of yielding to a will which she felt to be stronger even than Olive's was not of long duration."[23]

James recognizes that not all women are as docile or desirous of pleasing a man as Verena is—Olive, first and foremost. "Olive was intelligent enough not to have needed to be morbid, even for purposes of self-defense," he observes.[24] But, he shows that she lives in a constant state of tension between what her intellect tells her about the differences among human beings and "a theory she devotedly nursed, . . . which bade her put off invidious distinctions and mingle in the common life."[25] Although she avidly supported reform, she "found herself so often wishing that reformers were a little different."[26]

For example, she thought there was something grand about Mrs. Farrinder, when she meets the renowned advocate of women's suffrage. But Olive detected a false note when Mrs. Farrinder spoke to Olive about the ladies in Beacon Street. "Olive hated to hear that fine avenue talked about as if it were such a remarkable place, and to live there were a proof of worldly glory. All sorts of inferior people lived there." But Olive instantly reminded herself that it is "wretched to be irritated by such mistakes."[27]

Instead of criticizing artificial or false understandings of social class distinctions and guiding her own actions by the true and accurate differences she perceives among individuals, Olive believes it is the height of moral purity not to draw any distinctions at all. So when Miss Birdseye spoke as if she were a "leader of society," Olive could forgive her even that odious expression, because . . . one never pretended that she, poor dear, had the smallest sense of the real. She was heroic, she was sublime, the whole moral history of Boston was reflected in her displaced spectacles.[28]

James seems to agree that Miss Birdseye's failure to see human beings as they are reflects the essential character of the moral reform movements that grew up in America after the revolution, especially in Boston. But he does not take Miss Birdseye to be a moral exemplar. On the contrary, he writes:

She belonged to the Short Skirts League, as a matter of course; for she belonged to any and every league that had been founded for almost any purpose whatever. This did not prevent her being a confused, entangled, inconsequent, discursive old woman, whose charity began at home and ended nowhere, whose credulity kept pace with it, and who knew less about her fellow-creatures, if possible, after fifty years of humanitary zeal, than on the day she had gone into the field to testify against the iniquity of most arrangements.[29]

If Olive clearly perceives the differences among human beings, good and bad, why does she embrace a form of moral reform that denies such differences? James explains:

Olive had often declared . . . that her conception of life was as something sublime or as nothing at all. The world was full of evil, but she was glad to have been born before it had been swept away. . . . When the great reforms should be consummated [she wondered], would not life perhaps be rather poor and pale?[30]

The "most secret, the most sacred hope of her nature was that she might some day . . . be a martyr and die for something."[31] Olive thus admires her brothers' deaths in the Civil War, but she does not believe fighting will bring justice. Gentler means are needed. She has concluded that women not only can but must lead the last, only true crusade, for they alone know what it is to suffer.[32]

Olive fervently embraces the women's movement because it allows her to unite the two elements at war within her—her discriminating tastes and her democratic principles—into one passion. Thus far, men have ruled based on superior physical strength that makes them brutal, insensitive, and vulgar. Olive can prove her superiority by elevating "daintiness to a religion."[33] But she cannot take the leading role to which she aspires, because her internal emotional turmoil often leaves her speechless. She thus seeks to make Verena, an inspired, beautiful young speaker, her closest collaborator and friend.

Admiring the high-minded, impersonal moral passion of the New England reform tradition she sees embodied in Miss Birdseye, Olive has tried to repress, if not deny, the personal needs she finds illegitimate. Like most human beings, she wishes to love and be loved in return. Although some critics have suggested that she is a lesbian, Olive admits that she can imagine a man she would like very much. Unfortunately, there is none present—and she would not allow herself to be loved by a man in any case, because she thinks that would constitute an admission of her own inferiority and dependence.

Like Olive, James shows, the female physician who treats Miss Birdseye also lives a resolutely single life. But Dr. Mary Prance has no more sympathy for "the agitation" on behalf of women than Basil does.[34] However, the reasons she does not are somewhat different. Unlike Basil, Dr. Prance is not animated by any desire to reform the reformers. "Men and women are all the same to me," she tells him. "There is room for improvement in both sexes."[35] According to Dr. Prance, they all talk too much. Having devoted her life to caring for her patients and acquiring more knowledge about the human body, Dr. Prance does not feel the need for anyone to teach her what a woman can do. She does not cultivate "the sentimental side," as she calls it: "There's plenty of sympathy without [hers]. If they want to have a better time," she supposes, "it's natural; so do men." But it does not appeal to her "to make sacrifices for it; it ain't such a wonderful time—the best you *can* have!"[36]

Educated and able to practice a profession that makes her economically independent, Dr. Prance has achieved the major goals of the first generation of suffragists who argued that inalienable natural rights of women should be secured the same way those of men were. Basil sees that she was "bored with being reminded, even for the sake of her rights, that she was a woman—a detail that she was in the habit of forgetting, having as many rights as she had time for." He concludes: "Whatever might become of the movement at large, Doctor Prance's own little revolution was a success."[37]

In Dr. Prance we see what James meant by "the decline of the sentiment of sex."[38] He is referring not merely to the instinctive drive that brings the sexes together to procreate or the pleasure associated with it, but to the way in which individual human beings understand themselves and their relations to others, both their similarities and differences.

The history of the women's movement in the United States, both its achievements and its frustrations, has often been described in terms of the divisions that emerged among the female participants. Yet if we think about political activity, even when it was limited to men, as it was for most of human history, we see that it is always characterized by divisions. What distinguishes "the agitation on behalf of women" is that it makes the meaning and consequences of the sexual difference between men and women *the* issue. In Basil Ransom, Olive Chancellor, and Mary Prance, James depicts the three basic alternatives: Men are superior and should rule women, women are superior and should rule men, or men and women are basically the same and should be treated the same way. But he shows that none of these alternatives is apt to be personally satisfying for the individuals involved.

The power of sexual attraction may not have been adequately understood in late 19th-century America, when it was not considered to be a proper subject of conversation in polite society. But sex is only one of the forces that draws individuals together—or apart; it is not sufficient to define or satisfy anyone. As Tocqueville observed, Americans tend to understand themselves and others in terms of general ideas. What Tocqueville did not emphasize, but James does, is the way in which Americans tend to articulate their personal desires as general political ideas or theories and the way in which adherence to such general theories narrows and distorts their views of possible forms of human achievement and happiness.

That is the reason James suggests not merely that Olive is morbid but that her morbidness is typical. Her egalitarian democratic beliefs lead her to deny the legitimacy of her desire to achieve something great or even merely to be appreciated and loved for herself, intensely and exclusively, by another individual. She seeks relief from her inner turmoil not merely by joining a political movement but by seeking to find a kind of salvation through it.

In opposition to a later slogan adopted by some feminists, James would remind us, the personal is not the political. Democratic politics necessarily operate on a general level. Laws and institutions can guarantee rights and protect individuals from certain kinds of suffering, but, as James suggests in his depiction of Dr. Prance, the securing of such rights and protections will not suffice to make individuals happy. In this age of ever more intense partisanship, when Democrats cannot comfortably talk to Republicans, much less marry them, it may be well to be reminded of the many ways in which personal relations can be perverted, if not destroyed, by politics.

Notes

1. US Const. amend. XIX.
2. Henry James, *The Bostonians* (Modern Library, 1956).

3. Abigail Adams to John Adams, March 31, 1776, Massachusetts Historical Society, Adams Family Papers, https://www.masshist.org/digitaladams/archive/doc?id=L17760331aa.

4. National Parks Service, "Declaration of Sentiments," https://www.nps.gov/wori/learn/historyculture/declaration-of-sentiments.htm (emphasis added).

5. National Parks Service, "Declaration of Sentiments."

6. Equalrightsamendment.org, "Equal Rights Amendment," https://www.equalrightsamendment.org/.

7. Henry James, "The Speech of American Women," reprinted in *French Writers and American Women Essays* (Compass Publishing Co., 1960), 33.

8. James, "The Speech of American Women."

9. James, *The Bostonians*, 464.

10. James, *The Bostonians*, 5.

11. James, *The Bostonians*, 16–17.

12. James, *The Bostonians*, 11.

13. James, *The Bostonians*, 192–93.

14. James, *The Bostonians*, 194–95.

15. James, *The Bostonians*, 197–98.

16. James, *The Bostonians*, 193.

17. James, *The Bostonians*, 344.

18. James, *The Bostonians*, 345.

19. James, *The Bostonians*, 346.

20. James, *The Bostonians*, 344–46.

21. James, *The Bostonians*, 396.

22. James, *The Bostonians*, 62.

23. James, *The Bostonians*, 337.

24. James, *The Bostonians*, 156.

25. James, *The Bostonians*, 23.

26. James, *The Bostonians*, 34.

27. James, *The Bostonians*, 199.

28. James, *The Bostonians*, 35.

29. James, *The Bostonians*, 27.

30. James, *The Bostonians*, 159–60.

31. James, *The Bostonians*, 13.

32. James, *The Bostonians*, 185–86.

33. James, *The Bostonians*, 177.

34. James, *The Bostonians*, xi.

35. James, *The Bostonians*, 42.

36. James, *The Bostonians*, 42–43.

37. James, *The Bostonians*, 41.

38. James, "The Speech of American Women," 33.

10

The Centrality of the Constitution in the Civic Education of Americans

WILFRED M. MCCLAY
September 17, 2021

Q ueen Elizabeth II is now the longest-reigning monarch in British history, having easily surpassed the formidable 63-year rule of Queen Victoria and continuing to add to her record numbers at the time of this writing, in the summer of 2021. Her achievement has been widely celebrated in the American news media, partly because we Americans seem to feel a great fondness for Elizabeth and an enduring fascination with the British royal family.

Just why is that? This seems like rather strange behavior for a country that came into being through a revolution against one of Elizabeth's predecessors. Not to mention being a country whose Constitution—the 234th anniversary of which we celebrate in 2021—incorporated the principle that "no title of nobility" would be granted by the United States and that every state in the Union was to have a "republican" form of government—meaning "no kings and queens allowed."

There are probably more elements to that puzzle than there is space in these remarks. But surely part of the answer lies in the durable bonds that still link our two nations, in the form of shared language, customs, laws, and culture. Our country may have been born in rebellion, but our Constitution's form and contents are deeply indebted to the British precedents and influences that shaped it, especially following the long and often bloody struggles for power during the 17th century culminating in the constitutional arrangements established in the Glorious Revolution. More generally, the "special relationship" between our two nations has proved deep and enduring, despite our occasional differences. There can be no doubt about it; we Americans have a rooting interest in the Queen's well-being.

But something else is at work too. The Queen's most important role in her own country is an impersonal one, her office as a disinterested and trans-partisan symbol of the United Kingdom (and the Commonwealth). Elizabeth performs that role with superlative grace and is arguably the single most compelling symbol of political stability and unity in today's world. Despite all the changes and fissures that have afflicted British society since her reign began in 1952, including a radical transformation of the nation's international status and its demographic makeup, not to mention the endless foibles of the royal family, her matronly but commanding presence reassures her people—and those of us who care about them—that the essential things will carry on, year in and year out. Whether that essential British core will survive the British nation's eventual loss of this extraordinary woman is anyone's guess, but the odds are high that the monarchy she sought to preserve will endure so long as a reasonably coherent British nation also endures.

There is something enviable in that. We Americans often feel the absence of such unifying personal symbols in our own contentious nation, and many of us yearn for them—especially at the present moment, when so much in our national life seems to be fiercely contested and when the presidency itself, no matter who occupies that office, seems more often to be an avenue of division rather than a symbol of abiding unity. Seeming to lack the symbols of unity, we fear that we may be losing the thing itself. It is not an unjustified fear.

But in fact we do not lack for unifying symbols, if we are willing to avail ourselves of them. Ever since George Washington gallantly refused the office of monarch, we have been on a different path—a path on which our commitment to impersonal laws and impartial procedures overrides our commitment to any one man or woman as our symbolic head. For us it is a document, our Constitution, that plays the role of democratic monarch and thereby serves as the chief and most durable symbol of our national unity and our commitment to one another as one nation.

That is not all the Constitution does, of course. It is first and fore-most a legal document, a written expression of the supreme law of the land, establishing the fundamental structure of the national government, broadly delineating its relationship to the state governments, and explic-itly protecting certain individual and collective rights against the power of the national government. As such, it is not in any obvious way an equiv-alent to a monarch. And like most legal documents, it also is a rather dry affair. Unlike the Declaration of Independence, the Constitution contains, apart from its Preamble, almost no stirring language proclaiming the sweeping idealism of its claims.

But its symbolic function is nevertheless an absolutely crucial part of what it has been for us. We have lived under its authority for the entire span of our nation's history, apart from a brief prelude under the Articles of Confederation.[1] Hence, our national identity is difficult to conceive apart from it. To do so would mean entry into utterly uncharted waters. By contrast, the French have over the centuries cycled through a mul-titude of regimes—monarchies, republics, and empires—and yet French identity has never been reliant for its existence on any particular form of government. We think of the United States as a young country, and per-haps we are right to do so. But the established life of the American nation has not existed apart from its Constitution, which happens also to be the world's oldest constitution. Hence it is especially proper at a time of such intense contention in our national life that we pause to remember and reflect on the meaning of that fact.

* * * *

That of course doesn't mean that the Constitution and its longevity have always been seen as a cause for celebration. There have always been detractors, impatient with the impediments to change that are built into the constitutional structure. One of our most distinguished Founders, Thomas Jefferson, was often dismissive of the Constitu-tion's enduring importance and mocked those who "look at Constitu-tions with sanctimonious reverence, & deem them . . . like the ark of the covenant" and "ascribe to the men of the preceding age a wisdom more than human."[2]

He was not entirely wrong in this attitude. The Constitution should never be treated as the equivalent of Holy Writ, complete and unalterable, and its Framers never intended that it should be so regarded. But Jefferson was wrong to disparage our instinct to venerate the Constitution, and the fact that we have changed it in so many ways since his time—sometimes improving it, sometimes battering it, sometimes elaborating on it, and other times deviating from it—does not change matters. We need our sprightly 234-year-old Constitution now more than ever.

We need it primarily as the foundational charter of our liberties and our organizational plan for a limited government. But we also need it as an anchor for our national life, a focal point of legitimacy in times of conflict, and an educative instrument that demonstrates to those under its sway the kinds of restraint that are required of a free people living under the rule of law—the ways that the wants and desires of free citizens can be so directed as to make possible a good and orderly society. It is striking how often, in a time of crisis, our national debates revolve around rival interpretations of what the Constitution says. The right interpretation may be in doubt, but the necessity of looking to the Constitution for vindication of that interpretation is presumed.

As such, the Constitution must stand at the center of any civic education worthy of the name, as a model whose example is felt in all the activities of American citizenship. It is admittedly far less charming and personable than Queen Elizabeth, and it lends itself poorly to occasions of pomp and ceremony. But it has proved far more durable than any queen or king, and its health is the key to our continued unity and prosperity as a people.

Civic education should serve the function of unlocking the secrets behind that document's power. To learn about the complex structure of the federal and state government and come to understand the elaborate system of checks and balances that thwarts the natural tendency toward excessive concentration of power—this need not be a dry exercise in rote memorization. Understood rightly, the Constitution is nothing less than a profound reflection on human nature, just as James Madison said it was.[3] It conveys the hard truth that, given the flawed timber of human nature, a free and good society will also always be a contentious society, in which interests inevitably collide with other interests, and in which lawful rules of engagement for the adjustment and adjudication of conflict, and the institutions to embody them, are absolutely necessary.

Not everyone agrees. One of the arguments commonly adduced against the centrality of the Constitution is the social pluralism of today's American society. In this view, an 18th-century document designed for the governance of a relatively homogeneous and largely agrarian society of white Protestant English speakers could not possibly be adequate to the far more complex, increasingly diverse society in which we find ourselves today. What can the Constitution tell us about how to deal with issues like internet hacking, identity theft, or the rights of surrogate parents? Or more generally, how does the study of the Constitution help us think concretely about problems of which the Framers could not possibly have dreamed?

The argument can be extended further. Perhaps the very idea that there is a unified American national identity is itself a delusion; perhaps we are too diverse today to think of ourselves in that way any longer. If so, then, civic education should not concern itself with inculcating and reinforcing a national commonality that no longer exists. Instead it should concern itself with empowering subcommunities and marginalized groups, as means of expanding the reach of a more truly democratic ethos, "a more perfect union." Teaching the citizenry about theories and structures of governance is a waste of time. As some political theorists have argued, the essence of citizenship is activity; the citizen is the person who asks the question: What *should* we do?[4] And who then mobilizes to *do* it.

But this argument silently presumes a great deal. It presumes in the first place that nothing is to be gained from referring present-day technological puzzles back to older constitutional principles and categories. But that is certainly not true; if anything, such referring backward can be a potent source of illumination, precisely because it forces the reconsideration of particulars within the context of a larger and more abstract concept. Questions of internet security are clarified by reference to the principles of the Fourth Amendment; issues of Big Tech censorship are usefully developed by asking whether Google, Facebook, and Twitter are "common carriers," in the common-law sense of the term. We are forced to consider present-day instances in light of more enduring, even perennial, features of human relations.

The argument also presupposes that there is sufficient cultural homogeneity in present-day American society to achieve meaningful consensus about what it means to say that something *should* be done and how one acts lawfully in doing it. But proponents of this argument err, I fear, in saying that the question of "what should be done" is an empirical one. "Should" is never a simply empirical term; it necessarily implies the introduction of some anterior set of values, some conception of the moral universe that influences the course of human actions. The art of deliberation, too, is impossible without a whole set of prior commitments to the principles of integrity, rationality, and mutuality, which do not arise spontaneously in human beings but require education in shared values that are inculcated well in advance of the act of deliberating.

The pragmatistic premises of "action civics" are different.[5] They presume that civic education is kinetic, that one learns to deliberate by the act of deliberating, learns to make political judgments by the act of making political judgments. This is not entirely wrong, and the example of the elevating effect of jury service is powerful—or would be, if it were not an example that applies to adults rather than school-age children. But one cannot deliberate or judge until one has come into possession of the moral tools to do so and of knowledge independently acquired to make dispassionate and rational judgments. Otherwise one will simply be engaged in political action based entirely on what others tell one that he or she "should" be doing. When high school students are urged to participate in public demonstrations on behalf of complex issues—climate change, open borders, tax policy, or the proper role of the police—about which they cannot possibly have made an independent and informed judgment, that is exactly what is happening. They are being exploited rather than educated. This is a mockery of civic education.

The question of cultural diversity, too, can lead in a very different direction than the exponents of a New Civics would take it.[6] As Samuel Goldman argues in his engaging new book, *After Nationalism: Being American in an Age of Division*, given the formidable obstacles to a revived and intensified sense of national identity, we might be far better off if we concentrated on strengthening our "institutions of contestation"—foremost of which is the Constitution itself, along with the contestatory institutions it created and the system of courts and other juridical bodies—rather than chase the phantom of a more cohesive culture. In other words, give the people sparring rings to fight out their differences, rather than try to iron those differences out through a more comprehensive civic education.[7]

I am not sure I can agree with every element of this analysis, since it seems clear that an embrace of constitutionalism is *itself* a value commitment, a commitment to the idea that "what we should be doing" has to be pursued in conformity with the desiderata of a higher law, of previously established legal and constitutional norms and commitments, which include among them respect for those who think "we should be doing" something else and those who think "we should" leave them alone. But Goldman makes an important point: that a firm commitment to respect the institutional procedures of contestation (rules of evidence, right to counsel, etc.) without insisting in advance on particular substantive outcomes could be a minimal but essential basis for holding a highly pluralistic society together.

But how minimal? How much is enough? How can such unquestioned respect for our procedures be maintained, unless the Constitution itself is something to be venerated, something that brings respect to the government and contributes to its stability and endurance and that provides a bond that connects the people to the nation?

The Constitution's Framers seemed inclined to agree. Consider these words of Madison in *Federalist* 25:

Wise politicians . . . know that every breach of the fundamental laws, though dictated by necessity, impairs that sacred reverence which ought to be maintained in the breast of rulers
towards the constitution of a country, and forms a precedent
for other breaches where the same plea of necessity does not
exist at all, or is less urgent and palpable.[8]

If Madison is right, the dignity of the law should be understood as a
seamless web, for which an unattended tear in one area (especially the
area of the highest and most general law) can present a more general loss
of confidence in the law's efficacy and worthiness. A loss of reverence for
the highest law in the land cannot help but undermine the way law and
lawful behavior are understood on subordinate levels. It would undermine the efficacy and authority of "institutions of contestation."

But I do not think we should be ready to accede to such a thin understanding of what it means to be an American citizen. It is unfortunate that
the word "citizenship" has lost much of the noble luster it once had, just as
"civics" has wound up demoted to a kind of "user's guide" to the machinery of government.[9] Both words deserve better. Citizenship is not merely
about voting but also about membership in a society of civic equals—
citizens, not subjects, whose respect for one another's equal standing
under the law is a guiding moral premise of the democratic way of life.[10]

Civic education rightly understood, then, extends far beyond the
mechanics of how a bill becomes a law. It should promote a vivid and
enduring sense of our belonging to one of the greatest enterprises in
human history: the astonishing, perilous, and immensely consequential
story of our own country. Both things involve fostering that sense of felt
connection to our past and of appreciation for the good things that we
have inherited, along with a feeling of responsibility for the tasks of preserving them and improving on them. Hence a civic education is more
than a guidebook for practical action and more than an initiation into
a canon of ideas, although it should be both those things. It is an initiation into a community—and not just a community of the present, focused

narrowly on "what we should do" in the here and now, but also a community of memory, a long human chain linking past, present, and future in shared recognition and, one hopes, in gratitude.

Ultimately then, although it is wildly unfashionable for me to say so, a civic education should be an education in love. The love in question, needless to say, is something different from romantic or familial love or any other kind of love. And although we need to find ways to teach it, at the same time it cannot be imposed by teachers, schools, or government edicts, least of all in a free country. It must be embraced freely and be strong and mature enough to coexist with the elements of disappointment, criticism, dissent, opposition, and even shame that come with moral maturity and open eyes. But it is love all the same. Love can coexist perfectly well with a critical acknowledgment of faults and imperfections; do we not see that same coexistence every day, in a great many of our most important relationships with other people? The highest love is not blind.

But without encouraging the development of love for the nation, there will be less and less willingness by citizens to make sacrifices for the invisible and anonymous others making up the nation, whether those sacrifices are made on the field of battle or in the equitable provision of health care or the formulation of welfare policy. We already can see the development of an entitlement mentality that sees government merely as a vending machine for benefits, a dispenser of funds. Without the deeper foundation that love and memory supply, a people's sacrificial capacity will soon be exhausted, and their republic will perish.

* * * *

Let me give a concrete example of what a richer consciousness of the past—and of the Constitution's centrality in it—can provide. It is a particularly consequential one, since it involves a great American leader who possessed an enormously powerful sense of connection with the past, though he was largely self-educated: Abraham Lincoln.

We all know that Lincoln was a voracious reader. He had essentially no formal education and acquired his peerless sense of the English language from reading, including Shakespeare's plays and the King James Bible. It appears that he read almost no history in his younger days. The sole exception that we know of was his reading Mason Weems's 1799 biography of Washington, a tome that few would consult today, and certainly not for its accuracy.[11] It is the book that gives us the fable of young George chopping down the cherry tree.

The mature Lincoln would develop a far more informed and sophisticated understanding of history. And yet essential traces of Weems's book stayed with him all his life, an enduring deposit in his mind and heart that would influence his view of the American Revolution and the Civil War and reflect his fundamental values. We know this because in February 1861, 40 years after he first read Weems's book, Lincoln drew upon it explicitly.

He was on his way from Illinois to Washington to be inaugurated as president. It was a time of extraordinary tension, as Southern states were voting to drop away from the Union one after another in response to Lincoln's election. There was real reason to believe the nation was disintegrating.

Lincoln stopped in Trenton, New Jersey, on his way to Washington and gave a short but powerful speech to the New Jersey State Senate, in which he recalled how Weems's book affected him as a young man. He particularly remembered Weems's account of the Battle of Trenton, one of the pivotal moments in the American Revolution, stating, "I remember all the accounts there given of the battle fields and struggles for the liberties of the country, and none fixed themselves upon my imagination so deeply as the struggle here at Trenton, New-Jersey." Lincoln continued:

> The crossing of the river; the contest with the Hessians; the great hardships endured at that time, all fixed themselves on my memory more than any single revolutionary event; and you all know, for you have all been boys, how these early impressions last longer than any others. I recollect thinking then, boy even though I was, that there must have been something more than common that those men struggled for.[12]

That "something more than common" was, he said, "something even more than National Independence; that something that held out a great promise to all the people of the world to all time to come." Lincoln was "exceedingly anxious that this Union, the Constitution, and the liberties of the people shall be perpetuated in accordance with the original idea for which that struggle was made," and he hoped that he could be "an humble instrument in the hands of the Almighty, and of this, his almost chosen people, for perpetuating the object of that great struggle."[13]

That is a lot for a youthful story to do. It shaped a boy's mind and soul in ways that would have such enormous consequences for the man—and for all of us. That story, those "early impressions," helped him form a compelling vision of the American past—a vision both inspiring and true that would sustain him through the dark days to come. And it need hardly be pointed out that the generation of '76, the founding of the nation, and the establishment of the Constitution occupy the center of that vision, as they so often did in Lincoln's oratory.

So what are we to conclude from this example? Do we historians need to retool and start writing inspiring fables like those of Weems instead of hardheaded and dispassionate factual accounts of the past, based on careful and methodical research? Of course not. History must be based on truth, not on myth. We do ourselves and the young no favors by prettifying or oversimplifying the past and failing to give an honest account of our failures and our triumphs.

But we also do no favors to ourselves or the truth if we fail to honor the magnificent achievements of our history and leave them out of the accounting entirely, as has become too often the case. We need to remember that one of the civic functions of history, one of the chief reasons we endeavor to record the past and teach it to the young, is to serve as a vessel of shared memory, imparting to each generation a sense of membership in its own society, a sense of living connection to its own past—one that can unite us and sustain us in hard times.

Lincoln brought that very connection to many of his best wartime speeches, most notably to his speech at the dedication of the Soldiers'

National Cemetery in Gettysburg, Pennsylvania, on November 19, 1863. Just as he had done in Trenton, so he did in Gettysburg, even as war raged around him, reaching back to the nation's birth in 1776—"four score and seven years ago"—as one of the great achievements in human history, a precious legacy to whose preservation the deeds of the present should be dedicated. He found in the American founding a source of renewed courage and determination, a steadying influence in a time buffeted by chaos and fear.

* * * *

So can it be for us today. Our young people deserve nothing less. We are failing them, and the country, so long as we fail to give them a rich and sustaining sense of their past, one that is both truthful and inspiring. Consider the alternative. If a story of estimable things can give us courage and hope in a hard time, does it not stand to reason that a story of relentless failure, mendacity, and despoliation can have the opposite effect? For this inglorious story, too, is a kind of civic education.

We are solicitous of the "safety" of students who may be exposed to ideas or words that they may find upsetting. But why do we not think about the effects of the inglorious story that they are taking in? Doesn't their picture of the world profoundly affect their sense of life's possibilities and prospects? Shouldn't we consider whether the remarkably high indicators of unhappiness among the young—and not only them—are partly traceable to a massive loss of morale and hope? Suicides among Americans age 10 to 24 increased by nearly 60 percent between 2007 and 2018.[14] A Pew study found rising rates of depression, especially among teenage girls, and that 70 percent of teens think anxiety and depression are major problems for their peers. Roughly 50 percent see alcohol and drug addiction as major problems.[15] The list of pathologies could be extended much further.

I am deeply concerned about these statistics, as any sensible person should be. It is hard not to think they presage a kind of general moral collapse. No one would deny that there are material factors, such as the dizzying changes in the structures of the national and world economy, at work in these trends. But the morale of a nation is ultimately a question of spirit rather than matter. By moving into the vacuum left by the absence of a genuine civic education, the decline of traditional religion, and the decay of traditional structures of family life, the inglorious story has been gaining the upper hand; playing a significant role in sustaining our low morale; saturating the young in debilitating ideas about the past, present, and future; and leaving them isolated and anxious.

In an otherwise noncommittal recent story in *USA Today* about the suicide epidemic, one finds this statement: "Many children, experts say, are struggling to imagine their futures."[16] Indeed they are. But this should be no mystery to us. The great Austrian psychiatrist Viktor Frankl, himself a survivor of the Nazi concentration camps, observed that humans can bear almost any kind of deprivation—except for the deprivation of meaning. Those with a reason to live, a task or a goal toward which their strivings can be directed, a "why" that animates their lives—they can bear up under almost any hardship. But without that "why," almost any "how" can defeat us.[17]

To be sure, such matters take us far deeper than civics, as we have conventionally understood that subject. But properly understood, civics involves us in a consideration of human nature itself and of what is the best set of arrangements to cope with human nature as we find it. And it teaches us about our relationship and indebtedness to the past. It seeks to instill in us a sense of continuity with generations gone before and, by doing so, begins the process of locating one's life in a meaning larger than oneself. An approach to civics that is relentlessly pragmatic and present-minded and that fails to draw upon our treasure of unifying symbols—notably that of our Constitution—will fail to engender these things and will serve only to reinforce the shortsightedness and self-absorption that we already have in hyper-abundance.

Notes

1. The question of exactly when the Constitution became the law of the land is surprisingly complex. An excellent and fairly dispositive treatment of the matter is found in Gary Lawson and Guy Seidman, "When Did the Constitution Become Law?," *Notre Dame Law Review* 77, no. 1 (2001), https://scholarship.law.nd.edu/ndlr/vol77/iss1/1/.

2. Thomas Jefferson to "Henry Tompkinson" (Samuel Kercheval), July 12, 1816, https://founders.archives.gov/?q=samuel%20Kercheval&s=1111311111&r=9.

3. The reference here, of course, is to James Madison's *Federalist* 51 and particularly to these words: "It may be a reflection on human nature, that such devices should be necessary to control the abuses of government. But what is government itself but the greatest of all reflections on human nature?" *Federalist*, no. 51 (James Madison), https://founders.archives.gov/documents/Hamilton/01-04-02-0199.

4. Peter Levine, *We Are the Ones We Have Been Waiting for: The Promise of Civic Renewal in America* (Oxford University Press, 2013), 163.

5. National Action Civics Collaborative, website, http://actioncivicscollaborative.org/.

6. A discussion of the term "New Civics" can be found in David Randall, *Making Citizens: How American Universities Teach Civics* (National Association of Scholars, 2017), 56–165.

7. Samuel Goldman, *After Nationalism: Being American in an Age of Division* (University of Pennsylvania Press, 2021).

8. *Federalist*, no. 25 (James Madison), https://avalon.law.yale.edu/18th_century/fed25.asp.

9. Victor Davis Hanson, *The Dying Citizen: How Progressive Elites, Tribalism, and Globalization Are Destroying the Idea of America* (Basic Books, 2021), 1–18.

10. The most cogent English-language exponent of the connection between citizenship and membership was the late Roger Scruton, in many works in his voluminous oeuvre. See especially Roger Scruton, *England and the Need for Nations*, Civitas Institute, January 2004, https://www.civitas.org.uk/pdf/EnglandAndTheNeedForNations.pdf.

11. Mason L. Weems, *The Life of Washington*, ed. Marcus Cunliffe (Harvard University Press, 1962).

12. Abraham Lincoln, "Address to the New Jersey State Senate," Abraham Lincoln Online, February 21, 1861, http://www.abrahamlincolnonline.org/lincoln/speeches/trenton1.htm.

13. Lincoln, "Address to the New Jersey State Senate."

14. Sally C. Curtin, "State Suicide Rates Among Adolescents and Young Adults Aged 10–24: United States, 2000–2018," *National Vital Statistics Reports* 69, no. 11 (September 11, 2020), https://www.cdc.gov/nchs/data/nvsr/nvsr69/NVSR-69-11-508.pdf.

15. A. W. Geiger and Leslie Davis, "A Growing Number of American Teenagers—Particularly Girls—Are Facing Depression," Pew Research Center, July 12, 2019, https://www.pewresearch.org/fact-tank/2019/07/12/a-growing-number-of-american-teenagers-particularly-girls-are-facing-depression/.

16. Alia E. Dastagir, "More Young People Are Dying by Suicide, and Experts Aren't Sure Why," *USA Today*, September 11, 2020, https://www.usatoday.com/story/news/health/2020/09/11/youth-suicide-rate-increases-cdc-report-finds/3463549001/.

17. Viktor E. Frankl, *Man's Search for Meaning: An Introduction to Logotherapy* (Beacon Press, 2006). The book has appeared under several different titles since it originally appeared in German in 1946. A short and revelatory interview with Frankl is featured here: Noetic Films, "Viktor Frankl: Why Meaning Matters," YouTube, April 19, 2019, https://www.youtube.com/watch?v=BB8X-Go7lgw.

11

Our Constitutional Moment:
The Danger to the Rule of Law

LIZ CHENEY
September 19, 2022

On January 6, as I walked into the room where members of Congress were being evacuated, my phone beeped. I was receiving a text message from a young woman named Jenna Lifhits. She was sending me Abraham Lincoln's Lyceum Address. Its message of the importance of reverence for the law could not have been timelier. It is a notion that I think of often.

I also think often about what it means to be a patriot. Since this is the Walter Berns Constitution Day Lecture, I looked back at Professor Walter Berns's wonderful book, *Making Patriots*, in which he gives us the following definition of a patriot. He says, "A patriot has to be more than a citizen or mere inhabitant of a nation; he has to be devoted to his nation and be prepared to defend it."[1] And over the past 20 months or so, all of us have had the occasion—more occasion than we would have imagined—to think about what it really means to be patriots and what it really means to be citizens of a free nation, what it means to live in a constitutional republic.

When we think about where we are in our history today, I think it is important to remember that most people in most times in history have not lived in freedom. They have not had the opportunities that we have had to decide who leads us, how our laws are written, and what those laws are or how to control their destiny. Before I was elected to Congress, I spent a good deal of my career working around the world in countries that either were not free or perhaps had been free for only a fleeting moment in time—or, in the case of nations that had previously been behind the

Iron Curtain, that were just learning what it meant to be free. I have had the opportunity to see firsthand how powerful and how fragile freedom is.

I stood outside a polling place in Kenya as an election observer almost 30 years ago. We watched as men and women filed up to vote even as government soldiers arrived and chased them away. And we thought to ourselves, on this bipartisan election observation team, "Well, we're not going to have anything to see because the voting isn't going to happen here." About an hour later, people started streaming back in again to the polling place because they were willing to risk everything for the right to vote.

I sat across a table in 1992 in Nizhny Novgorod, Russia, from a young man who loved freedom—a young man who believed in freedom and believed in freedom for his people. A young man named Boris Nemtsov. Nemtsov was later assassinated by Vladimir Putin's thugs because he posed such a threat to Putin, because of his defense of and his dedication to freedom.

I also worked in Kyiv in about that same era, supporting young people who were trying to help their country throw off the shackles of the Iron Curtain and Soviet domination. One of the young women I worked with later became the finance minister of Ukraine. Today, we are all watching, helping, and defending the Ukrainians as they again are on the front lines of the battle for freedom. They are engaged in a war they must win, a war that the world needs them to win, and we must continue to help them.

Three people in my life have told me that it was the words of Ronald Reagan and the model of America that led them to seek freedom here. One was an immigrant who grew up in Fidel Castro's totalitarian regime. Another was a young man who grew up behind the Iron Curtain and became his country's minister of defense. He told me that he would secretly listen to Reagan's speeches at night on Finnish television, and he understood that America was a place he wanted to join. And I've known a man who spent years in the Soviet gulag, who again said it was the miracle of America and our freedom that convinced him of what was possible and what he needed to strive for.

I have seen the power of faith and freedom. I was in Kenya when St. John Paul II spoke there in 1985. A few years later, I was with my mom and dad at the Vatican—my dad was then the vice president—and John Paul grabbed my dad's hand and shook it as he said to him, "God bless America."

I know God has blessed America. We all know that we are incredibly blessed. But this freedom that we have been blessed with, this freedom that is defended and guaranteed by our Constitution, only survives if we recognize threats to it when they arise. And today, we are facing such a threat. It is a threat we have never faced before: It is a former president who is attempting to unravel our constitutional republic.

We are to this day living through the impact of a president who has abandoned his oath. If you think about our history, we have had presidents of both parties, men of goodwill (some much better than others), but all who fulfilled their oath. All except one.

We must be clear in this time of testing, at this time of challenge, that when men and women in positions of public trust defend the indefensible and make excuses for Donald Trump, they compromise the principles of our democratic republic. And each individual compromise to defend the conduct of one man incrementally changes that republic.

Excusing behavior that is clearly wrong or unlawful erodes the rule of law. It chips away at our nation's foundation. And make no mistake: Once this conduct is excused, it becomes permissible.

Think about the trajectory of the moment. The elected leaders of the Republican Party downplay the violence of January 6, and they demand that all others do the same. This has become a litmus test. It is as if the hundreds of serious injuries to Capitol police officers who defended our Capitol that day were inconsequential.

Over the past year, I have spent considerable time with Capitol police officers, some of whom are in this room tonight. I can definitively tell you that they defended this nation and they prevented a far worse constitutional tragedy, and I can tell you how they feel about what happened that day.

The same leaders who tried to minimize the violence also sometimes try to rationalize President Trump's refusal to instruct his supporters to leave the Capitol when the attack was underway. I hope that you all heard the testimony of Pat Cipollone in our Select Committee to Investigate the January 6th Attack on the United States Capitol hearings, corroborated by Cassidy Hutchinson and others on President Trump's White House staff. They revealed that President Trump was the only person who refused to respond to desperate calls for help, even from his own congressional allies. He refused to come to their aid. And if you watched our hearings closely, you know that Mike Pence was essentially the president for most of that day. White House staff knew it, and so did every other Republican and Democratic leader in Washington. How could Trump's refusal to act and his betrayal of our republic, our Constitution, and our principles come at no cost?

Many of the same elected officials who rationalized Trump's conduct also continue to spread the toxic lie that the 2020 election was stolen, even though they know that is a lie. For anyone who is even remotely on the fence about that issue, I urge you to download and watch our second hearing from the Select Committee last June and listen to the Republicans on President Trump's campaign, in his Justice Department, and in his White House. Listen to what they all said. They all said his claims were false, that they were complete BS. He knew it; they told him. "We all knew it."

We also today are watching members of my party excuse President Trump's decision to ignore the rulings of more than 60 courts as if those rulings were irrelevant. Apparently, in this view, a president is no longer obligated to faithfully execute the laws of the United States as required by the US Constitution. Will future presidents respect and enforce the rulings of our courts if we excuse this behavior with Trump?

Some leaders even argue that the vice president of the United States can reject or refuse to count electoral votes and thereby select the president. This is a legal absurdity. No honest person with any legal training would believe that. But now this view is embraced by millions and promoted by those who know it is false. Some elected Republicans even defend President Trump's decision to summon tens of thousands of supporters to Washington—knowing that they were angry and that many were armed—and instruct them to march to the Capitol.

It is apparently, in this view, OK to ignore the fact that the White House ignored intelligence that those coming to Washington intended to invade the Capitol and occupy it. Every one of us watching what President Trump was doing and saying knew that violence was likely. And yet, many now pretend it was a surprise.

On top of all of that, those who are protecting Trump—elected leaders of my party—are now willing to condemn FBI agents and Department of Justice officials and pretend that taking top-secret sensitive compartmented information documents and keeping them in a desk drawer in an office in Mar-a-Lago or in an unsecured location anywhere was somehow not a problem. They are attempting to excuse this behavior. They are attempting to say that it was normal, that it was a storage issue.

A number of people in this room have worked in national security positions in our federal government. You all know this is a grave problem. And apparently, the Department of Justice has evidence that Trump lied about having these documents and that he lied repeatedly. This has now become excusable, too, if you judge by the actions of the elected officials in my party.

Does defending Trump now mean excusing obstruction of justice? How many of our elected officials today are willing to do that? Bit by bit, excuse by excuse, we are putting Trump above the law. We are rendering indefensible conduct normal, legal, and appropriate—as though he were a king.

And now, Trump has been suggesting—not even subtly—that any legal action against him could result in violence. Our former president is apparently now suggesting that if he is prosecuted, his supporters should put aside our constitutional order and the rule of law. They should stand up and, through whatever means are needed, prevent his prosecution and prevent the application of the law. It is hard to see this as anything but a direct threat to our Constitution, to our republic—and a credible one at that. One can only wonder: Is this where the Republican Party will go next? Is prosecution inappropriate just because MAGA will violently oppose it?

All of us have an obligation to acknowledge what is happening. The activities that I have just listed for you are the erosion of the rule of law, and they are the undermining of our constitutional system. Our constitutional system has been defended and handed down to us by every generation since 1789. It comes to us with a duty of inheritance. It does not belong to us. It belongs to our children and our grandchildren, and we must not be the generation that allows it to unravel.

My friends, I say this to you as a conservative. I believe deeply in conservative policies. I believe in limited government. I believe in low taxes. I believe in a strong national defense. I believe that the family must be the central building block of our society. And I share the concerns that many of us have—justifiable concerns about radical liberalism and "wokeness."

But those concerns cannot justify what the Republican Party is doing now. The means do not justify the ends. This is how democracies fail. That cannot happen, and it must not happen. Stopping this erosion requires men and women of goodwill showing courage and remembering that no office is worth holding if you enable, through your action or your inaction, the dismantling of our republic.

All these issues must be above politics. We have an obligation to preserve the structure of our Constitution and our nation, exactly what many of us have sworn to do before God, and that requires leadership.

Over the past 20 months, we have seen acts of cowardice. We have seen acts of craven political ambition. But we have also seen incredible acts of courage, valor, and patriotism. And we must choose courage. We must choose the Constitution.

I want to leave you tonight with one other thought. Last month on a beautiful summer night on a ranch outside of Cody, Wyoming, I happened to be speaking to the mother of 11 children. Now, I have five children, and as Phil can attest, that is a lot of kids. So, I stood in silent awe of this mother of 11. She pulled me aside, and she paid me what might be the highest compliment I can imagine. She said to me, "I think you fight so hard for this country because you have a mother's love for her." It was such a moving and humbling idea, and it is one that every single one of us, whether we are parents or not, understands. We love our country.

To paraphrase Lincoln, we love America not just because she is ours. We love her because she is free. And millions of us are dedicated to ensuring that our children and their children inherit this tremendous blessing of freedom.

Notes

1. Walter Berns, *Making Patriots* (University of Chicago Press, 2001), 1.

12

Pluralism and the American Constitution

NEOMI RAO
September 18, 2023

O ur public discourse today often focuses on the divisions in American political and social life. We hear a lot about polarization, the decline of trust, and the breakdown of our institutions.

America is one of the most diverse and vibrant countries in the world, with a long tradition of religious and economic liberty. Yet there are signs everywhere that we are less able to appreciate and respect differences and, importantly, less thoughtful about what such diversity requires from our government and our courts.

And so, on this occasion, I want to recover the relationship between pluralism and our constitutional tradition. By pluralism I mean the inherent differences between individuals, which may be expressed through their interests and talents, their religious beliefs, and their chosen work.

The Framers of our Constitution recognized the inevitability of human differences in the pursuit of happiness. This fact of pluralism was deeply connected to individual liberty and served as an important animating principle behind the specific form of government established by the Constitution.

Tonight, I elaborate on this theme in three parts.

First, those who shaped our Constitution had firm and passionate beliefs about what was true in religion and politics. They were certainly not relativists. But they recognized that others, perhaps in error, would invariably hold different firm and passionate beliefs. For instance, James Madison recognized that "as long as the reason of man continues fallible . . . different opinions will be formed."[1] Because it is inevitable that the American people will hold different opinions, interests, and beliefs, the Constitution was designed to accommodate pluralism by protecting individual liberty and establishing political processes for representing and negotiating the varied interests across society.

Second, I will discuss the vitality of pluralism in our constitutional tradition and in the Supreme Court's jurisprudence. Just this past term, the Court struck down Harvard's affirmative action program, holding that such racial discrimination runs afoul of the Equal Protection Clause. Justice Clarence Thomas explained that maintaining a pluralistic society requires equal treatment by the government, not divisive and arbitrary racial preferences.

And finally, I will consider how the administrative state has undermined the constitutional protections for pluralism. The original progressive faith in expertise is fundamentally at odds with pluralism. Moreover, moving lawmaking out of Congress and into executive agencies has unraveled one of the primary institutions for negotiating pluralism. Agencies cannot replicate the democratic legitimacy of our representative legislature. When private ordering is replaced with public ordering, local control replaced by national control, and legislative control replaced by administrative edicts, those whose ideals are not reflected in the regulatory policy of the day invariably feel alienated.

The penetrating reach of regulation into all manner of social, religious, and economic activity often occurs with little regard for pluralism. When legislative majorities are lacking, the administrative process may intensify political distrust and polarization and strain the shared enterprise of our constitutional democracy. Restoring the legislative power to Congress would help realign the administrative state with the original Constitution. This would further the rule of law, and it may also reinvigorate the political processes necessary to peacefully accommodate pluralism in our diverse and vibrant nation.

The Founders' Pluralism

Let me begin with the Founders' understanding of pluralism. The Founders acknowledged and accepted the inevitability of human differences. They wrote a constitution that accounted for pluralism by structuring and limiting government to protect individual liberty, property rights, and minority interests.

The political philosophers influential on the Framers recognized the inevitability of human differences across matters of conscience and economic interest. For instance, John Locke described and recognized the deep pluralism within and across human societies. It was a fact "necessarily assumed."[2] He maintained that although there are objective principles of natural law, human consensus on moral and legal matters is unlikely.

It is precisely for this reason that individuals must come together and establish a government that can mediate their differences peacefully, through a legislative process aimed at the general welfare. Inevitable human diversity also required protection for private property and individual rights. Similar ideas about the social contract and the necessity of law were expressed by William Blackstone, Montesquieu, and Thomas Hobbes, to mention just a few.[3]

To be sure, neither the Founders nor the natural rights theorists they relied on were relativists, and they did not always agree about the benefits or burdens of pluralism.[4] Yet they recognized that diversity was inherent in human nature and reflected in our varied interests, beliefs, and pursuits.[5]

This diversity was particularly manifest in matters of conscience, which required free exercise of religion. As Madison emphasized, "The Religion . . . of every man must be left to the conviction and conscience of every man" because "it is the right of every man to exercise it as these may dictate."[6] George Washington stressed that "the conscientious scruples of all men should be treated with great delicacy and tenderness" and "extensively accommodated."[7]

Pluralism was also apparent in individual talents and interests. As Madison explains in *Federalist* 10:

> The diversity in the faculties of men, from which the rights of property originate, is not less an insuperable obstacle to a uniformity of interests. The protection of these faculties is the first object of government. From the protection of different and unequal faculties of acquiring property . . . ensues a division of the society into different interests and parties.

The latent causes of faction are thus *sown in the nature of man*.[8]

The primary accommodation for such pluralism was ultimately structural and political. The Constitution begins with Article I, which vests all legislative power in a collective Congress, a representative legislature in which different viewpoints could be expressed, debated, and ideally harmonized into a legislative solution "consonant to the public good."[9] As I have elsewhere explained, in much greater detail, the Constitution vests legislative power "in a collective Congress in order to create a government that brings together all the disparate interests of society and creates laws that further the general good, avoid corruption, and protect the rights of individuals."[10]

Political theorists and historians have long debated whether the Founders envisioned that the legislative process would identify an objective common good or simply negotiate different interests.[11] But either way, there was widespread recognition that Congress was the central institution for mediating diverse and plural interests across society.

While the legislative power was essential for negotiating pluralism, the Constitution established other structural protections for personal liberty. These include federalism and the separation of powers, a unitary executive with a national constituency, and an independent judiciary to uphold the rule of law. These structural safeguards were supplemented by the careful enumeration of specific individual rights, such as freedom of speech and religious exercise, as well as protections for private property.

Pluralism is a deep fact of the human condition. The Framers didn't seek to level out pluralism. Rather, in the spirit of liberty and prudence, they established a constitutional government designed to secure the welfare and prosperity of a growing and diverse nation.

Judicial Review Preserves and Protects Individual Liberty and Pluralism

Next, I want to explore the essential connection among individual liberty, constitutional rights, and pluralism that runs through many of the Supreme Court's decisions. Individual liberty and pluralism are two sides of the same coin; we care about individual rights precisely because each person is unique and "all men are created equal" and "endowed by their Creator with certain unalienable Rights."[12]

By upholding the structure of the Constitution and enforcing individual rights against the government, the judiciary can help maintain a peaceful pluralist society that protects each individual's life, liberty, and pursuit of happiness. A few examples demonstrate the vitality of pluralism in our constitutional tradition and in the Supreme Court's jurisprudence.

The theme frequently runs through the decisions upholding the First Amendment's protections for freedom of speech and religion. As the Supreme Court famously stated: "No official, high or petty, can prescribe what shall be orthodox in politics, nationalism, religion, or other matters of opinion."[13]

This past term, in *303 Creative v. Elenis*, the Court held that Colorado could not require a website designer to create expressive designs for same-sex couples. Justice Neil Gorsuch proclaimed, "The First Amendment envisions the United States as a rich and complex place where all persons are free to think and speak as they wish, not as the government demands."[14] The Constitution requires the government's evenhandedness and tolerance of different viewpoints. The government may speak as it chooses, but it cannot dictate the speech and expression of individuals or interfere with the free "marketplace of ideas."[15] Freedom of speech is particularly important for unpopular ideas and, as Justice Oliver Wendell Holmes Jr. said, to protect the speech we hate.[16] Maintaining free and open debate promotes robust democratic deliberation.

Pluralism also animates many of the Supreme Court's religious liberty cases. Free exercise cases frequently invoke the importance of protecting minority religions. While Establishment Clause jurisprudence for many years promoted secularism rather than religious pluralism, in recent years the Court has emphasized that the government cannot force religion underground or promote policies hostile to religion.[17]

For example, in the 2019 case *American Legion v. American Humanist Association*, the Court upheld the display of a "Peace Cross" that was part of a World War I memorial. As Justice Samuel Alito explained, "the Religion Clauses of the Constitution aim to foster a society in which people of all beliefs can live together harmoniously."[18] From a somewhat different perspective, Justice Elena Kagan's concurrence emphasized *"this Nation's pluralism*, and the values of neutrality and inclusion that the First Amendment demands."[19]

Consider also the 14th Amendment, which extended the constitutional commitment to equality and pluralism that was promised, but not fully realized, in the original Constitution. The Equal Protection Clause protects pluralism by prohibiting government discrimination and forbidding the creation of racial castes among citizens.

The Supreme Court decisions in this area have been somewhat mixed. But last term, in *Students for Fair Admissions v. President and Fellows of Harvard College*, the Court invalidated Harvard's affirmative action program. As Chief Justice John Roberts explained, the Equal Protection Clause prohibits discrimination on the basis of race, and "eliminating racial discrimination means eliminating all of it."[20]

In his soaring concurrence, Justice Thomas explicitly linked equal protection of the laws to pluralism.[21] He noted that our Constitution protects individuals, not racial groups or classes.[22] The Declaration of

Independence set forth our national creed that all men are created equal and therefore must be treated equally by the government.[23] Affirmative action was simply "naked racism" that promoted "a factionalism based on ever-shifting sands" of skin color and racial categories.[24] Justice Thomas continued, "Rather than forming a more *pluralistic* society . . . [affirmative action] strip[s] us of our individuality and undermine[s] the very diversity of thought that universities purport to seek."[25]

By upholding the equal protection of the laws, the Court protects the rights of individuals. And it prevents the factionalism that results when the government divides up its citizens and distributes benefits and burdens on the basis of race.

The Constitution's structural protections—federalism and separation of powers—are also inextricably linked to individual rights and accommodating what Madison called the "great variety of interests, parties, and sects" across our republic.[26] As the Court has said,

> The federal structure allows local policies more sensitive to the diverse needs of a heterogeneous society, permits innovation and experimentation, enables greater citizen involvement in democratic processes, and makes government more responsive by putting the States in competition for a mobile citizenry. *Federalism secures the freedom of the individual.*[27]

In a pluralist society, federalism provides more opportunities for representative politics and leaves space for important issues to be worked out by individuals in their local communities. In *Dobbs v. Jackson Women's Health Organization*, the Supreme Court recognized that Americans held a wide range of viewpoints about the morality of abortion and the appropriate scope of abortion regulation. In overturning *Roe v. Wade*, Justice Alito explained that the Constitution was silent on the matter of abortion. He emphasized:

> It is time to heed the Constitution and return the issue of abortion to the people's elected representatives. The permissibility

of abortion, and the limitations, upon it, are to be resolved like most important questions in our democracy: by citizens trying to persuade one another and then voting. That is what the Constitution and the rule of law demand.[28]

Through the proper exercise of judicial review, the Article III courts help preserve a vibrant pluralism by upholding constitutional rights and maintaining the structural limits on the federal government. The Supreme Court, however, has failed to uphold the structure of the Constitution with respect to perhaps the most essential protection for pluralism: the vesting of all legislative power in Congress.

Congress provides the mechanism for umpiring our inevitable disputes and resolving them through the lawmaking process of bicameralism and presentment.[29] Representation of different interests in the House and Senate promotes deliberation and ultimately the identification of policies that will serve the general welfare.[30] The legislative process in Congress may not be perfect, but it's fundamentally legitimate, representative, and accountable in a way that executive lawmaking can never be.

The Administrative State Undermines Pluralism

This brings me to the modern administrative state and my final point about the particular ways in which the administrative state threatens the peaceful pluralism protected by the Constitution.

To begin with, the progressive ideology behind an expansive administrative state is at odds with pluralism. The original progressives who advocated and advanced the modern administrative state—Woodrow Wilson, Frank Goodnow, and others—began with the faith that experts could find the "right" answers to social and economic problems. And having found the "right" answers, experts could, and should, impose them on the American people.[31]

The progressives did not concern themselves with *individuals* and the inherent differences between individuals that were part of the human condition. Instead, they emphasized *social* problems and reaching the "best" social policy and organization.[32] The original progressives candidly advocated sidelining the messy and unscientific legislative process and weakening judicial review.[33] For administration to succeed, Americans would have to move beyond the Constitution's archaic protections for individual liberty and private property.[34]

In short, the administrative zeitgeist is fundamentally at odds with pluralism and the protection for individual liberty that accommodates diverse interests, opinions, religious beliefs, and economic pursuits. The Founders emphasized moderation, fallibility, and individual liberty; the progressives pressed for science, certainty, and government control.

But the threat here is more than theoretical.

The administrative state's constitutional problems, I trust, will be familiar to this audience. My focus today is on how these constitutional problems exacerbate polarization and factionalism. Reaching into nearly every facet of social and economic endeavor, the modern administrative state has unraveled the Constitution's structural protections for peaceful pluralism.

At the most fundamental level, the administrative state has shifted policymaking from Congress to the executive branch. The Constitution vests all legislative power in Congress. Yet in practice, what looks very much like legislative power is today primarily exercised by administrative agencies.

Why is this a problem? There are many reasons, but one is that Congress was designed to represent and mediate the many different interests and concerns across our diverse society. Disputes would be channeled into legislative politics that were widely representative of many intersecting and competing interests. Because securing such agreement would be difficult, federal intrusion would be minimal, and most decisions would be left to private ordering or state and local regulation.

Lawmaking is hard and was designed to be so. As Justice Gorsuch explained in his concurrence in *West Virginia v. Environmental Protection Agency*, lawmaking was vested in the people's representatives "so that those who make our laws would better *reflect the diversity* of the people they represent and have an 'immediate dependence on, and an intimate sympathy with, the people.'"[35]

Executive branch agencies lack this type of representation. Agencies are staffed by subject matter "experts" and bureaucrats drawn from a narrow knowledge class. Siloed in their areas of expertise, agency staff often act as policy partisans. They simply do not represent the diversity of interests across American society. And they are institutionally not well situated to recognize the broader economic and social trade-offs of regulatory policy.

To be clear, it's not necessary to vilify the bureaucracy to recognize that their experience and sphere of action are narrow, specialized, and aimed at particular bureaucratic ends, rather than a holistic consideration of the general welfare. Modern proponents of the administrative state stress that it can promote so-called constitutional values, even when running afoul of the actual Constitution.[36]

But the reality is that the regulatory process can't come close to approximating the representative politics of Congress.[37] Sure, notice-and-comment rulemaking allows the public to weigh in. But the process usually involves only those with deep pockets and the most intense interests. Cozy regulatory capture is prevalent. And in any event, proposed rules often change little before becoming final rules, irrespective of the hundreds or thousands of filed comments.

Agencies often impose a singular solution on deeply contested matters, without the political deliberation, negotiation, and legitimacy of congressional action. Those who disagree with an administration's policies have little opportunity for representation in the regulatory process and little hope of stopping policies that trample on their beliefs or interfere with their economic livelihood. Agencies are structured to allow the energetic pursuit of an administration's policies without the compromises of congressional lawmaking.

While unitary and energetic *execution* is part of the constitutional design, energetic *lawmaking* is not. The government now intrudes into *more* areas of private life and with *less* political legitimacy. An expanding administrative state that imposes one-size-fits-all solutions to contested questions raises the stakes of disagreements in a pluralist society.

Consider a few examples in which the Supreme Court has found that agencies invaded individual rights or exceeded their legal authority.

Regulatory policy often blithely fails to accommodate religious exercise. For instance, the contraception mandate imposed by the Department of Health and Human Services (HHS) required employers to provide contraceptives, with no exemptions for those with religious or moral objections. The Supreme Court held that imposing the mandate on private employers with sincerely held religious objections to such contraception violated the Religious Freedom Restoration Act.[38] As the Court said,

> Arrogating the authority to provide a binding national answer to this religious and philosophical question, HHS . . . in effect tell[s] the plaintiffs that their beliefs are flawed. For good reason, we have repeatedly refused to take such a step.[39]

Agencies also often stretch or exceed their statutory power. For instance, during the COVID-19 pandemic, the Centers for Disease Control and Prevention (CDC) imposed a nationwide eviction moratorium, which the Supreme Court invalidated. The Court explained that the moratorium went well beyond what Congress had authorized, intruded on the landlord-tenant relationship regulated by the states, and claimed an unprecedented federal power.[40] As the Court said, "Our system does not permit agencies to act unlawfully even in pursuit of desirable ends."[41] The Court stressed that "Congress, not the CDC," had "to decide whether the public interest merits further action."[42]

The Supreme Court also invalidated the recent regulatory plan to forgive student loans because the policy exceeded the authority granted by Congress.[43] The chief justice explained that under the government's interpretation, "the Secretary [of Education] would enjoy virtually unlimited power to rewrite the Education Act . . . [and] unilaterally define every aspect of federal student financial aid."[44] Furthermore, the Court noted that

> this is a case about one branch of government arrogating to itself power belonging to another. But it is the Executive seizing the power of the Legislature. The Secretary's assertion of administrative authority has "conveniently enabled [him] to enact a program" that Congress has chosen not to enact itself.[45]

These cases dealt with issues of great importance, involving contentious moral questions and matters of social and economic significance. The Court recognized that such "major questions" must be addressed in the first instance by Congress.

Nonetheless, so far at least, the Court has shied away from a more robust enforcement of the nondelegation principle. Some justices have cited stare decisis and other practical considerations for avoiding nondelegation. None of these reasons, however, addresses the fundamental fact that the Constitution vests the legislative power in Congress—not some of it, but all of it.

As I have explained in my scholarship, widespread delegations have undermined the collective Congress and its incentives for checking executive branch agencies.[46] This failure of the political process further bolsters the need for judicial review to restore the constitutional limits on administration.

Justice Thomas and Justice Gorsuch have called for the Court to check the delegation of legislative power to the executive.[47] If the Court enforces Article I's vesting of all legislative power in Congress, it would uphold the separation of powers and protect individual liberty, all the better to serve the needs of our diverse and heterogeneous society.

Concluding Thoughts

Americans will inevitably disagree about many social, political, economic, and religious matters. As the Founders recognized, such disagreement is sown in the nature of man. Madison said it would excite "astonishment" and "admiration" if Americans could "peaceably, freely and satisfactorily . . . establish one general government, when there is such a diversity of opinions, and interests."[48]

So, on Constitution Day, it is worth recalling that the Founders recognized the inevitability of human diversity. They accepted pluralism as a social and political fact. And they responded to its challenges by establishing a government structured to promote individual liberty and the general welfare. At the center of this structure was Congress, a legislature carefully designed to represent the nation's diverse opinions and interests through collective lawmaking.

But the ubiquity of administrative action and the lassitude of Congress have strained our political mechanisms for mediating differences. The erosion of the original Constitution, the breaching of its limits on government, the blurring of the separation of powers, and the reversal of the federalist structure all make it harder for a diverse society to function and identify shared goals.

Restoring the constitutional limits on the administrative state would be good in itself. And it just might go a long way to restoring a more peaceful pluralism in America.

Notes

1. *Federalist*, no. 10 (James Madison), https://avalon.law.yale.edu/18th_century/fed10.asp.

2. John Locke, *Questions Concerning the Law of Nature*, ed. Robert Horwitz and Jenny Strauss Clay, trans. Diskin Clay (Cornell University Press, 1990), 193 ("Nor is there any reason to be surprised at the diversity of men's opinions concerning what is right and virtuous given the fact that they disagree on even the most fundamental principles, and

god and the immortality of the soul are called into doubt. These, although they are not practical propositions or laws of nature, must, nevertheless, be necessarily assumed for the existence of the law of nature, for there can exist no law without a legislator.").

3. See, for example, William Blackstone, *Commentaries on the Laws of England*, 1:125 ("Every man, when he enters into society, gives up a part of his natural liberty, as the price of so valuable a purchase; and in consideration of receiving the advantages of mutual commerce, obliges himself to conform to include the preservation of our civil immunities in their largest and most extensive sense."); Thomas Hobbes, *Leviathan*, 4th ed. (1651; George Routledge & Sons, 1894), 82; and Baron de Montesquieu, Charles de Secondat, *The Spirit of the Laws* (1748; Colonial Press, 1899), 1:20.

4. Compare, for example, "Cato No. III" in *Essays on the Constitution of the United States: Published During Its Discussion by the People, 1787–1788*, ed. Paul Leicester Ford (Historical Printing Club, 1892), 256–57 (arguing "in large republics, the public good is sacrificed to a thousand different views"); and Thomas Jefferson to Peter H. Wendover, March 13, 1815, in *The Writings of Thomas Jefferson*, ed. H. A. Washington (Taylor & Maury, 1854), 6:447 (maintaining that "difference of opinion leads to inquiry, and inquiry to truth").

5. See, for example, *Federalist*, no. 10 (Madison) (observing that "a zeal for different opinions concerning religion, concerning government, and many other points . . . have, in turn, divided mankind into parties"); and Forrest McDonald, *Novus Ordo Seclorum: The Intellectual Origins of the Constitution* (University Press of Kansas, 1985), 185–86, 293 (noting that although the delegates at the Constitutional Convention thought of themselves "as representatives of different political societies" and had "personal or group prejudices or interests," they came together to "institutionalize the pluralism with which they worked").

6. James Madison, "Memorial and Remonstrance Against Religious Assessments," in *The Papers of James Madison*, ed. Robert A. Rutland and William M. E. Rachal (University of Chicago Press, 1973), 8:295, 299.

7. George Washington to the Religious Society Called Quakers, October 1789, in *George Washington on Religious Liberty and Mutual Understanding: Selections from Washington's Letters*, ed. Edward F. Humphrey (1932), 11.

8. *Federalist*, no. 10 (Madison) (emphasis added).

9. *Federalist*, no. 10 (Madison).

10. Neomi Rao, "Why Congress Matters: The Collective Congress in the Structural Constitution," *Florida Law Review* 70, no. 1 (2018): 31, https://scholarship.law.ufl.edu/flr/vol70/iss1/1. See also Neomi Rao, "Administrative Collusion: How Delegation Diminishes the Collective Congress," *New York University Law Review* 90, no. 5 (2015): 1463.

11. See, for example, Joseph M. Bessette, *The Mild Voice of Reason: Deliberative Democracy & American National Government* (University of Chicago Press, 1994), 2–5 (describing Congress as a forum designed for deliberation between different interests); Colleen A. Sheehan, *James Madison and the Spirit of Republican Self-Government* (Cambridge University Press, 2009), 169 (arguing that James Madison believed

popular government could "[harmonize]" "various views of justice"); and James T. Kloppenberg, "To Promote the General Welfare: Why Madison Matters," *The Supreme Court Review* 2019 (2019): 355, 365 (claiming Madison believed that "two-way communication between representatives and their constituents might . . . bring into being the closest approximation of the common good that flawed human beings could create").

12. Declaration of Independence para. 2 (US 1776).

13. West Virginia Board of Education v. Barnette, 319 US 624, 642 (1943).

14. 303 Creative v. Elenis, 143 S. Ct. 2298, 2322 (2023).

15. See, for example, Red Lion Broadcasting Co. v. Federal Communications Commission, 395 US 367, 390 (1969); and Abrams v. United States, 250 US 616, 630 (1919) (Holmes, J., dissenting) ("The best test of truth is the power of the thought to get itself accepted in the competition of the market, and that truth is the only ground upon which their wishes safely can be carried out. That at any rate is the theory of our Constitution.").

16. See United States v. Schwimmer, 279 US 644, 654–55 (1929) (Holmes, J., dissenting).

17. See, for example, Lemon v. Kurtzman, 403 US 602, 612 (1971) (requiring government action to have a "secular legislative purpose"), overruled by Kennedy v. Bremerton School District, 142 S. Ct. 2407, 2427–28 (2022).

18. American Legion v. American Humanist Association, 139 S. Ct. 2067, 2074 (2019). Justice Samuel Alito cited the First Congress's decision to start each session with a prayer, which "stands out as an example of respect and tolerance for differing views, an honest endeavor to achieve inclusivity and nondiscrimination, and a recognition of the important role that religion plays in the lives of many Americans." *American Legion*, 139 S. Ct. at 2089.

19. *American Legion*, 139 S. Ct. at 2094 (Kagan, J., concurring) (emphasis added).

20. Students for Fair Admissions v. President and Fellows of Harvard College, 143 S. Ct. 2141, 2161 (2023).

21. *Students for Fair Admissions*, 143 S. Ct. at 2177 (Thomas, J., concurring).

22. *Students for Fair Admissions*, 143 S. Ct. at 2202 (Thomas, J., concurring).

23. *Students for Fair Admissions*, 143 S. Ct. at 2193–94, 2207–8 (Thomas, J., concurring).

24. *Students for Fair Admissions*, 143 S. Ct. at 2201–2 (Thomas, J., concurring).

25. *Students for Fair Admissions*, 143 S. Ct. at 2202 (Thomas, J., concurring) (emphasis added).

26. *Federalist*, no. 51 (James Madison), https://avalon.law.yale.edu/18th_century/fed51.asp.

27. Bond v. United States, 564 US 211, 221 (2011) (cleaned up) (emphasis added). See also National Federation of Independent Business v. Sebelius, 567 US 519, 536 (2012) ("The independent power of the States also serves as a check on the power of the Federal Government . . . [and] protects the liberty of the individual from arbitrary power.") (cleaned up).

28. Dobbs v. Jackson Women's Health Organization, 142 S. Ct. 2228, 2243 (2022) (cleaned up). See also *Dobbs*, 142 S. Ct. at 2305 (Kavanaugh, J., concurring) ("The

Constitution is neutral [on the question of abortion] and leaves the issue for the people and their elected representatives to resolve through the democratic process in the States or Congress—like the numerous other difficult questions of American social and economic policy that the Constitution does not address.").

29. See US Const. art. I, § 7.

30. See Rao, "Why Congress Matters," 32–33.

31. See, for example, Neomi Rao, "The Hedgehog & the Fox in Administrative Law," *Daedalus*, no. 3 (Summer 2021): 220, 222 ("The Progressives celebrated this fact: rather than follow outmoded concerns for individual liberty and private property, the new agencies would focus on expertise and government control for the social good."); and Ronald J. Pestritto, "The Progressive Origins of the Administrative State: Wilson, Goodnow, and Landis," *Social Philosophy & Policy* 24, no. 1 (January 2007): 16, 21, 28.

32. See, for example, Frank Goodnow, "The American Conception of Liberty," in *American Progressivism: A Reader*, ed. Ronald J. Pestritto and William J. Atto (Lexington Books, 2008), 62–63 ("Social efficiency probably owes more to the common realization of social duties than to the general insistence on privileges based on individual private rights.").

33. See, for example, Roscoe Pound, "Justice According to Law," *Midwest Quarterly* 1 (April 1914): 223 (explaining that "the present generation seems eager to reject the idea of a fundamental law . . . [and] is eager to unshackle administration, to take away judicial review of administrative action"); Steven G. Calabresi and Gary Lawson, "The Depravity of the 1930s and the Modern Administrative State," *Notre Dame Law Review* 94, no. 2 (2018): 821, 829, https://ndlawreview.org/wp-content/uploads/2019/01/7-Calabresi-Lawson.pdf ("[The Progressives] believed . . . there were 'experts' . . . who should administer the administrative state as freely as possible from control by representative political institutions."); and Philip Hamburger, "Exclusion and Equality: How Exclusion from the Political Process Renders Religious Liberty Unequal," *Notre Dame Law Review* 90, no. 5 (2015): 1919, 1946–47, https://scholarship.law.nd.edu/cgi/viewcontent.cgi?article=4615&context=ndlr ("The goal of administrative power was to escape representative accountability and the underlying political process. Woodrow Wilson . . . unctuously explained . . . 'the error of trying to do too much by vote' . . . writing that 'the reformer is bewildered' by the need to persuade 'a voting majority of several million heads.'") (quoting Woodrow Wilson, "The Study of Administration," *Political Science Quarterly* 2, no. 2 [1887]: 197, 208, 214).

34. See Goodnow, "The American Conception of Liberty," 62 ("While insistence on individual rights may have been of great advantage at a time when the social organization was not highly developed, it may become a menace when social rather than individual efficiency is the necessary prerequisite of progress.").

35. West Virginia v. Environmental Protection Agency, 142 S. Ct. 2587, 2617 (2022) (Gorsuch, J., concurring) (quoting *Federalist*, no. 52 [James Madison], https://avalon.law.yale.edu/18th_century/fed52.asp) [emphasis added]).

36. See, for example, Gillian E. Metzger, "1930s Redux: The Administrative State Under Siege," *Harvard Law Review* 131, no. 1 (2017): 1, 78, https://harvardlawreview.

org/print/vol-131/1930s-redux-the-administrative-state-under-siege ("[The] features of the administrative state . . . carry constitutional significance, both in satisfying constitutional structural requirements and in ensuring that broader separation of powers principles retain force in the world of contemporary governance."); Cass R. Sunstein and Adrian Vermeule, *Law & Leviathan: Redeeming the Administrative State* (Harvard University Press, 2020), 8–9 (arguing that administrative agencies are guided by principles of "morality" that "address many of the concerns that critics of the administrative state tend to lump together under headings such as 'the rule of law'"); Emily S. Bremer, "The Unwritten Administrative Constitution," *Florida Law Review* 66, no. 3 (2015): 1215, 1219, https://scholarship.law.ufl.edu/cgi/viewcontent.cgi?article= 1198&context=flr (arguing that the "unwritten administrative constitution . . . has evolved to become the primary means through which fundamental constitutional values are extended into the modern administrative context"); and John A. Rohr, *To Run a Constitution: The Legitimacy of the Administrative State* (University Press of Kansas, 1986), 171 (explaining "the career civil service en masse heals the defect of inadequate representation in the Constitution").

37. See Rao, "The Hedgehog & the Fox in Administrative Law," 220–22.

38. Burwell v. Hobby Lobby Stores, 573 US 682 (2014).

39. *Burwell v. Hobby Lobby Stores*, 573 US at 724.

40. Alabama Association of Realtors v. Department of Health and Human Services, 141 S. Ct. 2485 (2021).

41. *Alabama Association of Realtors*, 141 S. Ct. at 2490.

42. *Alabama Association of Realtors*, 141 S. Ct. at 2490.

43. Biden v. Nebraska, 143 S. Ct. 2355 (2023).

44. *Biden v. Nebraska*, 143 S. Ct. at 2373.

45. *Biden v. Nebraska*, 143 S. Ct. at 2373 (internal citations omitted) (alteration in original).

46. See Rao, "Administrative Collusion," 1503–4 ("Since members exercise only collective power, their personal ambitions can be furthered only through the institutional strength of Congress and its power in relation to the other branches. . . . Open-ended delegations of authority undermine these structural safeguards by fracturing the collective Congress and separating the interests of individual legislators from the interests of Congress.").

47. See, for example, Gundy v. United States, 139 S. Ct. 2116, 1235 (2019) (Gorsuch, J., dissenting); and Department of Transportation v. Association of American Railroads, 575 US 43, 86 (2015) (Thomas, J., concurring).

48. James Madison, "Ratification Without Conditional Amendments," in *The Papers of James Madison*, ed. Rutland and Hobson, 11:172.

13

How to Take the Constitution Seriously

YUVAL LEVIN

September 17, 2024

It's a great honor to deliver this 13th annual Constitution Day Lecture. I've gotten to attend all the prior dozen lectures, and so when Gary Schmitt suggested I be the speaker this year, I was both daunted and honored. The prior speakers set a bar I can only aspire to.

But it's an honor above all because the lecture is named for Walter Berns, one of my heroes. I got to know Walter a little in the last decade or so of his life, though I certainly didn't know him personally nearly as well as some others here. But I've spent an enormous amount of time with Walter's writing—learning from him in the way that you can only really learn from the written words of a profound and brilliant thinker.

I've learned from Walter about patriotism and civic education, about John Locke and Thomas Hobbes and the nature of the liberal society. But I have especially and above all learned from Walter about the US Constitution.

Some of what he taught me was substantive and particular. He was right about the First Amendment half a century ago, for instance, and the fact that constitutional and judicial thought (including on the right) has taken a different path reflects poorly on that different path and reflects well on Walter. His understanding of the question has become only more relevant in the age of the internet and social media, and the sooner his insights on that front are rediscovered, the better.

But above all, I have learned from Walter about *how* to think about the Constitution, or maybe it would be better to say that I have learned from him about just *what* the Constitution is. Walter was a constitutional scholar, but he was not a lawyer. He was part of a cadre of political scientists—political theorists, really—who made the Constitution their subject in the middle decades of the 20th century. Along with the likes of Herbert Storing, Martin Diamond, Robert Goldwin, and even Walter's sometimes nemesis Harry Jaffa, Walter insisted that the Constitution was more than just law and should be studied by more than just lawyers.

Lawyers are important, and constitutional law is a vital portion of constitutional theory and practice. But Americans have left too much of our constitutionalism to lawyers.

The result of that, Walter argued, was that "the Constitution came to be seen not as the embodiment of fundamental and clearly articulated principles of government but as a collection of hopelessly vague and essentially meaningless words and phrases inviting judicial construction."[1]

Walter wrote those words in the conclusion to a collection of his writings published in 1987 called *Taking the Constitution Seriously*. And ultimately, that is what he has taught me to do: to take the Constitution seriously, by seeing what it really is in whole.

And that's what I want to lay out for you tonight: my sense of just what the Constitution actually is. This is my sense, not Walter's, and so I can't claim his authority for this conception of our governing charter. But the pursuit of it—the conviction that our Constitution is law but also more than law and that to take it seriously would require us to see it in full—I certainly do owe to him.

So let's consider the Constitution in Bernsian terms and see how we might take it seriously.

* * * *

"What is the Constitution?" is a strange question. On its face, the US Constitution is a fairly short document, about 7,500 words with all the amendments, that describes the goals, powers, institutions, and key rules of a system of government.

But of course, the Constitution is more than a document. It is also that system of government itself, brought into being by the words on the page but embodied in a set of offices, officials, laws, norms, habits, and traditions. It is the essence of the American regime, which is by now the world's oldest and most durable democratic republic. And it decisively shapes the political ethos of our society and even the character and dispositions of the American people.

The Constitution can be all these things because it is in essence a framework—a structure or form that matches means to ends.

To try to capture its key facets, we can think about the US Constitution roughly as composing a five-part framework: It is a legal framework, a policymaking framework, an institutional framework, a political framework, and a framework for union and unity.

These are not alternative descriptions. They are all true of our constitutional system. But at different times we tend to prioritize them differently, with serious consequences for how we understand our common life.

To really take the Constitution seriously, it would help to consider each of these in its own terms briefly.

So first, we might think of the Constitution as a *legal* framework—a text duly enacted that establishes a set of rules that can be put into effect by public officials and interpreted by judges in response to cases and controversies. The Constitution describes itself as "the supreme Law of the Land," and it certainly is first and foremost a legal document in this sense.

But understood as law, the Constitution is above all a set of constraints or structured boundaries on power. Some of these are expressed as personal rights, in effect defining protected spaces around individuals and communities into which others, or the government, may not enter. And some are expressed as definitional constraints on the institutions of government—placing a broad category of governing powers (like "the executive power") in an office, but then shaping and defining the structure of that office to channel and contain that power.

In both cases, the Constitution as law defines boundaries, and then judges (as interpreters of the Constitution as law) patrol those boundaries and insist on their enforcement. There is a vast space for public and private action within the boundaries sketched out by the Constitution, a space meant to be filled by the lawful actions of both public officials and citizens. But broadly speaking, the Constitution as law is a negative or protective instrument, a shield more than a sword.

And this makes sense, since the judge (unlike other constitutional officers) can only be called into action when a complaint or case presents itself—when someone can reasonably claim that a boundary has been transgressed.

That is not to say that the Constitution even as law is therefore purely procedural or devoid of substantive purpose. Limits necessarily speak of a purpose—they are there for a reason, and that reason is deeply rooted in an understanding of the ends of government. And the work of the judge, the interpretation of both statutes and the Constitution itself, is among the most important influences on the public life of our free society.

So the Constitution's standing as our foundational legal framework is the first and foremost grounds of its significance for us. And yet there is no question that a view of the Constitution that takes in exclusively or largely its legal character would be a blinkered view. It would suggest that our system of government is at its heart a system of limits on government and that the problems with the constitutional system in our time are essentially functions of people doing things they shouldn't in ways that judges ought to stop.

That is not what some of our most significant constitutional problems actually involve today. Much of what is wrong with our constitutional practice is not illegal, and the tendency to leave American constitutionalism to judges alone is frequently a form of dereliction.

Ultimately, the Constitution is far more than a set of procedural boundaries not only because it is our highest written law but also because it is more than just law. Ironically, contemporary critics (particularly on the right) who argue that limiting the judiciary largely to policing procedural boundaries would lead to a constitutionalism devoid of moral substance have too narrow a conception of constitutionalism themselves. They identify the Constitution entirely with law and constitutional practice with the work of the judge.

But judicial restraint is actually a means of protecting the space for legislative, executive, and civic action, and such action is far from morally neutral. To confuse the work of judges with the entire work of living out the Constitution is to undermine both the judiciary and the rest of our system.

The Constitution's role as law is essential to its fuller purpose, and it is reasonable to view the system as first and foremost a legal framework. It sets the boundaries of what our federal government may do, and those boundaries cannot be violated for the sake of other constitutional ends. But what happens within those boundaries is also constitutionalism, even if it isn't always law.

* * * *

Second, therefore, we might think of the Constitution as a *policymaking* framework—a set of tools and authorities that enable a government to address practical problems by enacting statutes and implementing them, raising revenue and spending it, creating public programs and administering them, and taking policy action in response to needs and events.

Our Constitution was adopted above all because its predecessor, the Articles of Confederation, was grossly inadequate as a policymaking framework, and the new system certainly established a far better one.

Policymaking is much of the substance of everyday governing. In this arena, the judge's role is muted, and the legislator and executive come to the fore. Their objective is to make law and carry it out in pursuit of substantive public goals. They are bound by the limits the Constitution imposes on the uses of government authority, but within those limits they are meant to deploy that authority. The Constitution as a policymaking framework is therefore primarily a set of *powers*. Policies and programs direct those powers to meeting public needs and satisfying public desires, and officials are judged as policymakers by how well they do that.

The Constitution is rooted in an understanding of the great importance of effective governance, and the case for it has always put great emphasis on policymaking. Its Framers believed that governmental incompetence undermines a society's self-confidence and, with it, the capacity for self-rule.

There is clearly a tension between the Constitution as a legal framework and the Constitution as a policymaking framework. A view of the Constitution that prioritizes government's capacity to act must naturally chafe against a view that prioritizes boundaries on action. And so policy-minded constitutionalism has always clashed with legally minded constitutionalism and insisted that any system of government assigned goals as ambitious as those assigned to our Constitution must be granted powers sufficient to achieve those goals.

But like a legalistic constitutionalism, this kind of policy-minded approach to our system tends to monopolize our thinking about the Constitution and crowd out other priorities. Approaching the Constitution as a policy instrument is plainly justified and crucial up to a point. Our system exists to enable a government to address public problems and meet national needs.

But there is much more to government than policy. Government also exists to secure basic rights and structure political relations, for example, and that requires us to think about the Constitution in terms other than policymaking. Arguments from policy, like arguments from law, cannot always simply trump other modes of constitutionalism. The authors of the Constitution clearly recognized this, and the American system in particular actually tends to de-emphasize policymaking in relation to its other goals.

The kinds of parliamentary democracies that prevail in Europe tend to prioritize muscular policy action. They often empower the majority coalition in the legislature to act fairly quickly and efficiently as long as its majority holds. That majority was chosen by the public to wield power, and so for them it should govern and then be judged again by voters.

The American system almost never simply empowers any majority in that way, but rather insists on restraints that slow and structure decision-making and require broad and durable coalitions both within and across institutions.

One implication of this distinctly American constitutionalism is that it deprioritizes substantive policy outcomes and instead prioritizes structured decision-making and broad accommodations. It assumes that addressing a public problem is a matter of finding not the best technical solution but a solution that is most satisfactory to the relevant community on the whole. The goal is to address a problem in a way that people are happy with and feel is reflective of some understanding of their wishes and desires.

For this reason, the American system often implicitly prefers doing nothing over enacting aggressive policy programs by narrow legislative margins. All four of the other ways of thinking about the character of the Constitution—as a legal, institutional, political, and unifying framework—militate in favor of that kind of policy restraint.

Frustration with that restrained or gridlocked character of the system often leads people to try to elevate policy outcomes above procedural constraints and institutional boundaries. Even constitutional officers themselves do this.

The courts might prioritize Congress's *goals* (in health care legislation, for instance) over the letter of the laws it writes or over the separation of powers. A president might decide that his administration must change the immigration system or forgive student loan debt even if Congress won't. Members of Congress might create a federal program that can fund itself without requiring regular appropriations. In each case, the people involved treat our system of government as a means to a policy end at the expense of its character or limits.

Sometimes these actions are illegal. Sometimes they are just contrary to the spirit of the Constitution. Either way, they express a desire to treat the Constitution exclusively as a policy instrument. It is such an instrument, but not exclusively.

* * * *

Now, although the legalistic and the policy-centric approaches to the Constitution are in tension in many respects, both focus above all on the powers that the system grants its different parts—whether with an eye to the limits or the uses of those powers.

But if you consider the questions taken up by the Framers at the Constitutional Convention, you will find that they spent more time thinking about structures than about powers. They were obsessed with institutional design.

Third, therefore, we might approach the Constitution as an *institutional framework*—a set of formalized bodies (a congress, a presidency, and courts) that each has a distinct structure and character and carries out a particular kind of work. Our constitutional system is made up of these interlocking institutions, and it's given its shape by their forms.

We are not used to thinking of political forms this way. Our usual approach to the separation of powers leaves us imagining that that there is a fungible commodity called "power" that the different branches of our government exercise, so that the question is who has more or less of it.

But our system does not just divide the power of the national government into three. It divides it among legislative, executive, and judicial institutions, each of which is expected to exercise its authorities differently and for a different purpose.

Congress generally frames and authorizes government action. It makes the laws that channel public power and allocate public resources. In a complex society like ours, this kind of framing work is necessarily the product of accommodation and compromise, and the work of the Congress is therefore necessarily plural: It is a work of many and involves conciliation among them.

The presidency, meanwhile, generally acts within the structures established by the laws that Congress frames. The office's purpose is action, and its institutional design reflects that. The president also reacts to events, adjusts to pressures, and makes concrete choices among permissible options in complicated situations. Action like that is necessarily a singular endeavor, not a group activity, and to be carried off well, it requires energy, boldness, steadiness, focus, and ambition. The executive branch of our government is meant to enable those virtues in the individual chosen to exercise the power it possesses.

The judiciary then steps in after laws have been framed and actions have been taken and reviews them in response to cases and complaints to make sure that general rules have been applied appropriately in particular circumstances. It neither makes laws nor acts to execute them but assesses the behavior of others.

It is only a slight exaggeration to say that the Congress is expected to frame for the future, the president is expected to act in the present, and the courts are expected to assess the past.

These boundaries are not perfectly clean, of course. In fact, as James Madison noted in *Federalist* 48, to achieve the primary purpose of the separation of these branches—which is preventing abuses of power—it is actually necessary to intermix the branches a little at the margins.

So the president not only has a veto power over legislation but also is invited in the text of the Constitution to occasionally think like a legislator and recommend to Congress "such measures as He shall judge necessary and expedient." Congress is given a role in foreign policy and exercises oversight over the entire federal bureaucracy, and the Senate has to approve treaties and confirm key presidential appointments. The courts are more constrained to their own sphere, but they exercise a kind of oversight, too, and can strike down both legislative and executive actions found to violate the Constitution or the laws.

This mixing of authorities is marginal though. And rather than give each branch a real share of the kind of work the others do, it gives each branch some modest means to restrain the others in their own domains, as a defensive measure. This intermixing is therefore intended ultimately to preserve the separation between the branches and insist on the differences between them.

The most crucial of these differences are not about who has more or less power; they are fundamental distinctions of purpose, structure, and form. So they are best understood in institutional terms.

That means we need to assess the health of our system by not only whether its various players are transgressing the boundaries established around their powers and using those powers to good policy effect but also whether they are playing the sorts of roles assigned to them and exercising the *kind* of power they were given.

When an administrative agency exercises an open-ended power to make general rules and enforce them in specific circumstances, it is acting legislatively and judicially even though it lacks a legislative or judicial form—and so is violating the structure and logic of our Constitution. This is one way to describe what is wrong with much of the modern administrative state: legislative or judicial actions without legislative or judicial forms.

When a president says, "If Congress won't act, I will," he is threatening to violate the constitutional order. There are no properly legislative actions that an executive could properly carry out instead.

When a judge creates a novel policy or right of action, he is acting in ways that may be permitted to other constitutional officers but not to judges. He is exercising a share of the power of the government, but in a form not appropriate to the particular institution of which he is part.

Even if actions like those are allowed by statutes or justified by loopholes that clever lawyers can describe to eager judges, they turn out to be counter-constitutional when we consider the Constitution from an institutional and not just a legal or policymaking point of view. The institutional structures established by the Constitution call for certain forms of action and restraint by their occupants, and those constitutional officers should be judged by how they play their parts.

Crucially, this means that an institutional approach to our system of government could help us see not only when one of the branches overreaches but also when it underreaches and so fails to do its necessary work.

Congress today is plainly underactive. Its members often want to shirk responsibility for hard decisions and tend to favor vague legislative mandates that describe popular goals but leave the tough governing details to bureaucrats and judges. That's generally not illegal, and courts can't do all that much about it. But an institutional perspective shows it to be a constitutional dereliction that does serious harm to our system of government.

An institutional perspective can also help us understand the complicated balance that the Constitution strikes between the need to empower the government to govern effectively and the need to restrain it and avert abuses of power.

On this point, Walter Berns is an especially helpful guide. As he showed, that balance is ultimately maintained not by limits on the quantity of power granted to government but by the structures, forms, and formalities built into the institutions that deploy that power.

The structural complexity that is so often frustrating to energetic reformers aims to both moderate and legitimate uses of power, just as formality does in our social lives. Formalities are indirect, and constitutionalism seeks various means of making government action less direct or, as Walter put it in *Taking the Constitution Seriously*, "of doing properly what has to be done politically."[2]

And ultimately, formalities like that also shape the character of our polity, the political personality of our society. And so they point us toward the next facet of constitutionalism.

* * * *

Fourth, then, we might approach the Constitution as a *political* framework. This is the most capacious if also the most nebulous of the modes of constitutionalism we have considered. It refers to politics in its highest sense, not as a contest for power but as the common life of a community.

And so it comes closest to the classical notion of a constitution, which is not so much the written charter of a government but, in Aristotle's terms, "a certain ordering of the inhabitants of the city" and "the way of life of a body of citizens."[3] In this sense, the Constitution is almost analogous to the soul of a polity, and it describes the innermost character of our society and the meaning of citizenship and authority in its life.

To understand the Constitution in such political terms is therefore, for one thing, to contemplate the character of the regime we have.

As the University of Virginia's James W. Ceaser has written,

> Political constitutionalism . . . understands the Constitution
> as a document that fixes certain ends of government activity,
> delineates a structure and arrangement of powers, and encour-
> ages a certain tone to the operation of the institutions. By this
> understanding, it falls mostly to political actors making politi-
> cal decisions to protect and promote constitutional goals.[4]

It is by this light, by considering these kinds of questions about the proper tone of the operation of our institutions, that we can see some of the dysfunctions of our politics in recent years as constitutional problems. Failures of responsibility that involve constitutional officers behaving like performers or seekers of celebrity, for instance, are increasingly common in all our political institutions. They don't always involve a violation of formal boundaries, and so they generally can't be addressed by litigation, but they nonetheless result from fundamental constitutional deformations—derelictions of responsibility and corruptions of political culture.

Violations of constitutional norms that are not legally enforceable fall into this category too. Confronted with that kind of behavior, we have to ask ourselves not only "is this technically permissible?" but also something more like "does this belong in our kind of politics?" That's a question that demands to be answered in terms of the purpose and goals of the Constitution, the sort of government it was aimed to create, and the sort of society it governs.

Answers to it will be anchored in the ideals that shape our civic aspirations and in the common historical experiences that have forged us into a nation. They won't be as precise or confident as answers given by the courts to strictly legal questions, and they may be open to more debate and adjustment. But they are no less crucial for that.

Often what is at issue when the political character of the Constitution is at stake is not any one particular provision of the document but its overall tenor—what Montesquieu called "the spirit of the laws." This spirit, or general genius, of the American republic can be hard to pin down sometimes, but it has a few broad characteristics we can certainly discern.

It is, for one thing, rooted in the principles articulated in the Declaration of Independence—truths that are foundational to the character of our society. The Constitution does not restate these truths, but they are a starting point for its essential republicanism.

That does not necessarily mean the Declaration can be used as an interpretive instrument by judges seeking to apply the Constitution in particular cases. There are rare occasions when this may be appropriate. But the Declaration is most essential to the Constitution understood as a political framework, not a legal framework. It makes sense of the spirit of the whole.

The spirit of our Constitution is also given form by the ambitions laid out in its preamble. These also generally aren't enforceable as law but are political ambitions in the very highest sense. They describe the goods our government seeks to provide to its society, which are presumably the preconditions for that society thriving. And they remind us to think about our system of government not only in negative terms (in terms of what it protects us from and commits not to do to us) but also and more so in positive terms (in terms of what it offers us, demands from us, and commits to secure for us).

The spirit of the Constitution is also plainly democratic, in our modern sense of the term. It assumes that power is ultimately rooted in the people. Some historians have argued that the Constitution took a step away from the more radically democratic character of the Declaration of Independence, since it restrains majority power and recoils from any kind of radical or revolutionary politics.

But the Constitution is actually much more democratic than the Declaration, which after all did not specify any particular form of government, made no reference or commitment to majority rule, and suggested that a wide variety of regimes could be legitimate if they began with the public's consent. The Constitution is plainly committed to majority rule through representation sustained by regular elections. It builds on the Declaration of Independence and completes it in a democratic direction. And it therefore stamps our political culture with an emphatically democratic temperament.

At the same time, though, the Constitution is also clearly committed to protecting minority rights and freedoms, and so it does seek to restrain the uses of majority power. This, too, is evident in every one of its institutions and provisions and is integral to the spirit of the regime it constitutes.

The tension between the imperative to empower majorities and the imperative to protect minorities (what we now might call the democratic imperative and the liberal imperative) and the attempt to combine the two is responsible for a lot of the Constitution's structure and character.

At both the conceptual and the practical levels, the tension between democracy and liberalism is often also mediated in the constitutional system by republicanism. This is another essential element of the political framework of American constitutionalism, but one that has become less familiar to us over time.

Republicanism is sometimes identified with its procedural implications, and especially with representative as opposed to direct democracy. But republicanism, in both its classical and modern forms, runs far deeper than that. It is a civic ethic, not a system of government.

At its heart is an idea of the human being and citizen that emphasizes our responsibilities to one another and to the common good. It counterbalances the democratic ethos because it values not just what we each want but what is good for all of us. It counterbalances the liberal ethos because it values not just rights but obligations.

Such republicanism is the deepest political wellspring of the Constitution, but it has been largely lost to us. It has become so unfamiliar that we often mistake the consequences of its absence for symptoms of an excess of those ideas it was meant to counteract—and so we argue that we have become too liberal when it might be more accurate to say that we are not republican enough.

American constitutionalism requires a distinctly republican virtue and cannot do without it. To be a free people able to take advantage of the sort of system of government established by our Constitution, we need also to be a people with the kind of civic virtue that might, as Madison argued in *Federalist* 55, "justify a certain portion of esteem and confidence."[5] The character of the souls of our citizens and leaders matters immensely and is of great concern to the constitutional system.

A recovery of some sense of the meaning of republicanism will be necessary for any constitutional renewal, and such a recovery will require in turn a grasp of the Constitution as a political framework. But the political facet of the Constitution is not just the result of a collection of ideas and abstractions. It is also the product of an accumulated national history.

America is not just an idea, although it is an idea. America is also a nation, filled with men and women who live together and share a set of experiences, roots, and loves that render them into fellow citizens. The battles won and lost, challenges overcome, achievements and failures, triumphs and tragedies that fill the chronicles of American history also fill the hearts and minds of the American people. And our political character cannot help but be formed and framed by that life lived in common.

All of this is more vague and fuzzy than stark legal doctrines and institutional blueprints. It serves a different purpose than those do. But it is no less crucial to the meaning of our Constitution and to its effectuation in practice—not by judges but by the rest of us.

The character of our Constitution as a political framework begins to help us see the enormously complicated and contradictory ambitions of our system of government. The Framers sought a government that would be energetic but restrained, effective but limited, democratic but liberal and republican, responsive yet reflective, representative of a vast and fragmented society yet able to focus on national challenges and address them. They approached the task by treating each of these seeming contradictions as a potentially creative tension—a source of vigor and balance.

That sort of approach has risks, of course. And maybe the foremost risk inherent in it is the risk of disintegration. And so the Constitution was designed to pursue these varied ends in ways that explicitly avoided disintegration and sought greater consolidation and unity. This is why the

Constitution also has to be understood as structuring our solidarity—describing what it is that constitutes us as a people.

* * * *

So fifth and finally, we might think of our Constitution as a framework for *unity*. This idea is inherent in the very notion of a constitution and in the very term, which describes a whole constituted by constituent parts.

It is evident, too, in the very first ambition articulated in the preamble, which is "to form a more perfect Union." And it is apparent in the first-person plural in which the document presents itself, beginning with the fact that its first word is "we."

But that "we" is aspirational as much as it is empirical. Like the opening of the Declaration of Independence—which describes the Americans as "one people" connected by political bands with "another" and so implies that it speaks for an already existing distinct nation rather than a new one being created—the Constitution opens by speaking on behalf of a united people when in fact the unification of that people is among its foremost goals.

It is a goal the Framers and the public knew would not be easy to achieve. The fearful prospect of disunity and even war among the states was very real to late-18th-century Americans.

And the need for union was often the first and foremost argument advanced by champions of the Constitution at the various state ratification debates. The first 23 of the 85 Federalist Papers were explicitly devoted to the need to preserve the union, and almost all the rest touch on that subject too.

Sometimes, the case for unity was advanced through aspirational descriptions, like the opening of the preamble, which insisted the Americans were already united but had to work to remain so. Charles Pinckney, a delegate to the Constitutional Convention from South Carolina, insisted to the delegates that "the people of the United States are perhaps the most singular of any we are acquainted with" because "among them there are fewer distinctions of fortune, and less of rank, than among the inhabitants of any other nation."[6] They were, to a unique degree, one people. John Jay said much the same in *Federalist* 2.

But there was more than a hint of wishful thinking in these assurances. It was no coincidence that unity was put forward as the first ambition of the reformed American regime in the preamble. Throughout the deliberations over the Constitution, a dark cloud of disunity hung in the air—disunity among the states and among the people.

That challenge had to be kept in sight. And the Constitution does keep it in sight. It was built with a keen awareness of the plurality and fractiousness of the American nation. It was offered as a way to live with the reality of our diversity and divisions, aiming to mitigate their downsides without harboring the utopian illusion of eliminating them. The key Framers of the system hoped that the multiplicity of American life did not have to mean that Americans would be irredeemably alienated from each other, embittered and in conflict.

They did not deny the reality of the diversity of interests and opinions in our country, but they refused to believe that it had to mean that unity was impossible or not worth pursuing. Rather, the system they constructed presumes an idea of unity that takes that multiplicity for granted and attenuates disunity through common action.

All the other facets of the Constitution contribute to this one. Through the institutions it constructed, the boundaries it set, the ambitions it held out, and the spirit of the polity it helped instantiate, the system was plainly intended to help *forge* common ground in American life and not just occupy such ground. It seeks to enable social peace, which cannot be taken for granted under modern conditions of pluralism.

Social peace can offer a stable backdrop for political life. In a free society, it is not quiet but raucous. It can't be achieved by conquest or surrender but only by mutual accommodation. It is the condition of differing without rejecting one another's legitimacy—of disputing without being at war.

The very idea of a written Constitution that stands apart from regular legislation as the framework of a regime is rooted in the ambition to establish some such common ground in a permanently fractious polity. By distinguishing between views about the system of government and views about policy and interests, it stakes out space for agreement that can allow our disagreements to be dealt with more constructively.

Our system can withstand a lot of discord, provided we share a general understanding of the character and purpose of the Constitution itself. That is why some restoration of such an understanding is an essential precondition to the recovery of our civic culture. But that culture, even in moments of relative unity, is a culture of disagreement.

The breakdown of political culture in our day is not a function of our having forgotten how to agree with each other but a function of our having forgotten how to *disagree* constructively. And this is what our Constitution can better enable us to do. As a framework for unity, the Constitution functions as a means of rendering disagreement more constructive.

It does this above all by rendering disputing factions in our politics into parties to a substantive debate about how to proceed together.

* * * *

To engage in that debate, to participate in the intense, dynamic struggles that constitute American political life, is to practice constitutionalism. It is the work of citizens and, in their name, also the work of public officials.

The work of judges is above all intended to sustain the space for that civic life, not to occupy or overtake that space. And in that sense, the role of law in the American constitutional vision is vital but limited—it exists to limit, and therefore it must itself be limited.

This, too, was a core insight that Walter Berns illuminated through his vital work. To take the Constitution seriously, we have to take it in full, to see what it demands of us as citizens of a republic. Constitutionalism is everyone's work.

That is an insight that cannot be repeated too often. It's an insight that we who are Walter's successors here at AEI have tried to make into a guiding light for our work. We are proud to notice and to show that we learned it from Walter, and we teach it in no small measure in his name.

Walter's last lecture here at AEI was a celebration of Abraham Lincoln on his 200th birthday. It's online and really worth your while. In his concluding words in that lecture, the final words he offered us as an AEI scholar, Walter said this:

> We say that a man can be known by the company he keeps. So I say that a nation, a people, can be known and judged by its heroes, by whom it honors above all others.

> We pay ourselves the greatest compliment when we say that Abraham Lincoln is that man for us.[7]

I think the same can be said of this institution. We pay ourselves the greatest compliment when we say that Walter Berns was our teacher on all things constitutional. That's a summary of what this lecture has been, and it's no coincidence that we have named this series of lectures for him.

That, above all, is why I'm honored to be here tonight, repeating and restating things I learned from Walter Berns.

Notes

1. Walter Berns, *Taking the Constitution Seriously* (Madison Books, 1987), 214.
2. Berns, *Taking the Constitution Seriously*, 184.
3. Aristotle, *Politics*, trans. Carnes Lord (University of Chicago Press, 2013), 63, 118.
4. James W. Ceaser, "Restoring the Constitution," *Claremont Review of Books* 12, no. 2 (2012), https://claremontreviewofbooks.com/restoring-the-constitution.
5. *Federalist*, no. 55 (James Madison), https://avalon.law.yale.edu/18th_century/fed55.asp.
6. James Madison, *Notes of Debates in the Federal Convention of 1787* (Ohio University Press, 1966), 281.
7. Walter Berns, *Lincoln at Two Hundred: Why We Still Read the Sixteenth President* (AEI Press, 2009), 16.

Afterword:
Walter Berns and the Constitution—
A Celebration

WALTER BERNS, CHRISTOPHER DEMUTH,
LEON R. KASS, AND JEREMY A. RABKIN
September 20, 2012

*I*n *this volume's concluding chapter, we include three presentations on Walter Berns's scholarship that were delivered during AEI's first Constitution Day celebration in 2011. We present the remarks in the sequence they were given—beginning with Jeremy A. Rabkin, who at the time was professor of law at George Mason University School of Law, followed by Leon R. Kass, who was then the AEI Madden-Jewett Chair. Then former AEI President Christopher DeMuth spoke, and the event concluded with Walter's own brief response to their presentations.*

Remarks by Jeremy A. Rabkin

It is an honor to be speaking here today. But as a student of Walter Berns, it is also somewhat daunting. Nearly 40 years ago, I enrolled in a graduate seminar with Professor Berns. He was not the sort of professor who tried to ingratiate himself with students. He did not say, "Call me Walter."

Even a few years later, when I was already an assistant professor, Professor Berns did not hesitate to clarify my place. We were both at the same social gathering. As the conversation turned to a particular topic, I piped up, "I have a story about that." Berns cut me off: "You are too young to be telling stories." I hope I am old enough now to tell some stories. But, just in case, I will try to stick to the published record here.

Walter Berns waited some 50 years to tell (or, anyway, to publish) stories about his early encounters with Frieda Lawrence in Taos, New Mexico. He confides in a recent essay on the subject that, as a young man, he hoped to become a novelist and had no idea of becoming a political scientist.[1] Anyone who browses through his collected essays can see that he retained at least a knack for sketching a word picture with telling—or devastating—details.

In the 1970s, Berns published an article in the *National Review*, sharing some unflattering stories about Father Daniel Berrigan, SJ.[2] The main story concerns his debate with an unnamed professor of government at Cornell University, where Berrigan had been the Catholic chaplain in the late 1960s and Berns at the time was a professor of government. When I reread this piece recently, I concluded that it must have shamed Father Berrigan into withdrawing altogether from public life. A quick check on Wikipedia informed me that he has, over the past decades, remained active in antiwar protest—but in Staten Island, which is probably not a Division I contender in the antiwar protest leagues.

Alas, the Berns treatment did not have quite the same impact on the international human rights community as we may hope that it had on the Jesuit order. Still, no one who reads Berns's 1983 essay on the UN Human Rights Commission can think of the Universal Declaration of Human Rights without recalling this line—and wincing:

> One does not have to be an historian to imagine the response of mankind (to whose opinions they were paying "decent respect"), if Jefferson and his colleagues of 1776 had written: that all men are created equal, that they are endowed by their creator with certain unalienable rights, that among these are life, liberty, and a paid vacation.[3]

But I don't mean to suggest that the contributions of Walter Berns to constitutional studies were primarily those of a literary takedown artist. Actually, what most strikes me now, browsing through his occasional essays of four decades, collected in two different volumes, is how "high toned" they are. Contributions to op-ed pages or opinion magazines tend to lose their punch with the passing of years. The original targets of their spleen or ridicule come to be justly forgotten. An author still railing against them (in a later collection) will seem to be throwing darts against the wind. But almost all of Walter Berns's occasional pieces remain engaging and often quite charming, even decades later. He did not waste his words, even in short essays, on mere point scoring. (But I can attest, from conversations over the years, that his private stance was not one of serene detachment.)

Sometimes, even in a short piece or brief passage, Berns could elicit a palm slap to the forehead: "Why didn't I think of that?"—followed by the consoling, "Why didn't *anyone else* think of that?" In a short 2004 piece, Berns addressed the question, "Why a vice president?"—a question that, right up to this moment, continues to trouble observers of Joe Biden.[4] Berns explains that the Framers gave two votes to each elector in the Electoral College on the assumption that most electors would vote for their home state candidate, so with two votes, the odds improved that someone would get a majority—and the runner-up could then be recognized as vice president. The rationale seems obvious once it's explained. But you won't find the explanation in James Madison's *Notes of Debates in the Federal Convention of 1787* or in the pages of *the Federalist Papers*. You won't find it in any of the most recent full-length histories of the Founding, either.

To take another example, Berns's 1987 book, *Taking the Constitution Seriously*, points out that during the American Revolution, the Continental Congress invited Quebec to join the other rebellious colonies—despite misgivings about joining hands with a French-speaking and predominantly Catholic province. What they did not do was invite any islands of the West Indies to join, even though Jamaica alone had twice the population of Quebec and was English-speaking and Protestant and generated much more revenue for Britain. But, as Berns points out, to embrace such places at the time would have meant embracing more slave territories.[5] Two generations later, that was an attractive prospect for political advocates in Southern states (who cast covetous eyes, for example, on Cuba). But at the time of the American Revolution, there seems to have been a clear understanding that more entanglement with slavery was more trouble for the new republic.

As a trained social scientist, I gathered some data for this talk. I checked the Lexis inventory of law review articles for citations to Walter Berns. Among the most frequently cited Berns works, in fact, are his articles on early debates about the First Amendment, demonstrating that even Jefferson and Madison seem to have conditioned their defenses of freedom with one eye on what would avert challenges to slavery. He showed that the most avid defenses of freedom in the Founding era were not simply about freedom.

Walter Berns was not a conventional conservative. His scholarship gave little attention to constitutional debates about property or contract rights. He did not even devote much attention to federalism—except to repudiate states' rights doctrines that might justify the secession of Southern states in 1860. He was not much interested in debates about the New Deal. He was not even much interested in defending "tradition" as such. In his first book, *Freedom, Virtue and the First Amendment*, he spoke rather dismissively of the "so-called conservative movement": "This contemporary political theory of conservatism may be characterized by the fact that it concludes its inquiry at the point where, historically, political philosophy began. Its contributions to our political understanding may be judged accordingly."[6]

Berns's writings do not enter into details of case law or legal "doctrine." He was interested in "contributions to our political understanding." In that first book he says:

> A reasonable jurisprudence would be guided by the knowledge that freedom and justice are not always compatible. This knowledge, however, is denied to those who find comfort in a "confined philosophical imagination" since to consider the problem of how freedom and justice can be reconciled, one

must have knowledge of justice. To provide this knowledge is the function of political philosophy.[7]

He even says that

> the purpose of the Supreme Court cannot be described as making justice conform to the Constitution. It is rather to make the Constitution conform to justice. Supreme Court justices seek to make the law of the Constitution conform as closely as possible to what is right as they see the right. As long as they exercise the power of judicial review, there can be no alternative to this.[8]

It might seem quite a distance from these early pronouncements to the stance he takes in later writings. Clearly, Berns was provoked by the activism of the Warren and Burger courts. He thought the country was getting far too much bending of the Constitution to "what is right as [the justices] see the right."[9] The Berns work most cited in law reviews is his 1982 article in *The Supreme Court Review*, "Judicial Review and the Rights and Laws of Nature." Here is the central point:

> The new natural law [of the 17th and 18th centuries] merely commanded men to seek peace, in Hobbes' case, or, in Locke's, to find the arrangement under which men might preserve both themselves and others. Natural law in this modern sense is not a legal discipline. Lawyers, simply as lawyers or even as judges, have no competence in it, and courts have no jurisdiction over it. As for natural rights themselves, or the powers that men enjoyed in the state of nature, with the exception of the right of self-defense, they had to be renounced or transferred to the sovereign.[10]

Berns was still more forthright in deprecating claims to a higher justice in "Constitutionalism and Multiculturalism":

Every such accusation [about America's faults] presupposes a law . . . something like a holy law against which political life is to be measured. One might think that life in the United States could be heaven, or was supposed to be heaven; but the Founders promised no such thing. What they promised was liberty, including the liberty to tend to the salvation of our own souls, and the country they established was the first in all of history to make, and to keep, that promise. By keeping it . . . they made "corruption voluntary to an appreciable degree."[11]

The contrast between these statements might suggest that Berns changed his outlook over time, becoming ever more wary of appeals to "justice." But there is not such a sharp contrast between early and late Berns. In 1979, Berns published a defense of the death penalty with the forthright title *For Capital Punishment: Crime and the Morality of the Death Penalty*. He agreed to have it reprinted in 1991. It is among the most cited of his works, because so few serious scholars have advanced this sort of moral defense of capital punishment.

The book does not merely argue that the Framers of the Constitution (and those of the 14th Amendment) plainly contemplated capital punishment for at least some crimes, so judicial activists are wrong to read it out of the Constitution. Berns engages the deepest moral questions. He goes to some trouble to show that the strongest argument against capital punishment was already advanced by the Marquis Beccaria in the 18th century. Reasoning from the Hobbesian premise of a state founded in the self-interest of each citizen, Beccaria concluded that no one would consent to a social contract arming the state with the power to impose this ultimate penalty. Berns rejected the conclusion by challenging the premise:

Criminals are properly the objects of anger and the perpetrators of terrible crimes—for example, Lee Harvey Oswald and

James Earl Ray—are properly the objects of great anger. They have done more than inflict an injury on an isolated individual; they have violated the foundations of trust and friendship, the necessary elements of a moral community, the only community worth living in. A moral community, unlike a hive of bees or a hill of ants, is one whose members are expected freely to obey the laws and, unlike a tyranny, are trusted to obey the laws. The criminal has violated that trust and in so doing has injured not merely his immediate victim but the community as such. He has called into question the very possibility of that community by suggesting that men cannot be trusted freely to respect the property, the person and the dignity of those with whom they are associated. If men are not angry when someone else is robbed, raped or murdered, the implication is that there is no moral community because those men do not care for anyone other than themselves.[12]

So I don't think Berns changed his mind about freedom and justice. From his earliest to his latest works, he has always shown a clear-eyed appreciation for the promise of the modern perspective on politics without losing sight of its limitations. There is something liberating in the outlook of John Locke or Thomas Jefferson—and also something that threatens to diminish the human spirit. Berns emphasized the fundamentally liberal premises of the Constitution (in the classical, Enlightenment sense of "liberal")—without pretending that either classical liberalism or the Constitution itself offers a neat, simple, or entirely satisfactory answer to every political challenge. An opinion column he published in *The Wall Street Journal* in 1981 acknowledges, forthrightly, the danger of letting ideology displace all thought:

What characterizes a political problem is the absence of a solution, in the strict sense of the term, and what characterizes the Soviet Union is its proclivity for solutions, including simple if not yet final solutions. It is not an accident, as Marxists would say, that we do things differently.[13]

If it is "conservative" to doubt the reach of political solutions, Berns was certainly a conservative throughout his career. But he was never content to venerate the Constitution simply because it is old. When he argued for letting established arrangements remain—as he did, for example, in defending the Electoral College—he insisted on probing the constitutional argument, not merely praising the adequacy of the result.[14]

Now I hope I can tell a story in his presence. I recently had a conversation with a 2008 graduate of Cornell. Asked about his teachers, he said, "Some were very capable instructors. You could learn technical skills and technical subjects from them. But my classmates could not take seriously the idea that our professors were purveyors of wisdom." Students of Walter Berns took that idea for granted—that Berns was, in fact, a purveyor of wisdom. He showed us the wisdom of the American Founders, while reminding us that not all wisdom can be fitted within the limits of a modern constitution.

Remarks by Leon R. Kass

I am both pleased and humbled to be able to offer words of tribute to Walter Berns at this commemoration of Constitution Day: pleased, because I welcome a chance to express my enormous regard for Walter—as scholar, citizen, and gentlemanly human being; humbled because, in this distinguished gathering that includes so many of Walter's students, there are people vastly more qualified than I to speak knowledgably about his scholarship. Still, as a reader, admirer, and friend of nearly 30 years, perhaps I can offer something of value for your consideration.

It is absolutely fitting and proper to honor Walter Berns in connection with Constitution Day. The United States Constitution, and the underlying ideas and ideals of "constitutionalism," have been the central focus of Walter's intellectual life. In his teaching and writings, he has expounded their foundational and enduring significance for the American polity, and he has defended their wisdom against the depredations of famous law professors and Supreme Court justices. Right from the start, Walter showed his capacity and courage for swimming against the stream in the cause of the right and the good. The guiding spirit of his career was heralded already in his first academic publication, in 1953, in which this untenured assistant professor, in the name of justice and due process of law, offered a rigorous and spirited critique of Oliver Wendell Holmes's Supreme Court's opinion in *Buck v. Bell*, upholding involuntary eugenic sterilization of the mentally retarded and celebrated in Holmes's smug dictum, "Three generations of imbeciles are enough."[5]

As his writings over a lifetime make plain, Walter's devotion to constitutionalism goes deeper than the written document and the institutions it created, and his appreciation of the Constitution itself is richer than that of jurists who must interpret it and lawyers who look to it as the bedrock law of the American polity. Like his friends and remarkable fellow teachers of American constitutionalism, Robert Goldwin, Herbert Storing, and Martin Diamond—all fellow students of Leo Strauss at the University of Chicago during its golden age—Walter's work has always been informed by the lifelong study of political philosophy and, therefore, also by a sensitivity to and a concern for certain extra-constitutional yet constitutive conditions, cultural and spiritual, for the flourishing of the American constitutional order: civic virtue, love of country, and the education of the young. Time permits but the briefest glance at some of Walter's writings on each of these crucial subjects.

Mindful of the difficulty of cultivating virtue in a polity that emphasizes rights over duties and whose citizens are encouraged, by the march of equality, to shed traditional moral teachings that counter self-absorption, Walter, without a touch of moral preening or priggishness, has written often about the importance of virtue for a self-governing people. In the 1960s and 1970s, when the issue was acutely joined, Walter was a vigorous upholder of the, in my view, correct but—alas—losing side of the legal and cultural debate about the limits of freedom of speech in relation to obscenity and pornography. (His first book, based on his doctoral dissertation, was titled *Freedom, Virtue and the First Amendment.*) Exactly 40 years ago, in a prescient article in *The Public Interest* titled "Pornography vs. Democracy: The Case for Censorship," Walter offered a subtle and sophisticated defense of censorship in the name of the mores necessary for the survival of a free people.[16] Pointing out that the pleasure we derive from the arts not only forms our tastes but also "helps determine the kind of men we become, and helps shape the lives of those with whom and among whom we live," he raised some unfashionable questions about art and politics:

> Is it politically uninteresting whether men derive pleasure from performing their duties as citizens, fathers, and husbands or, on the other hand, from watching their laws and customs and institutions being ridiculed on the stage? Whether the passions are excited by, and the affections drawn to, what is noble or what is base? Whether the relations between men and women are depicted in terms of an eroticism wholly divorced from love and calculated to destroy the capacity for love and the institutions, such as the family, that depend on love? Whether a dramatist uses pleasure to attach men to what is beautiful or to what is ugly?[17]

Walter then proceeded to show that the political effect, if not also the intended purpose, of the newly fashionable obscenity, licensed by revisionist First Amendment jurisprudence, was to make us shameless, oblivious to the distinction between public and private, and therefore hostile both to the protection of the delicate sphere of human love and to politically relevant self-command:

There is a connection between self-restraint and shame, and therefore a connection between shame and self-government or democracy. There is, therefore, a political danger in promoting shamelessness and the fullest self-expression or indulgence. To live together requires rules and a governing of the passions, and those who are without shame will be unruly and unrulable; having lost the ability to restrain themselves by observing the rules they collectively give themselves, they will have to be ruled by others. Tyranny is the natural and inevitable mode of government for the shameless and self-indulgent who have carried liberty beyond any restraint, natural and conventional.[18]

Not content to show that the liberty demanded by the arts is not necessarily good for civil society, Walter then showed why the unwillingness to distinguish between the obscene and the non-obscene also destroys our ability to distinguish between art and trash and, finally, also between good and evil, the true and the false, the noble and the base. Looking at the changes in American popular culture and American mores since this article was written in 1971, who would dare say that Walter was mistaken?

The virtues of civic life, beginning with self-command and reaching toward public-spiritedness, although especially important for self-governing citizens, are not peculiarly American. Closer to what makes us a nation, and the exceptional nation in human history, is the fact of our founding on philosophical principles, expressed in the Declaration of Independence: equal and unalienable natural rights, to be made secure by government, which governs legitimately only by consent of the governed. Yet, as Walter, among others, have stressed, these American principles, even as stated in 1776, are in fact universal, capable of gaining the rational assent of any thoughtful human being. Something more fundamental than mere cognitive agreement with our principles is required for the attachment of the citizens and for the well-being and, indeed, the very survival of the American polity. These depend on love of country, and, when push comes to shove, on the willingness of its citizens to defend and, if necessary, to give their lives for her. Patriotism is the second extra-constitutional theme of Walter's scholarship, and the subject of his superb little book *Making Patriots*.

Written shortly before 9/11, for a general audience, Walter's *Making Patriots* seeks to educate his fellow Americans both in the need for patriotism and in the difficulties in securing it today. Unlike ancient republics like Sparta, where all male children were reared for warfare and no distinction existed between citizen and patriot, legal citizens of the United States may enjoy the privileges and immunities of citizenship at little personal cost and without any obligation to serve or even love their country. In fact, patriotic devotion among us is, paradoxically, rendered more difficult precisely because of several blessed features of the American Republic for which, in truth, we citizens should feel grateful to our country: the protection of individual rights of life, liberty, and the private—and privatizing—pursuit of happiness, each according to his own idea of happiness; religious freedom and the right to worship—or not worship—a God whose moral teachings need not always square with the demands of American law and who commands us to love him "with all your heart and with all your soul and with all your might"; and, at the same time, the encouragement of commerce and the love of private gain, a more solid foundation for civic peace and prosperity than the higher moral demands of duty, piety, and virtue, but one that tends to produce self-serving entrepreneurs rather than self-sacrificing patriots.[19] Walter carefully and subtly takes up these and other permanent challenges to the cultivation of patriotic attachment in modern America, and then turns to the area where our novel circumstances give the greatest cause for concern: the education of the young or, one should rather say, their miseducation.

Patriots are not born, they are made. Their formation is even more a matter of the heart than of the head, and it takes place from the earliest ages. Although the Constitution is silent on education—this was a matter left to the states—the Founders were very concerned about the education of citizens for self-government. Jefferson proposed a system of universal public education that would render our children "worthy to receive, and able to guard the sacred deposit of the rights and liberties of their fellow citizens."[20] Walter reviews the efforts associated with such names as Noah Webster and William McGuffey, among others, to inculcate belief in God, moral virtue, and love of country, along with the teaching of reading, writing, and arithmetic, efforts that lasted, successfully, well into the early 20th century.

And then things began to unravel. Supreme Court decisions in the 1940s, applying to the states for the first time the First Amendment's separation of church and the national state, began the inexorable secularization of public education. How were virtue and love of country to be promoted once religious teachings were banished from the public education of the young? It was from there but a short decline into the belief that public schools should not be promoting patriotism at all, should not be arguing for the superiority of one way of life above another, should instead be teaching the young that preferential love of your own was indefensible and dangerous, that patriotism was in fact the last refuge of scoundrels.

To begin to remedy these educational diseases, Walter suggests that we must pay renewed attention to the lives of those Americans who have not only grappled with the nation's gravest troubles but whose words have helped their fellow countrymen understand and appreciate the gift that is American citizenship. Walter gives us splendid and inspiring chapters on Abraham Lincoln and Frederick Douglass, men whose words and deeds can still be a beacon for budding—and aging—patriots.

Education of the heart is more the work of poets than of philosophers and statesmen, and this is especially true for the making of patriots. Fortunately for the American Republic, our greatest statesman has also been our greatest national poet. Abraham Lincoln has been a lifelong preoccupation of Walter Berns, who grew up—as I did—in Chicago, where Lincoln was the American most to be admired. Walter has many times taught courses on Lincoln's life and thought and written repeatedly about him. To celebrate the bicentennial of Lincoln's birth, Walter gave his last public lecture in this room, titled "Lincoln at Two Hundred: Why We Still

Read the Sixteenth President."[21] In this moving tribute, Walter offered us additional reasons for sharing his regard for Lincoln, finishing with special attention to Lincoln's greatest speeches: the last paragraph of the first inaugural address, the Gettysburg Address, and the second inaugural address. As Homer was poet or maker of the Greeks, so Walter's Lincoln is poet or maker of the Americans, both by teaching us, in memorable words, who we are and what we as a nation nobly aspire to and also, by his own heroic and self-sacrificing example, what it takes to defend, preserve, and live up to the highest principles of our common life.

Walter finished that beautiful lecture as follows:

> We say that a man can be known by the company he keeps. So I say that a nation, a people, can be known and be judged by its heroes, by whom it honors above all others.

> We pay ourselves the greatest compliment when we say that Abraham Lincoln is that man for us.[22]

I would like to add that we at AEI pay ourselves a very great compliment indeed when we celebrate and honor our colleague and teacher, Walter Berns. His life and work, defending and honoring the American Republic and its great heroes, is a model and inspiration for all who have been blessed to know and to learn from him.

Remarks by Christopher DeMuth

In America today, the Constitution has come to mean constitutional law. Most Americans venerate their Constitution and realize that it is an important source of their liberties and their nation's success. But when they talk about it, or hear political leaders or the media talk about it, the subject is almost always what courts—especially the Supreme Court— have said in its name. We pay attention to our Constitution when the

Court holds that one of its provisions forbids, or does not forbid, a particular practice—banning violent video games, regulating corporate political contributions, suing funeral hecklers, or providing racial preferences in college admissions. Moreover, as Justice Antonin Scalia noted in his AEI Francis Boyer Lecture in 1989, these holdings are often treated as if they were policy decisions rather than constitutional decisions—even when they are not, in fact, policy decisions.[23] If the Court holds that Congress does not have the authority under the Interstate Commerce Clause to forbid the possession of guns in school zones by means of a statute with such-and-such provisions, the media report gravely that the Court has said people can take guns into schools.

It was not always this way. There was a time when the Constitution was understood to be a guide to political officials and even to citizens and voters. Consider the president, whose oath of office, prescribed by the Constitution, is pointedly spare—he will "preserve, protect, and defend" the Constitution. As Walter Berns has noted, in the 19th century all of our presidents invoked the Constitution in their inaugural addresses following the taking of that oath; moreover, constitutional arguments were central to many live political controversies, especially in Abraham Lincoln's speeches and debates on slavery and the union.

But in the 20th century, beginning with Theodore Roosevelt, constitutional appeals and references all but vanished from presidential inaugurals and also from political debates (one exception being FDR's arguments for his court-packing proposal). Modern presidents assuredly do not regard the Constitution as a guide to their own actions. They would not think of vetoing an act of Congress simply because they regarded it as unconstitutional, even though the veto power was intended as a safeguard against unconstitutional legislation. Instead, they sign the act into law and say that, while they may have their own opinion, it is of course up to the courts to decide the constitutional question, and then their Justice Departments proceed to advocate the act's constitutionality before those courts.

Congressional practice has become little different. Several decades ago, in the early years of Walter Berns's career, it was still the case that a few curmudgeonly senators would rise to ask what provision of the Constitution authorized the undoubtedly worthy bill under consideration and then vote against it in the absence of a satisfactory answer. No more. The Speaker of the House of the previous Congress, Nancy Pelosi, articulated the modern approach. Asked for the constitutional authority for a controversial piece of legislation, she said, "Are you serious?"[24] (This was not a question but an expression of contempt.) In the current session, the House leadership has reversed course and required that the source of constitutional authority be specified at the beginning of every bill—but to little avail. "General welfare," "necessary and proper"—these are good enough for congressional work. The Constitution as a guide to action is now just for judges in pronouncing on the actions of others.

Walter Berns's 50 years of scholarship stands in opposition to this shriveled conception of the Constitution. He is one of a line of AEI constitutional scholars distinguished for not being lawyers—a line that also includes his great friend, the late Robert A. Goldwin, and now his younger colleague, Michael Greve, and also departed members of the AEI extended family, such as Herbert Storing and Martin Diamond. I do not know that Walter, or any of them, would regard it as a badge of honor to be a member of the American Political Science Association rather than the American Bar Association. But it is certainly a distinguishing characteristic of their work that they regard the Constitution as a political document—one intended to provide serviceable solutions to enduring political problems such as succession, faction, corruption, and religious-political strife; to promote civility and restrain and channel the passions; and thereby to secure the blessings of liberty.

To perpetuate these blessings, the Constitution is to be studied in its own right, along with the Declaration of Independence and the Federalist Papers and the work of antecedent thinkers from the ancients through Hobbes and Locke. They are to be studied not as a source of slogans or prescribed solutions but rather of counsel—of wisdom—in understanding and coping with today's problems in our own ways. The reasoning and decisions of courts are an important part of this endeavor—the

Constitution is emphatically law and is to be respected as such—but they are not the only or even the most important part.

Walter Berns's work advocates and embodies this approach in three distinctive ways. The first, surely reflecting the influence of his teacher Leo Strauss, is scrupulous attention to the text. Walter is a man of firm opinions and sometimes a sharp tongue, and he is a brilliant polemicist when he wants to be—as in his devastating putdown of Garry Wills's interpretation of the Declaration.[25] But in dealing with the text of the Constitution or a court opinion, or the pronouncement of a philosopher or politician, he is unfailingly fair-minded, nuanced, and sympathetic, seeking to understand the constraints and purposes of the author in the best possible light. Especially when he disagrees with an argument, he is patient to discover the kernel of usable truth.

A striking feature of Berns's discussions of constitutional cases is that he will analyze the words and reasoning of the advocates, courts, and dissenters at length without getting around to mentioning how the case was actually decided. To a lawyer such as myself, this habit of emphasizing reasoning over result is infuriating, until you get the hang of it. When you do, you are liberated. The decision is what interests the litigants and gives the case its immediate drama, but it is the reasoning that lives on—affecting future behavior and the course of our constitutional order, often in unpredictable ways.

In a Berns essay, decisions are important mainly to illustrate the strengths and (more often) weaknesses of the reasoning Walter has been leading us through—as when this reasoning leads, in about the same breath, to the banning of *Memoirs of Hecate County* but not of a seamy crime magazine.[26] And Walter recognizes the tug of the immediate case upon reason and principle. A staunch opponent of extra-constitutional legislating by judges, he admits that he would have done his damndest to invalidate Virginia's compulsory sterilization law at issue in *Buck v. Bell*, even though the Constitution seems to say nothing on the matter.[27] His capacity to place himself in the shoes of his subjects extends even to his imagined self.

Second, Walter's attention to words and reasoning is coupled with a powerful opposition to excessive abstraction and formulae—especially to abstract "rights" that are supposed to override all other considerations. Should the democratic principle of "one man, one vote" lead us to abolish the Electoral College in favor of direct popular election of the president? No, says Berns, because that principle, important as it is, is not the only important consideration—we also want our presidents to attend to regional and other interests and want our succession contests to be resolved with clear and unambiguous results. The Electoral College has done these things rather well for more than two centuries, and almost certainly better than direct election would have done. And, come to think of it, the Electoral College promotes some valued aspects of liberal democracy that direct election would compromise—such as the protection of minorities, which are more influential at the state level than they would be in a single national electorate.[28]

Should the libertarian principle that individual freedom trumps all other considerations decide cases under the First Amendment? No, because that principle, important as it is, is not the only important consideration—few people are indifferent to the uses of freedom, and effective freedom depends on not only the absence of restraint but the nature of the culture in which it is exercised. And, come to think of it, our freedoms surely rest more on our constitutional structure and traditions of limited government than on absolutist extensions of the First Amendment: The whole Constitution is our Bill of Rights. Freedom, says Berns, is not an answer but rather a problem—it is a good in itself, and an instrument for virtue, in many circumstances but not in others. As a license for every individual to do exactly as he pleases, it can lead to its opposite, to tyranny.[29]

Which brings us to the third Bernsian emphasis: the importance of the polity, in particular the nation-state, enjoying the patriotic allegiance of its citizens. Neither freedom nor democracy nor any other desirable condition, not any Supreme Court doctrine or five-part balancing test, not any law professor's theory of how our institutions should be deconstructed and reconstituted, can exist except in the context of a living organic nation that protects and suffers them. A nation is in large part a historic accident; its course is not always open to persuasion, but the good in it cannot endure without considered patriotic commitment. The American nation, because it consists more than others of a set of political ideals as well as ties of blood and geography, depends more than others on the cultivation of patriotism and public-spiritedness. Freedom may be a problem, but it is one worth fighting for. If a sufficient number of citizens are unwilling to stand for freedom in the necessarily imperfect embodiment of our national inheritance, then all the clever theorizing on its behalf is for naught.

America has become vastly more democratic, heterogeneous, libertarian, and statist than it was 224 or even 50 years ago. Can the sort of informed constitutional inquiry that Walter Berns exemplifies make a practical difference anymore? Perhaps not, but it is important to note that, although Walter is opposed to many contemporary developments in law, policy, and society, his writing is not oppositional: He writes not as a dissenter but rather as a teacher.

A deep theme, a basso continuo, runs through his writings from his first book, *Freedom, Virtue and the First Amendment*, down to one of his most recent, *Making Patriots*. That theme is the necessity of civic education to the preservation of our constitutional liberties. He is not proposing the creation of a new categorical grant program for constitutional studies; he does not have a specific reform platform at all, and he understands the great difficulties of accomplishing what he has in mind. He insists only that if we cease to know our Constitution—to understand its theories and practices and appreciate its strengths and shortcomings—then its great achievements will not endure.

I believe that Walter's life's work is itself an essential part of the program he advocates. That our political leaders have taken their leave of constitutional reflection and advocacy is a great loss—in part because it has left federal judges with a monopoly on the enterprise, and monopoly is not good for anyone. But their monopoly is yet incomplete: Constitutional reflection and advocacy is not only for those in power but also for citizens and especially for scholars who specialize in it for the benefit of others. Walter's great contribution is in seeing the Constitution whole—as much more than a set of legal doctrines or parade of court decisions—and in showing that it can illuminate the most vexing contemporary problems and controversies. There is no better way to observe Constitution Day than to read Walter Berns.

Remarks by Walter Berns

Some three decades ago, I came to AEI and found my old friend Robert A. Goldwin in charge of the Constitution program here, and I joined that program. As a part of that program, foreign scholars and statesmen and stateswomen interested in the Constitution were invited to come here to discuss the American Constitution, its institutions, and its underlying principles, and a number of us—largely AEI scholars but not exclusively AEI scholars—went elsewhere and talked about the American Constitution in countries abroad. We visited Cyprus, France, Portugal, and, on a very important occasion, South Africa.

We also went to countries in this hemisphere—for instance, Chile, Brazil, and Mexico. Brazil was an especially interesting experience. Mind you, in each of these cases I was talking to people who, essentially for the first time, were involved in writing or considering a new constitution for their countries. Brazil in this case had just rid itself of a military dictatorship, and they were considering how to advance the cause of constitutional government there. I spoke in various places—usually before a law school audience—and I think it was in a law school at Recife where, after I finished my prepared remarks, an individual, probably a law professor—certainly an angry Brazilian—stood up and denounced not me but the person who'd invited me to speak. He said, and one can understand why he said it, "Why did you invite an American here? They've had only one Constitution. Why didn't you invite someone from Bolivia? They've had a hundred."

My principal experience in participating over the years in the program directed by Goldwin was a deep appreciation of the American Constitution. And I came away with a sense of the extraordinary achievement of George Washington, Thomas Jefferson, James Madison, Alexander Hamilton, Gouverneur Morris, and James Wilson as Founders. We are an extraordinary nation because no other country has had men or women like our Founders, and we should appreciate them, respect them, and study them—and in the process acquire an ever-stronger attachment to this country of ours.

Notes

1. Walter Berns, "Remembering Frieda Lawrence," in *Democracy and the Constitution: Essays by Walter Berns* (AEI Press, 2006), 203, https://www.aei.org/wp-content/uploads/2018/05/Democracy-and-the-Constitution.pdf?x85095. For the original publication, see Walter Berns, "My Days with Frieda Lawrence," *Commentary* 106, no. 2 (1998): 59–61, www.commentary.org/articles/walter-berns/my-days-with-frieda-lawrence/.

2. Walter Berns, "The 'Essential Soul' of Dan Berrigan," in *In Defense of Liberal Democracy* (Regnery Gateway, 1984), https://archive.org/details/indefenseofliberooooobern/page/308/mode/2up. For the original publication, see Walter Berns, "The 'Essential Soul' of Dan Berrigan," *National Review*, November 9, 1973, 1231–43.

3. Walter Berns, "Taking the United Nations Seriously," in *In Defense of Liberal Democracy*, 108. For the original publication, see Walter Berns, "Taking the United Nations Seriously," *Public Opinion* (April/May 1983).

4. Walter Berns, "Why a Vice President," in *Democracy and the Constitution*, 104–6. For the original publication, see Walter Berns, "The Insignificant Office," *National Review*, July 9, 2004, https://www.nationalreview.com/2004/07/insignificant-office-walter-berns/.

5. Walter Berns, *Taking the Constitution Seriously* (Simon and Schuster, 1987), 47–48.

6. Walter Berns, *Freedom, Virtue and the First Amendment* (Louisiana State University Press, 1957), ix.

7. Berns, *Freedom, Virtue and the First Amendment*, 46–47.

8. Berns, *Freedom, Virtue and the First Amendment*, 162.

9. Berns, *Freedom, Virtue and the First Amendment*.

10. Walter Berns, "Judicial Review and the Rights and Laws of Nature," *The Supreme Court Review* 1982 (1982): 66. Reprinted in Berns, *In Defense of Liberal Democracy*, 46.

11. Walter Berns, "Constitutionalism and Multiculturalism," in *Multiculturalism and American Democracy*, ed. Arthur Melzer et al. (University Press of Kansas, 1988). Reprinted in Berns, *Democracy and the Constitution*, 92.

12. Walter Berns, *For Capital Punishment: Crime and the Morality of the Death Penalty* (Basic Books, 1979; University Press of America, 1991), 155.

13. Walter Berns, "Who's Afraid of Agee-Wolf?," *The Wall Street Journal*, November 4, 1981. Reprinted in *In Defense of Liberal Democracy*, 111.

14. Walter Berns, "Let's Hear It for the Electoral College," *The Wall Street Journal*, January 8, 1981. Reprinted in *In Defense of Liberal Democracy*, 169–73.

15. Walter Berns, "*Buck v. Bell*: Due Process of Law?," *Western Political Quarterly* 6, no. 4 (1953): 762–75, https://doi.org/10.2307/443203.

16. See Walter Berns, "Pornography vs. Democracy: The Case for Censorship," *The Public Interest*, no. 22 (Winter 1971): 3–24, https://www.nationalaffairs.com/public_interest/detail/pornography-vs-democracy-the-case-for-censorship.

17. Berns, "Pornography vs. Democracy," 10.

18. Berns, "Pornography vs. Democracy," 13.

19. Deut. 6:5 (English Standard Version).

20. Thomas Jefferson, "A Bill for the More General Diffusion of Knowledge," June 18, 1779, Founders Online, https://founders.archives.gov/documents/Jefferson/01-02-02-0132-0004-0079.

21. See Walter Berns, "Lincoln at Two Hundred: Why We Still Read the Sixteenth President," AEI Bradley Lecture, February 9, 2009, https://www.aei.org/wp-content/uploads/2018/05/Lincoln-at-Two-Hundred.pdf.

22. Berns, "Lincoln at Two Hundred."

23. Antonin Scalia, "Antonin Scalia: Judicial Address," AEI Annual Dinner, aired December 6, 1989, on C-SPAN, https://www.aei.org/multimedia/antonin-scalia-judicial-address/.

24. See Damon Root, "ObamaCare on Trial," *Reason*, July 2012, https://reason.com/2012/06/11/obamacare-on-trial/.

25. Walter Berns, "In 272 Words," *Commentary* 94, no. 5 (1992): 54–57, https://www.aei.org/articles/in-272-words/.

26. Berns, *Freedom, Virtue and the First Amendment*, 41ff.

27. Berns, "*Buck v. Bell*."

28. See Walter Berns et al., *After the People Vote: A Guide to the Electoral College*, ed. John C. Fortier (AEI Press, 1992).

29. See Berns, *Freedom, Virtue and the First Amendment*.

Walter Berns's Biography

Walter Berns was born in Chicago on May 3, 1919. As a boy, he remembered watching survivors of the American Indian Wars march down Michigan Avenue during the Memorial Day parade. At school, he memorized the Gettysburg Address and revered Abraham Lincoln as "a genius . . . our greatest patriot." These beginnings sparked a love of country that led the political scientist throughout his long and distinguished academic career.

He received a bachelor of arts from the University of Iowa and studied as a nondegree student at Reed College. During World War II, Berns served in the United States Navy from 1941 to 1945.

After the war, he earned a master's and a doctoral degree in political science at the University of Chicago. He studied constitutional law with C. Herman Pritchett and political philosophy with Leo Strauss. He would later say,

> I owe a great deal to the University of Chicago. In a way I owe much of the happiness in my life to the university. It was there that I became aware of what my career should be; it was there that I met my closest friends, who remained my friends; it was there that met my wife. . . . What can beat that?[1]

Berns taught in the political science departments at Louisiana State University, Yale University, Cornell University, Colgate University, the University of Toronto, and Georgetown University, where he was the John M. Olin University Professor. Soon after moving to Georgetown in 1979, Berns joined AEI as a resident scholar, working on topics in constitutional law, the American political system, and American statesmanship.

The author of numerous volumes and monographs—*Lincoln at Two Hundred* (2010), *Democracy and the Constitution* (2006), *Making Patriots* (2001), *After the People Vote: A Guide to the Electoral College* (2004, 1992), *Taking the Constitution Seriously* (1987), *The Writing of the Constitution of the United States* (1985), *In Defense of Liberal Democracy* (1984), *After the People Vote: Steps in Choosing the President* (1983), *For Capital Punishment* (1991, 1979), *The First Amendment and the Future of American Democracy* (1976), and *Freedom, Virtue and the First Amendment* (1957)—Berns's work on American governance and society also appeared in *Commentary*, *The Atlantic Monthly*, *The New York Times*, and *The Wall Street Journal*.

His government service included membership on the National Council on the Humanities and the Scholars Council of the Library of Congress, and in 1983, he was the alternate United States representative to the United Nations Commission on Human Rights. He held Guggenheim, Rockefeller, and Fulbright Fellowships and was a Phi Beta Kappa lecturer.

In 2005, President George W. Bush awarded him the National Humanities Medal for his scholarship on the history of the Constitution.

Walter Berns passed away on January 10, 2015.

Notes

1. Cynthia Barnes, "Walter Berns," National Endowment for the Humanities, 2005, https://www.neh.gov/about/awards/national-humanities-medals/walter-berns.

About the Authors

James W. Ceaser is the Harry F. Byrd Professor of Politics at the University of Virginia and director of the Program for Constitutionalism and Democracy there. His writings and scholarship have focused on American politics, presidential selection and elections, and political thought. Ceaser is the author of several books, including *Nature and History in American Political Development: A Debate* (2008) and *Presidential Selection: Theory and Practice* (1979). He is a frequent contributor in the popular press.

Liz Cheney served as the US representative for Wyoming's at-large congressional district from 2017 to 2023. Before her election to Congress, she served in the State Department as deputy assistant secretary of state and principal deputy assistant secretary of state for the Middle East. She is the coauthor—along with her father, former Vice President Dick Cheney—of *Exceptional: Why the World Needs a Powerful America* (2015). At the time of her Constitution Day lecture, Representative Cheney was serving in the House of Representatives.

Christopher DeMuth is a Distinguished Fellow in American Thought at the Heritage Foundation. Mr. DeMuth was president of the American Enterprise Institute from 1986 to 2008 and the D. C. Searle Senior Fellow at AEI from 2008 to 2011. He served in the Nixon administration in various capacities, and from 1981 to 1984 he was executive director of the Presidential Task Force on Regulatory Relief under President Ronald Reagan. He writes extensively on regulatory policy, law, and political economy.

Philip Hamburger is the Maurice and Hilda Friedman Professor of Law at Columbia Law School and a nonresident senior fellow at the American Enterprise Institute. In 2014, he established Columbia Law School's Center for Law and Liberty. His research has focused on constitutional issues related to religious liberty and contemporary debates about administrative law, constitutional interpretation, and free speech. He is the author of several volumes, including *The Administrative Threat* (2017) and *Is Administrative Law Unlawful?* (2014).

Leon R. Kass has served as dean of the faculty at Shalem College in Jerusalem since 2021 and is professor emeritus at the University of Chicago Committee on Social Thought. After serving as chairman of the President's Council on Bioethics from 2001 to 2005, he joined AEI as the Hertog Fellow in Social Thought and is currently a senior fellow emeritus at the American Enterprise Institute. His scholarship has ranged widely, involving issues in biomedical ethics, civic and liberal education, and biblical exegesis. His latest book is *Founding God's Nation: Reading Exodus* (2021). At the time of his Constitution Day remarks, Dr. Kass held AEI's Madden-Jewett Chair.

Brett M. Kavanaugh has served as an associate justice of the US Supreme Court since 2018. Before joining the Supreme Court, he was a judge on the US Court of Appeals for the DC Circuit from 2006 to 2018 and previously worked under President George W. Bush as assistant to the president and staff secretary in 2003 to 2006 and as associate counsel to the president in 2001 to 2003. He was serving on the DC Circuit Court when he gave the 2017 Constitution Day lecture.

Yuval Levin has served as the director of Social, Cultural, and Constitutional Studies at the American Enterprise Institute since 2019, where he also holds the Beth and Ravenel Curry Chair in Public Policy. Before joining AEI, he was a vice president and Hertog Fellow at the Ethics & Public Policy Center from 2007 to 2019. Dr. Levin is also the founder and editor of *National Affairs* and senior editor of *The New Atlantis*. His most recent book is *American Covenant: How the Constitution Unified Our Nation—and Could Again* (2024).

Wilfred M. McClay holds the Victor Davis Hanson Chair in Classical History and Western Civilization at Hillsdale College. Before coming to Hillsdale in 2021, Dr. McClay was the G. T. and Libby Blankenship Chair in the History of Liberty at the University of Oklahoma and the director of the Center for the History of Liberty. He served for 11 years on the National Council on the Humanities and is a member of the US Semiquincentennial Commission. His most recent book is *Land of Hope: An Invitation to the Great American Story* (2019).

Michael W. McConnell is the Richard and Frances Mallery Professor of Law and director of the Constitutional Law Center at Stanford Law School. He formerly served as a judge on the US Court of Appeals for the 10th Circuit from 2002 to 2009. He also was assistant general counsel of the Office of Management and Budget and assistant to the solicitor general in the Department of Justice. His latest book, coauthored with Nathan S. Chapman, is *Agreeing to Disagree: How the Establishment Clause Protects Religious Diversity and Freedom of Conscience* (2023).

Michael B. Mukasey is a retired partner and of counsel at Debevoise & Plimpton. He served as the 81st United States Attorney General from 2007 to 2009 under President George W. Bush and as a federal judge in the Southern District of New York from 1988 to 2006, including six years as chief judge. His career has focused on national security law and terrorism-related cases, and he received the Learned Hand Medal for excellence in federal jurisprudence by the Federal Bar Council in 2004.

Jeremy A. Rabkin was a professor of law at George Mason University's Antonin Scalia Law School from 2007 to 2024. Previously, Dr. Rabkin was a professor of government at Cornell University for over two decades.

He has served on the Council of Academic Advisers of the American Enterprise Institute and the Center for Individual Rights' board of directors. He has written extensively on topics in international law, state sovereignty, the Constitution, civil rights, and public law. His most recent book is *Striking Power: How Cyber, Robots, and Space Weapons Change the Rules of War* (2017), which he coauthored with John Yoo.

Neomi Rao has served as a judge on the US Court of Appeals for the DC Circuit since 2019. Previously, she was a professor of law at George Mason University's Antonin Scalia Law School from 2006 to 2017 and founded the law school's C. Boyden Gray Center for the Study of the Administrative State in 2014. She also was the administrator of the Office of Information and Regulatory Affairs from 2017 to 2019 and special assistant and associate White House counsel to President George W. Bush from 2005 to 2006.

Diana Schaub is a professor of political science at Loyola University Maryland and a nonresident senior fellow at the American Enterprise Institute. Her scholarship has centered on issues in political philosophy and American political thought and history—with a particular focus on Abraham Lincoln and Frederick Douglass—and the relevance of core American ideals to contemporary challenges and debates. She also was a member of the President's Council on Bioethics from 2004 to 2009 and is a contributing editor of *The New Atlantis* and a member of the *National Affairs* publication committee. Her latest book is *His Greatest Speeches: How Lincoln Moved the Nation* (2021).

Gary J. Schmitt is a senior fellow in the American Enterprise Institute's program on Social, Cultural, and Constitutional Studies. He has been a scholar at AEI since 2005, writing on and directing programs in national security and civic education. In government, Dr. Schmitt was a staff director on the Senate Select Committee on Intelligence and executive director of the President's Foreign Intelligence Advisory Board. In recent years, he has focused on the American presidency and constitutional issues. His most recent book is *McCulloch v. Maryland at 200: Debating John Marshall's Jurisprudence* (2020).

James R. Stoner is the Hermann Moyse Jr. Professor and director of the Eric Voegelin Institute at Louisiana State University (LSU), where he has taught since 1988. He also chaired LSU's Department of Political Science from 2007 to 2013. His academic research focused on topics in political theory, English common law, and American constitutionalism. From 2002 to 2006, he served on the National Council on the Humanities. His most recent book, coedited with Paul O. Carrese and Carol McNamara, is *Free Speech and Intellectual Diversity in Higher Education* (2023).

Catherine H. Zuckert is the Nancy Reeves Dreux Professor of Political Science Emerita at the University of Notre Dame and an advisory board member for the School of Civic and Economic Thought and Leadership at Arizona State University. She served as editor in chief of *The Review of Politics* from 2004 to 2018. She has written extensively on topics in political philosophy, literature, and the American regime's philosophical foundations. Her most recent book is *Machiavelli's Politics* (2017).

Michael P. Zuckert is the Nancy Reeves Dreux Professor of Political Science Emeritus at the University of Notre Dame and has been a clinical professor in the School of Civic and Economic Thought and Leadership at Arizona State University since 2019. His scholarship has focused on topics in political philosophy, modern natural rights, and American constitutionalism. He was the founding editor of *American Political Thought*. His latest book is *A Nation So Conceived: Abraham Lincoln and the Paradox of Democratic Sovereignty* (2022).

www.ingramcontent.com/pod-product-compliance
Lightning Source LLC
Chambersburg PA
CBHW062048270326
41931CB00013B/2994